FIELDS *of* RICH TOIL

O'er homes of the millions, o'er fields of rich toil,
Thy science shall shine as the Sun shines on soil,
And Learning and Labor — fit head for fit hand —
Shall crown with twin glories our broad prairie land.

— From a song written by John Gregory
for the inauguration of the
University of Illinois, March 11, 1868.

EUGENE DAVENPORT

Dean of the College of Agriculture, 1895–1922;
Vice-President of the University of Illinois, 1920–1922.

FIELDS *of* RICH TOIL

THE DEVELOPMENT OF THE UNIVERSITY OF ILLINOIS COLLEGE OF AGRICULTURE

Richard Gordon Moores

PUBLISHED FOR THE COLLEGE OF AGRICULTURE BY THE
UNIVERSITY OF ILLINOIS PRESS
URBANA, CHICAGO, LONDON

FOR

DR. TOM S. HAMILTON
DISTINGUISHED SCIENTIST AND GENTLEMAN

Preface

On July 2, 1862, President Abraham Lincoln signed the Morrill Act creating the land-grant universities. At that time, more than sixty percent of the population of the United States lived on farms, and the individual farmer produced only enough food and fiber for four and one-half people. Today, with less than six percent of the population on farms, he produces enough for twenty-seven people. Only nine percent of our labor force is engaged in food production, as compared with forty percent in Western Europe, forty-five percent in Russia, and from seventy to ninety percent in the underdeveloped countries. By releasing millions of people for work in other occupations, American agricultural technology has helped us to attain the highest standard of living in the world.

In the development of this technology the agricultural colleges of the land-grant universities have played a key role. *Fields of Rich Toil* is about one of these colleges — the College of Agriculture of the University of Illinois. Largely as a result of the research, teaching, and extension activities of its College of Agriculture, Illinois ranks first among the states in cash sales of corn and soybeans and second in sales of meat animals. Illinois also leads the nation in total dollar value of agricultural exports, and in the number of people employed in the farm machinery, flour and meal, confectionery products, soybean processing, and prepared meats industries.

In writing this book, I was faced with a special problem: how could I place the College within the larger context of the University without submerging the reader in a sea of facts that would obscure the real story I had to tell? My solution was to concentrate upon those people and events directly involved with the College of Agriculture. For example, only two presidents of the University are considered at length — John Milton Gregory, the first, because during his tenure the histories of the College and the University were essentially the same; and Andrew Sloan Draper, the third, for reasons that become apparent in the narrative itself.

My treatment of the College is also necessarily selective. I believe that the historian's principal function is to present as objectively as possible those events that occurred far enough in the past so that they can be viewed in clear perspective. For this reason, I have concentrated primarily here upon the earlier years of the College of Agriculture. The book deals with the College from its brave beginnings shortly after the Civil War, through its flounderings in the 1880s and 1890s, to its emergence during the 1920s into a true higher institution of agricultural learning. More recent developments in the College are summarized in Chapter Eleven.

I incurred many debts during the writing of *Fields of Rich Toil*, and I particularly wish to thank the following: Louis B. Howard, Dean of the College of Agriculture from 1954 to 1965, and Orville G. Bentley, the present Dean, for administrative encouragement and assistance; Maynard J. Brichford, the University Archivist, for his unfailing courtesy and helpfulness; Mrs. Sally McDermott, for making meaningful order out of my notes, and for solving several knotty research problems; Adrian Janes, head of the Office of Agricultural Publications, for granting me leave from my duties as an editor in that office, and for administering periodic doses of creative criticism; Professor D. E. Alexander of the Department of Agronomy for loaning me his records of the early corn-breeding work at the University, and for clarifying certain points arising from my study of those records; Professors J. Leonard Bates, D. A. Brown, George H. Douglas, Tom S. Hamilton, Lyle H. Lanier, Sherman Paul, Winton U.

Solberg, Margery Suhre, and John S. Titus for reading all or parts of the manuscript and offering valuable suggestions; Mrs. Judith Eskew and her assistants for typing the manuscript; and, especially, Elmer Roberts, Professor of Animal Genetics, Emeritus, for his work in assembling and classifying the materials in the College of Agriculture files over a period of many years, for tracking down literally hundreds of facts and sources for me, and, above all, for sharing with me his delightful recollections of the lives and work of some of the people who appear in these pages. The final responsibility for the book is, of course, mine.

R. G. M.
Urbana, Illinois

Contents

FIELDS *of* RICH TOIL

I shall soon die; you will soon die; we shall soon die; but these institutions will live — still live to learn their art and their duty, and to help the race, long after the oaks have grown, and fallen again, and rotted over our graves.

—JONATHAN BALDWIN TURNER

ONE

A New Kind of Education

IN THE MID-NINETEENTH CENTURY, American agriculture was still essentially a handicraft art. Cyrus McCormick's reaper was not yet widely used in most parts of the country, and many farmers rejected the horse-drawn rake because they believed that the horse's droppings spoiled the hay. Despite a growing interest in science, superstition continued to influence farming practices, and even enlightened farmers planted their crops according to the phases of the moon "just to be on the safe side."[1] There was no agricultural science worthy of the name, and in Illinois the very richness of the soil worked against the development of that science. The farmer in Michigan or Tidewater Virginia was lucky if he raised enough food for his family and livestock, but all his Illinois brother "had to do was tickle the earth with a hoe and it would laugh with a harvest."[2] Much of the best prairie land in the state had been classified as "swamp" by government surveyors and could be bought for fifty cents or less an acre. This virgin soil was so fertile that most farmers were convinced that it would never wear out. Others were not so sure, and among these were

---

[1] If the horns of the new moon pointed upward, the moon would hold water. This meant, depending upon the way one read the "signs," that the planting season would be wet or dry. Corn planted during the new moon would have large stalks but bear only a few ears; corn planted when the moon was old would yield heavily even if the stalks were small.

[2] Eugene Davenport, "Early Trials of the Agricultural Colleges and Experiment Stations," 1924. Typed manuscript in College of Agriculture files.

3

the men who joined Jonathan Baldwin Turner's crusade for the higher education of the "industrial classes" in Illinois.

The question as to whether Turner or Senator Justin Smith Morrill of Vermont deserves the most credit for the establishment of the land-grant universities seems likely to remain unresolved. Probably it can never be answered fully or to everyone's satisfaction. The important point is that each man in his own way — Turner, by first formulating a comprehensive plan for a national system of universities, and Morrill, by fighting for many years in Congress for passage of the act that bears his name — made a significant contribution to the movement for industrial education. But that movement itself was "not the invention of any reformer, but the logical outcome of the progress of science and art. . . ."[3] The passage of the Morrill Bill was simply the last act in a drama that had started many years before.

Jonathan Turner, one of the leading actors in that drama, was a transplanted Easterner. After attending Yale, he had come West in 1833 to teach rhetoric, Greek, and Latin at Illinois College in Jacksonville. Although Turner had been trained in the classics at Yale, the circumstances of his early life (the son of a poor Massachusetts farmer, he had paid his way through college by sawing wood and tending gardens) and the hardships he observed and experienced on the Illinois prairie made him unalterably opposed to the kind of education that encourages a man "to soar away to Greece or Rome . . . before he knows how to plant his own beans, or harness his own horse, or can tell whether the functions of his own body are performed by a heart, stomach, and lungs, or with a gizzard or gills."[4] After his retirement from Illinois College in 1847, Turner devoted many years of his life (he died in 1899 at the age of ninety-four) to the cause of industrial education.

---

[3] *First Annual Report of the Board of Trustees of the Illinois Industrial University* (Springfield, 1868), p. 175. Subsequent citations of the trustees' reports will contain only an abbreviated title and, for the initial entry, the year of publication. For a detailed discussion of the land-grant college movement and Turner's contribution to that movement, see Winton U. Solberg, *The University of Illinois 1867–1894: An Intellectual and Cultural History* (Urbana, 1968), pp. 22–58.

[4] *Report of the Commissioner of Patents for the Year 1851. Part II — Agriculture.* 33 Cong., 1 sess. Senate Exec. Doc. 118. Washington, 1852.

"As things now are," Turner said at a farmers' convention in Granville, Illinois, on November 18, 1851, "our best farmers and mechanics, by their own native force of mind, by the slow process of individual experience, come to know, at forty, what they might have been taught in six months at twenty; while a still greater number of the less fortunate, or less gifted, stumble on through life almost as ignorant of every true principle of their art as when the began." Towering above his audience, a giant of a man with deep-set, piercing eyes and a biblical beard, Turner looked remarkably like John Brown the abolitionist. He also resembled Brown in the radical intensity of his views. Like most converts to a new religion, Turner was violently opposed to what had once given him nourishment.[5] He told the farmers that

> All civilized society is, necessarily, divided into two distinct . . . classes . . . the 'professional' class and the 'industrial' class. . . . The one class have schools, seminaries, colleges, universities, apparatus, professors, and multitudinous appliances for educating and training them, for months and years, for the . . . profession which is to be the business of their life; and they have already created, each class for its own use, a vast and voluminous literature that would well-nigh sink a whole navy of ships. But where are the universities, the apparatus, the professors, and the literature specifically adapted to any one of the industrial classes?

The answer, of course, was that there were not any. Nor would there be any, Turner said, until they — the working people themselves — rose up and demanded a "system of *liberal* education for their own class, and adapted to their own pursuits. . . ." The problem could not be solved by any of the existing universities because they were specifically designed to meet the needs of the professional class; nor could it be solved by "an incidental appendage" attached to these universities" as a mere secondary department." The only solution was to establish "a University for the Industrial Classes in each of the States. . . ."[6] These new uni-

---

[5] Much of the Granville speech is an unreasoned and vitriolic attack on the classicists and other "pedantic fools." It was his own training in the classics that enabled Turner to attack the "old education" with such devastating effect.

[6] All quotations from Turner's Granville speech are from Mary Turner Carriel,

versities, which would teach every science and art known to man, would elevate the farmer and mechanic to that exalted position in human society that God meant for them to occupy. No student above a certain fixed age would be excluded, and he could attend the university for as long — "whether three months or seven years" — as he wished. A few months after the Granville speech, Turner published a letter in the March, 1852, issue of *Prairie Farmer* calling upon "the farmers and their friends" to "exert themselves" to "secure for this State and for each State in the Union, an appropriation of public lands adequate to create and endow in the most liberal manner, a general system of popular Industrial Education, more glorious in its design and more beneficent in its results than the world has ever seen before."[7]

Turner's plan, as Allan Nevins has pointed out, was not original. The concept of free education for the people was as old as the American Colonies themselves, and public lands had been granted for educational purposes since the ordinances of 1787. The first of these ordinances, passed by Congress on July 13, 1787, for the government of the Northwest Territory, did not grant public lands, but it contained a clause that was to have a far-reaching effect on public education in the United States. "Religion, morality, and knowledge being necessary to good government and the happiness of mankind," the ordinance stated, "schools and the means of education shall forever be encouraged." This clause, written with a force and felicity of expression common in our early history, became at once both the embodiment and the definition of American education. Ten days later, on July 23, 1787, Congress wrote into the ordinance for the sale of public lands to the Ohio Company the provision that section 16 in each township be set aside for common schools and "not more than two complete townships . . . be given perpetually for the purpose of a university." This ordinance can be considered the birthday of the state-university movement. All but four of the twenty-one states admitted into the Union before the Civil War received land grants for education, and by 1854, the national government had

The Life of Jonathan Baldwin Turner (n.p., 1911; 2nd ed., Urbana, 1961), p. 75. Hereafter cited as Carriel.

[7] *Prairie Farmer*, March, 1852, p. 114.

donated over sixty million acres of public lands for schools and over four million acres for state universities.

By the mid-nineteenth century, then, the precedent of granting land for education was well established. And in 1841, more than a decade before Turner spoke at Granville, Captain Alden Partridge of Vermont asked Congress (in what appears to be a clear forerunner of the Morrill Bill) to appropriate forty million dollars for education from the sale of public lands, the money to "be distributed among the States . . . in proportion to their representation on the floor of Congress." The concept of universities for the people was "in the air" — indeed, it had been in the air since Washington recommended "the institution of a national university" in his first message to Congress. Turner's major contribution to the cause of industrial universities was in crystallizing a vague, undirected impulse toward higher education into a national and workable project. His plan for a nationwide system of universities was printed in the report of the Illinois State Board of Agriculture, the United States Patent Office Report, and newspapers throughout the country. Public reaction was mixed. Many

Jonathan Baldwin Turner, one of the leaders in the fight for industrial education.

newspapers, including the *Philadelphia North American* and the *Southern Cultivator*, praised the plan, and Horace Greeley's *New York Daily Tribune* hailed it as "a noble step forward." But some newspapers, taking their cue from ministers, lawyers, and others with a vested interest in the old "classical" education, attacked the plan viciously. Magazines ran cartoons of silk-hatted professors awkwardly holding plow-handles in their kid-gloved hands, and the *Mount Morris Gazette* described Turner's "beautiful and practical plan" as "admirably calculated to ease the State of a few million, and establish at Jacksonville a mammoth workshop, a State farm of a few thousand acres, and huge model barns, sheds, cowyards, and cider-mills, where some salaried and skillful Professors, twirling ebony canes and shaded by silk umbrellas, might teach some hundred would-be farmers, (all but the labor,) how to farm scientifically."[8]

This image of the agriculture professor as a cane-twirling, silk-hatted charlatan was slow in dying. Indeed, it was perpetuated by the very people the "new" education was primarily designed to help — the farmers themselves. The average frontier farmer was "governed by established tradition which gave tolerable guidance for operations within human control and reconciled him to a fatalistic acceptance of the inscrutable and unmodifiable manifestations of nature."[9] He was enjoying apparent success in practicing an "extensive" system of agriculture based upon the exploitation of rich, cheap, and abundant land, and he bitterly resented the interference of "book farmers" into what he regarded as his private affairs. If he considered a higher education for his son at all, it was as an avenue of escape into one of the professions where he would not have to work as hard as his father had worked.

The resentment of farmers and the contempt of classicists were a part of the early history of nearly all the land-grant institutions, but the Illinois Industrial University (renamed the University of Illinois in 1885) was uniquely unfortunate in also having to face

---

[8] Burt E. Powell, *Semi-Centennial History of the University of Illinois I: The Movement for Industrial Education and the Establishment of the University, 1840–1870* (Urbana, 1918), pp. 40–41. Hereafter cited as Powell.

[9] Earle D. Ross, *Democracy's College: The Land-Grant Movement in the Formative Stage* (Ames, 1942), p. 18.

the active hostility of the very men who had struggled to bring her into existence. Jonathan Turner and his followers, who had fought for over three decades for the realization of their dream of a higher education for the industrial classes, believed that their dream had been betrayed. There were several reasons for this belief, but the most important one — and the one underlying all of the others — was the fact that the University was located in Champaign County, the lowest bidder of the four counties competing for the location.

The story of how Champaign County won the location of the University goes back to 1859. In January of that year, a Methodist minister and promoter named Jonathan C. Stoughton arrived in the towns of Urbana and West Urbana (the latter was renamed Champaign in 1860). The Reverend Mr. Stoughton represented a company composed of himself and several other gentlemen who were interested in establishing seminaries at various towns in the state. The company had already founded the Clark Seminary at Aurora, and settled upon the Urbanas as a likely location for another institution of the same kind. Stoughton proposed to buy two hundred acres of land between the two towns and erect a brick building upon it. Eight acres of this land would comprise the seminary campus; the remainder would be divided into town lots and sold to subscribers at an average price of two hundred dollars per lot. After the entire cost of the building and the eight acres had been paid for from the sale of the lots, the seminary and its grounds would be turned over to the subscribers. Stoughton's company would make its profit from selling the unsubscribed lots adjoining the seminary grounds. This proposal appealed to the local residents for several reasons. Undoubtedly the most important one was the profit to be expected from the increased value of the lots. But responsible citizens of both towns were anxious to heal the breach that had existed ever since the Illinois Central Railroad established the town of West Urbana several years before. Stoughton's project promised to narrow this " 'awful' gap," as well as to give the two communities "an educational institution of the first class."

Construction of the "Urbana and Champaign Institute" building was started in 1861, but the work was interrupted by the Civil

War. Neither Stoughton and his associates nor the local investors were able to carry out their side of the bargain, and all parties to the contract were anxious to dispose of the unfinished building as quickly as possible.[10] The passage of the Morrill Act gave them the opportunity they had been waiting for, and in 1867, Champaign County offered the Institute property as the major part of its bid to locate the state land-grant university in Champaign-Urbana. Of the four counties actively competing for the location of the University, Morgan County's bid of $491,000 (including the Illinois College property at Jacksonville) was the highest. McLean County, anxious to attach the new institution to the Illinois State Normal University at Normal, offered land, bonds, and free railroad freight valued at $470,000. Logan County offered the cash equivalent of $385,000 in an attempt to locate the University near Lincoln. Champaign County, representing the Twin Cities of Champaign and Urbana, offered the Institute property, 970 acres of farmland, $100,000 in county bonds, $50,00 worth of free freight on the Illinois Central Railroad, and $2,000 worth of shade, ornamental, and fruit trees "from the neighboring nursery of M. L. Dunlap, Esq." The total cash value of Champaign County's offer was estimated at $285,000.

Champaign County's success in securing the location of the University (by a legislative vote of 67 to 10) was due largely to the efforts of an adroit and not overly scrupulous politician named Clark Robinson Griggs. A former member of the Massachusetts legislature, Griggs had been an evangelist, an army provisioner during the Civil War, the owner of a bakery in Memphis, Tennessee, and a farmer at Philo, Illinois. After his right hand was injured in a corn sheller, Griggs gave up farming and devoted himself to politics and railroad promotion. He was elected state

---

[10] The building was commonly called "the Elephant" — a soubriquet based partly on its ungainly appearance and partly on the fact that it was a "white elephant" that the local citizens were anxious to have taken off their hands. It was still unfinished in 1867, when Champaign County was awarded the location of the University, and extensive remodeling was necessary to prepare it for the opening of classes the following year. A legislative committee estimated the cash value of the building (which Champaign County claimed had cost $120,000) at $75,000, but it was worth perhaps half that much. The first mayor of Urbana lived in part of the building for two years, and his wife gave birth to a daughter there.

representative on the Republican ticket with the understanding that he would do everything possible to obtain the location of the University at Champaign-Urbana. The members of the "Champaign ring," as the stockholders in Stoughton's original project came to be called by hostile newspapers, could not have chosen a better man for the job. Along with the ability to make friends easily and use them to advantage, Griggs possessed a sincere belief in the justice of his cause and a nice appreciation of the line between chicanery and outright illegality. During his campaign for the location of the University, Griggs repeatedly called attention to the fact that Jacksonville already had state institutions for the insane, the deaf, and the blind, that Bloomington had the normal school, that Chicago (which had even then a population of over a quarter of a million) would grow fast enough without the University, that eastern Illinois had not received any patronage from the state treasury, and that Champaign County comprised one of the richest and most exclusively agricultural sections of the state. He won the necessary votes for Champaign County by securing the backing of influential news-

The original University building.

papers and politicians of both parties, by logrolling with various sectional interests, and by supplying his fellow legislators with cigars, liquor, and lavish oyster suppers and quail dinners.[11]

Outraged by Griggs's success, Jonathan Turner excoriated the "Champaign ring" for "the scheme inaugurated in perfidy, which was destined, at last, to end in a degree of corruption, hypocrisy, drunkenness, and debauchery unparalleled in the history of Illinois legislation." He predicted that the University would "dwindle down to a mere boys' school for these Champaign villagers," and that "no men of talent or genius will ever gather around it . . .

---

[11] Clark Robinson Griggs to Wallace N. Stearns, April 23, 1906, Clark R. Griggs Memoir, Record Series 2/5/19, University of Illinois Archives. (Unless otherwise indicated, unpublished materials are located in the University of Illinois Archives.) See also "Clark Robinson Griggs and the Location of the University," *Alumni Quarterly and Fortnighty Notes* I (October 15, 1915): 17–22, and Allan Nevins, *Illinois* (New York, 1917), pp. 32–40. Nevins interviewed Griggs in 1915, when the latter was ninety-five years old.

Clark Robinson Griggs, the man most responsible for locating the University in Champaign-Urbana.

nothing above the level of the miserable scamps and scalawags, whose votes and services were bought up at the capital by promises of office or lots of cash — (some of them it was said for twenty-five dollars a head) most of whom could be named in advance of their formal appointment to the board" [of Trustees].[12] The ill-feeling created by Turner and his fellow agriculturists seriously hampered the progress of the University for many years. "Even now," Allan Nevins wrote in 1917, "it may be contended that the location of the University was a mistake. It went to two mere hamlets in a sparsely settled region regarded as little removed, in large part, from a marsh: the flattest, plainest, most monotonous section of Illinois."[13] But the University was founded, as its original name indicates, to "promote the liberal and practical education of the industrial classes. . . ." Although the term "industrial classes" was meant to include all those who worked with their hands — mechanics as well as farmers — there is no doubt that the leaders of the land-grant college movement were thinking primarily of farmers. Turner seldom mentioned mechanics in his hundreds of speeches on behalf of the new education, and Justin Morrill's many appeals to Congress for passage of his educational bills contain only one extended reference to the "mechanic arts."

In 1867, about eighty-five percent of the people in Illinois were living on farms. The University was founded principally for these people, not for their city cousins. Champaign County, whatever its scenic deficiencies, was then — and still is — one of the richest agricultural areas in the state, and it seemed admirably adapted to the purpose of teaching the sons of farmers the business of farming. Considering the reasons for which the University was originally founded, it seems likely that Thomas Jefferson himself would have approved of locating the new institution at Champaign-Urbana — if not, perhaps, of the methods through which that location was obtained. Whether Griggs's methods were different in kind or only in degree from those employed by the three other competing counties will probably never be known.

---

[12] *Jacksonville Journal*, March 16 and 18, 1867, account of "Report of Committee on Location of Industrial University" in Powell, pp. 492–505.

[13] Nevins, *Illinois*, pp. 40–41.

There is no written evidence, at any rate, to substantiate the charges of bribery. But moderation was never one of Turner's virtues, and the fiery old farmer-professor, incensed beyond reason at the location of the University, condemned everyone connected with the institution, including its first head, John Milton Gregory.

Gregory was elected regent (the title of president was rejected as smacking too much of the "old" education) at a meeting of the Board of Trustees held in Springfield on March 12, 1867. He accepted the position with the condition that his salary be raised from the proposed $3,000 to $4,000 a year. Even then he had reservations about assuming "the task before whose grandeur stronger hearts and brains than mine might have paused in modesty if not in dread."[14] But it is doubtful whether a better man for the job could have been found. As secretary of the Michigan board of education, Gregory had helped reorganize the curriculum of the Michigan Agricultural College (now Michigan State University), and he knew, as Turner and his disciples could not possibly know, the difficulties inherent in this new kind of education.

Certainly Gregory's background was humble enough to have satisfied even Turner's exacting requirements. Like Turner, Gregory was the son of an unsuccessful Eastern farmer, and he was brought up on the family farm and tannery near Sand Lake, New York. Gregory's father, a tyrannical hard-shell Baptist, had little use for the fripperies of an education. He believed that God was "hard, not easy," and he required his sons to work at home until they were twenty-one years old. But unlike Turner, who was as sturdy as the oaks he was fond of referring to in his speeches, Gregory was "the physically feeble member of a large family." Because of his precarious health, he was not of much help on the farm or in the tannery. "You may as well let him go," one of his older brothers told the father, ". . . he'll probably die if he stays."[15] And so, at seventeen, John Gregory received his father's

---

[14] *Seventh Annual Report* (1875), p. 66.

[15] Charles A. Richmond, "Dr. Gregory's Early Days," *Alumni Quarterly*, VIII (July, 1914): 149.

reluctant consent to leave home and obtain, through his own efforts and entirely at his own expense, an education.

After graduating from Union College in New York, where he came under the influence of its progressive president, Eliphalet Nott, Gregory studied law for two years and then entered the Baptist ministry. But his real interests lay in public education rather than in law or theology, and in 1854 he became editor and publisher of the *Michigan Journal of Education*. In 1859 he was elected superintendent of public instruction in Michigan, and he served three consecutive terms in this position before accepting the presidency of Kalamazoo College in 1865. Although unprepossessing in appearance, Gregory was intelligent, energetic, and enthusiastic, with a substantial reputation as an educator and lecturer. When he came to Illinois he was forty-five years old. If Turner had known Gregory at this time a great deal of needless opposition would probably have been avoided.[16] When the two men finally met, they discovered to their mutual surprise that they shared similar educational views as well as satisfactorily humble origins, and they quickly became friends. But in 1868, Turner, not prone to reasoned inquiry under the best of circumstances, was in no mood to investigate Gregory's qualifications for the regency.

---

[16] In his history of the University of Illinois, Allan Nevins states that Turner, upon learning of Gregory's election to the regency, exclamed: "O Lord, how long, how long? An ex-superintendent of public instruction and a Baptist preacher! Could anything be worse?" Nevins, *Illinois*, pp. 44–45. Although Nevins did not document this quotation, it has the true Turnerian ring.

TWO

Narrow-Gaugers versus Broad-Gaugers

Turner and the other men who fought in the battle for industrial education shared a common goal: the elevation of agriculture and the mechanic arts to the dignity and prestige of the learned professions.[1] Like revolutionaries before them, however, they disagreed as to the best path for reaching their goal. The adherents of a "narrow-gauge" path wanted to exclude all subjects from the University curriculum that did not contribute directly to the "practical" education of the farmer and mechanic. The "broad-gauge" group wanted to combine the new education with the old, to add to the curriculum rather than subtracting from it. Each group justified its point of view by citing the clause in the Morrill Act stating that "the leading object shall be, without excluding other scientific and classical studies, and including military tactics, to teach such branches of learning as are related to agriculture and the mechanic arts. . . ."[2] The narrow-gauge

---

[1] Contrary to popular opinion, this battle was not fought by the great mass of farmers, but by a relatively small group of educated and enlightened men in the agricultural societies. Most farmers, both before and for many years after the founding of the land-grant universities, were either indifferent to or openly contemptuous of the benefits of the new education.

[2] This clause was incorporated, in somewhat different form, in the state act organizing the University, but its ambiguity remained. For a comparison of the two clauses, see *First Annual Report*, pp. 2, 6.

group interpreted this clause to mean that the University's first and mandatory duty was to provide those subjects that dealt with agriculture and mechanics. Later, if conditions were favorable and "there were funds for the purpose," the classical studies might also be included in the curriculum. The broad-gauge group believed that the clause not only permitted the inclusion of the classical studies, but that "the language may not unreasonably be understood to imply that the latter studies shall not be excluded from the course."[3]

This was also the point of view held by John Gregory. "While we justly revolt against the old tyranny which compelled every seeker of liberal learning to study the classics," he said, "let us not establish a counter tyranny to decree that no one shall study the classics." As regent, Gregory automatically became president of the Board of Trustees and chairman of the committee on course of study and faculty. Although he was "in hearty sympathy with educational reform," his own training and tastes prevented him from following the narrow-gauge path to that Millennium of Labor prophesied by Jonathan Turner. "In laying the foundations of an institution which is to last through coming ages, and to affect all future generations," Gregory told the Board of Trustees on May 8, 1867, "we have need to plan wisely." Gregory believed that "the agricultural and mechanical arts are the peers of any others in their dignity, importance and scientific scope," but he envisioned a University that would "fit for society and citizenship, as well as for science and industry" — that would produce "broad-breasted, wise-hearted, clear-thinking men — men of rich, deep culture, and sound education."[4]

Gregory's plan for the University reflected both his own broad

---

[3] *First Annual Report*, p. 47. "We suppose," The *Chicago Tribune* commented on December 9, 1867, "that this is plainly an intimation that though Science, including special instruction in Agriculture and Mechanics, shall be the main objects of attention, there shall be a chance, if any young farmer or mechanic desires to make a ninny of himself by wasting his time on Greek, the odes of Horace and 'Cicero de Senectute,' for him to do so. We have no patience with such intolerable nonsense, nor with the men of whom it is begotten."

[4] Quotations from *First Annual Report*, pp. 180, 49. "A historian may be a reformer," Allene Gregory wrote of her father; "he is seldom a revolutionist." Allene Gregory, *John Milton Gregory: A Biography* (Chicago, 1923), p. 35.

educational interests and a desire to assuage the feelings of the narrow-gauge group by relating everything in the curriculum to the needs of agriculture. Even the intensely practical department of Trade and Commerce had to be justified in terms of its value to "the educated farmer." In addition to this department and to the required Agricultural, Polytechnic, and Military departments, Gregory proposed departments of Chemistry and Natural Science and of General Science and Literature. The Department of Chemistry and Natural Science was a course in applied science, such as the application of geology to mining, or of chemistry to the analysis of soils, and it included "extended and practical study of mineralogy, geology, and natural history in general, with the arts of collecting and conserving specimens, and of arranging cabinets and conducting geological surveys." The Department of General Science and Literature comprised "the general educational and college course." Its aim was "to furnish such a liberal education as may best fit students for either the mastery of the

John Milton Gregory,
Regent of the University,
1867–1880.

special courses in the arts [i.e., agriculture and mechanics], or for the special duties of life," and it offered courses in the pure sciences, mathematics, English, classical and foreign languages, philosophy, and political economy.

The Agricultural Department embraced "the study of common tillage, aboriculture, fruit growing, cattle and sheep husbandry, veterinary art, agricultural chemistry, and rural engineering and architecture."[5] This list sounds impressive enough, but Gregory knew from his experience at Michigan that few of these courses were of genuine University caliber. His solution was to allow students to complete their educations by supplementing the meager subject matter in agriculture with courses from the department of General Science and Literature. Aware that these courses were more "liberal" than precisely necessary for the training of farmers and mechanics, Gregory pointed out to the Board that "half the public value of a body of educated agriculturists and mechanicians will be lost, if they lack the literary culture which will enable them to communicate through the press, or by public speech, their knowledge and discoveries. . . ."[6]

By including the Department of General Science and Literature in his proposed curriculum, Gregory laid the foundations for a true university and performed the most important single act of his career. But this final heresy aroused the bitter antagonism of the narrow-gauge group. They had wanted a regent who was a "practical" educator; they were given a Baptist minister and former head of one of the hated classical colleges. They had wanted to adjust the level of instruction in the University to the standards of the district schools; they were given a curriculum that included the dead languages and mental and moral philosophy.

At the May, 1867, meeting of the Board of Trustees, Gregory presented a list of fifteen proposed professorships. This list was headed by the professorship of practical and theoretical agriculture, followed by horticulture, analytical and practical mechanics, military tactics and engineering, and civil engineering in that

---

[5] Quotations from *First Annual Report*, pp. 52, 50.
[6] *First Annual Report*, p. 49.

order. It is worth noting that ancient languages, the bugaboo of the narrow-gaugers, occupied thirteenth position in this list, and that mental and moral philosophy, Gregory's particular forte, was in last position. During the following nine months, Gregory made strenuous efforts to find a professor of agriculture, but these proved fruitless. All of the candidates for the position were either successful farmers with little knowledge of science or scientists who knew almost nothing about agriculture. The only man in the country who seemed to possess both the requisite scientific knowledge and practical farming experience was Dr. Manly Miles of the Michigan Agricultural College, and he was not available. By the early spring of 1868, only two of the professorships on Gregory's list had been filled. These were English language and literature (eleventh on the list) held by William Melville Baker, and history and social sciences (fourteenth on the list) held by George W. Atherton.[7]

The University opened on the windy morning of March 2, 1868. Baker, Atherton, and Gregory — the entire faculty — waited on the steps of the one University building to greet the fifty young men who enrolled on that first day.[8] Beyond the building stretched the prairie — limitless, eternal, and as flat as a man's hand. "No bush or shrub had ever grown upon that bare piece of prairie," Judge Joseph O. Cunningham, a member of the first Board of Trustees, was to recall more than fifty years later. "Not a path nor a drive had been prepared except those made by marauding teamsters. . . . in any and all directions around the building and across the grounds."[9] The first student to enroll was fifteen-year-old James Newton Matthews of Mason, Illinois, and he enrolled,

[7] Baker taught at the University until his death in 1873 at the age of fifty. He was buried in Mount Hope cemetery at Urbana. Atherton resigned from the University on January 1, 1869, to become professor of political economy and constitutional law at Rutgers. He was appointed president of Pennsylvania State College in 1882, and died at State College, Pennsylvania, in 1906 at the age of sixty-nine.

[8] Seventy students enrolled the first week, but two were "called home, one by sickness and one by business." Later enrollments increased the number to seventy-seven. Forty-five of these students were from Champaign County.

[9] Joseph O. Cunningham, "The Genesis of Our Campus," *Alumni Quarterly* IX (January, 1915): 19.

appropriately enough, in agriculture.[10] But the raw wind whipping across the prairie, lifting the long coattails of the three men standing on the steps of the Institute building, was like a reminder of past troubles and a presage of troubles to come.

Nine days later, on March 11, 1868, the inaugural ceremonies of the University were held in the chapel of the Institute building. Members of the Board of Trustees, local citizens, anxious to see and hear the new regent, and "distinguished guests from other parts of the State" crowded into the chapel until "serious fears were felt for its safety and extra supports were placed thick under its overburdened floors." The side walls of the chapel were decorated with American flags in honor of the occasion. Behind the flag-draped speakers' platform, a portrait of George Washington ("the great Farmer of the Revolutionary period") was flanked by American eagles. Above this portrait, the University motto, "Learning and Labor," was spelled out in letters made of evergreen boughs.

The exercises started at nine o'clock in the morning with a voluntary from "Cantata of the Haymakers" by George F. Root of Chicago, composer of "Rally Round the Flag, Boys" and the revivalist hymn "Come to the Saviour." The voluntary, aptly entitled "How Good is He the Giver," and conducted by Mr. Root himself, was sung by a fifty-voice choir accompanied by two pianos. (After the exercises one of these pianos was offered for sale — "a rare chance for some of our citizens to secure and keep among us this chef d'oeuvre of musical art.")[11] The voluntary was followed by "Selections of Scripture," prayers, a mixed quartet's rendition of "Lord, Forever at My Side," the reading of letters from guests unable to attend the ceremonies, including Governor Richard J. Oglesby and Senator Richard Yates, and the singing of the Uni-

---

[10] Matthews was graduated from the University in 1872, and received an M.D. degree from Missouri Medical College in St. Louis in 1878. He practiced general medicine in Mason until his death in 1910 at the age of fifty-eight. Matthews was interested in literature, and was one of the founders of the Western Association of Writers. A good doctor but a bad poet, he published two books of poetry — *Tempe Vale and Other Poems* (1888) and *Poems by Alonzo Hilton Davis, with Memoir* (1891). For a typical example of Matthews's verse, see "Twenty Years After" in *Illini*, March 26, 1888.

[11] Powell, p. 304.

versity anthem, written for the occasion by the regent and set to
music by the indefatigable Mr. Root:

> We hail thee! Great Fountain of Learning and light;
> There's life in thy radiance, there's hope in thy might;
> We greet now thy dawning, but what singer's rhyme,
> Shall follow thy course down the ages of time?

> O'er homes of the millions, o'er fields of rich toil,
> Thy science shall shine as the Sun shines on soil,
> And Learning and Labor — fit head for fit hand —
> Shall crown with twin glories our broad prairie land.[12]

Dr. Newton Bateman, state superintendent of Public Instruction and an ex-officio member of the Board of Trustees, then
launched into a lengthy recounting of the entire industrial educational movement in Illinois. Bateman's two-hour peroration was
distinguished by the speaker's apparent belief that adjectives are
not subject to the law of diminishing returns and (under the circumstances) an embarrassingly extended eulogy of Professor
Jonathan Baldwin Turner: "In the West, the man whose voice
rang out earliest, loudest and clearest, in this great movement —
whose words pealed and thundered through the minds and hearts
of the people, and the round shot of whose tremendous broadsides
of irrefragable facts and logic, and fiery rhetoric, plowed and
plunged and ricochetted through these prairies, with an energy
and vehemence that no bulwarks of ignorance or apathy could
withstand. . . ."[13] After Bateman subsided, the choir sang an
original ode "written by a lady," and General S. A. Hurlbut presented the regent with the keys to the University. Gregory then
delivered the Inaugural Address.

"I should be something more or less than human not to feel the
solemn pressure of this hour," Gregory began in the deep, resonant
voice that was to be remembered by his former students for decades after it was stilled forever. "Slowly a great want has struggled
into definite shape in the hearts of mankind. . . . It is labor
lifting its Ajax cry for light to guide its toil, and illuminate its

[12] *First Annual Report*, p. 154.
[13] *First Annual Report*, p. 156.

22

life. . . . The eyes of the nation have been turned toward the rising light, and vague, but mighty, hopes have gathered in the public mind. To us it is committed, here in Illinois, to realize these hopes. Rarely has a grander duty, nor, perhaps, a more difficult one, fallen to the lot of any body of men. We are the servitors of the age itself." The rich voice rolled on for nearly an hour, and the audience forgot, in the speaker's earnestness and eloquence, the short, slight figure and the homely, wide-mouthed, somehow unfinished-looking face. "Let us but demonstrate," Gregory said, "that the highest culture is compatible with the active pursuit of industry, and that the richest learning will pay in a corn field or a carpenter's shop, and we have made universal education not only a possible possession, but a fated necessity of the race. . . . The light which has heretofore fallen through occasional rifts, and on scattered hill tops, will henceforward flood field and valley with the splendors of the noontime sun, and the quickened intellect of

Agriculture students, 1868. Standing, left to right: John J. Davis, George Upstone, Samuel M. Newby; sitting, left to right: George B. Scripps, Edmund B. Hazard, Millard F. Porterfield.

23

the race will bloom with new beauty and burst into a richer fruit-age of industrial arts." [14]

The Inaugural Address was followed by the singing of "America" and the benediction. Most of the audience then "repaired to the University dining room below, where a plentiful repast had been provided by the ladies of Champaign and Urbana. The dinner was succeeded by toasts, sentiments, and speeches, and the assemblage dispersed in great good humor." [15] But at least one man in that assemblage was not "in great good humor." This man was Matthias Lane Dunlap, a member of the Board of Trustees, agricultural correspondent for the *Chicago Tribune*, and an outstanding orchardist and farmer. [16] A self-made man, Dunlap had achieved success through what Turner described as "native force of mind" and "the slow process of individual experience." During his long years of struggle, he had "often felt the want of a more scientific course of study," and he had fought first beside Turner for the establishment of a state land-grant university, and later, with other prominent citizens of Champaign County, for the location of that University in the Twin Cities.

At the first meeting of the Board of Trustees a year earlier, Dunlap had seen his own nominee for regent, Daniel Pinckney, passed over in favor of Gregory. Since that time, he had suffered defeat after defeat at the hands of his fellow Board members. Some of Dunlap's proposals, such as the one providing that any member of the state legislature was competent to hold the office of Regent, seem willfully wrong-headed and contentious, and deserved the summary treatment they received. But others, such as his resolutions for the admission of women students and against "the folly of attempting to carry on the farm and horticultural department by the labor of students," were not only worthy of serious consideration, but were proved sound by later events. [17] In the fall of

<hr/>

[14] *First Annual Report*, pp. 174, 175, 182.

[15] *First Annual Report*, p. 182.

[16] In his *Tribune* column, Dunlap discussed agricultural problems in a practical, straight-forward way that farmers could easily understand, and his handsome nursery near Savoy offered tangible evidence of the soundness of his views. Dunlap donated $2,000 worth of trees and shrubs from his nursery as part of Champaign County's bid for the location of the University.

[17] Women were admitted to the University in the fall of 1870, with Gregory

24

1867, Dunlap, writing under the pseudonym of "Rural," launched a concerted attack upon the University in the *Chicago Tribune.* Since he directed his most withering fire against the curriculum and especially against Gregory, the chief architect of that curriculum, it is tempting to characterize this attack as another example of narrow-gauge opposition to what was essentially a broad-gauge course of study. But as a trustee, Dunlap himself had approved the proposed curriculum, and as a member of the committee appointed to inform Gregory of his selection to the regency, he had recommended that Gregory's salary be increased from $3,000 to $4,000 a year.

The ambiguity of Dunlap's position is well illustrated by his "Rural" article in the *Chicago Tribune* of December 18, 1867. After stating that the damage to crops from weather and insects cannot be corrected "by reading Virgil, Homer, or Cicero, in their native dialects," he does an abrupt about-face, admits that "the course of study . . . will nearly comprehend our wants," and switches the attack to the faculty. Who, he asks, will teach the courses in agriculture and the mechanic arts?

> Certainly not the Regent, for his is but a classical and theological education; [18] not the professors elected, for one [Baker] is to ultimately have the choice of Greek, Latin and French, and the other [Atherton] is prepared for the social studies. . . . The great mistake of the Trustees was in the selecting of the head of the University. . . . If the right man is not in the right place, we may expect little of value from it until a change is made. . . . It is not expected that the Regent shall be a teacher of the several classes; yet he ought, at least, to know what should be taught. If he has experience as a cultivator of the soil, he will be better qualified for the duties before him. If, on the other hand, he has never given the practical sciences attention; if he knows little or nothing of prairie soils, of climate, or of culture; if for the first time he gazes out upon our rich domain of prairie on his way to direct the education of our youth in the several industries of which he knows nothing, it is easy to predict a failure.

---

himself casting the deciding vote. After years of comparative failure, the manual labor requirement for students was finally abandoned as impractical.

[18] Gregory's education was "classical," but he had no formal training in theology.

Dunlap continued his attack throughout the fall and winter of 1867–1868. Nor did he confine his activities to the pages of the *Tribune*. He loudly proclaimed "in public stores in Champaign" that he was the author of the "Rural" articles, he commended editors of other newspapers who also disapproved of the University, and he provided at least one of these editors with ammunition for further assaults. At the examinations for prospective students on February eighth, Dunlap attempted "by many false and disparaging statements" to dissuade students from attending the University. A few days later, at a horticultural meeting in Freeport, he "ridiculed and reviled the University" in a public speech. On February twenty-second, Professor Baker, riding on the train between Decatur and Champaign, heard Dunlap "bring ridicule upon the University and its course of instruction, falsely asserting that its faculty knew nothing of Agriculture and contrary to his own knowledge of the facts."[19]

Late in January of 1868, Dunlap wrote a letter to Dr. William Matthews in reply to the latter's inquiry about living expenses for his son James at the University. After informing Dr. Matthews that board was about four dollars a week, Dunlap gratuitously added that he was not going to enroll his own son in the University. "The Regent and his friends," he wrote, "ask for a trial of his plans and I suppose we shall have to sacrifice a year to convince them . . . that they are worthless."[20] When Matthews brought his son to Urbana on the day that the University opened, he also brought Dunlap's letter and gave it to Gregory.

Shortly after the first "Rural" article appeared in the *Tribune*, Gregory had written General Mason Brayman, one of his staunchest allies on the Board, that "there are men among us who are evidently determined to prey upon us," and he had asked Brayman to prepare a resolution "deprecating and disapproving of any member's communicating as a correspondent of any newspaper

---

[19] John M. Gregory Papers, 1838–1898, Record Series 2/1/1, Box 2. Memoranda in the Dunlap Case, March, 1868. Hereafter cited as Gregory Papers.

[20] M. L. Dunlap to Dr. William Matthews, January 23, 1868, Gregory Papers. James Matthews was the first student to enroll in the University. See footnote 10 above.

the proceedings of the Board."[21] Now, on the same day that he received Dunlap's letter to Dr. Matthews, Gregory wrote Brayman again. "Rural is still boisterous and abusive as ever . . . . I received today from Dr. Matthews, who came to bring his son here, the inclosed letter, which Dr. M. thought so wrong that he brought it along to show to us. It is a clear attempt to dissuade him from bringing his son here, and Dr. M. says it would have succeeded in its purpose if an earlier letter had not reached him from Prof. Atherton."[22]

Dunlap was not a stupid man — his success as a horticulturist and farmer and the clarity of his "Rural" articles on strictly agricultural subjects attest to his common sense and capability. How does one account, then, for his illogical — even irrational — opposition to policies for which he himself had voted? It can be accounted for on equally irrational and illogical grounds: Dunlap simply disliked Gregory. Whether one views his hostility to Gregory as that of an uneducated and ignorant man — a "hick" — toward his intellectual and cultural superior, or as that of a member of the landed gentry — the owner of 1,500 acres of choice farmland and orchards — toward a poor parvenu parading his learning before his betters, the important fact is that Dunlap wanted to get rid of the regent by any means that he could. Gregory had not fought in the battle for industrial education, and Dunlap felt for him the kind of contempt that a combat infantryman feels for a rear-echelon soldier. Like many self-made men, Dunlap distrusted those who talked rather than acted. The regent, like many physically small men, was preeminently a talker, and his effusions about "the hungry eyes of toiling millions" and the "cultured mind . . . linked to a brawny hand" must have driven the old orchardist almost to distraction. Dunlap's sudden changes in point of view, fence-straddling, and wily withdrawals to attack from

---

[21] John Gregory to Mason Brayman, November 22, 1867, Gregory Papers. Brayman was a former Union officer and scholarly lawyer who had revised the state statutes several years earlier. The printed trustees' reports do not contain any reference to the proposed resolution, but this fact is not conclusive. All evidence of Dunlap's defection was carefully expunged from these reports.

[22] John Gregory to Mason Brayman, March 2, 1868, Gregory Papers.

another quarter were all part of a grand strategy: to depose Gregory and those sympathetic to him.

The trustees sympathetic to Gregory included many of the "cultivators of the soil" on the Board, as well as the "merely literary doctors, lawyers, and clergymen." The most prominent of these farmer-trustees was Willard Cutting Flagg of Madison County. Like Dunlap, Flagg was a successful orchardist, but, except for a common interest in horticulture, no two men could have been less alike. Dunlap was blunt, narrowly practical, and quick to anger, with the appearance of a disgruntled Santa Claus. Flagg was a graduate of Yale, cultured, soft-spoken, and darkly handsome — a perfect example of the gentleman farmer in the George Washington tradition. With the exception of Gregory himself, Flagg did more than any other man to put the infant institution on its feet. As corresponding secretary of the Board of Trustees (a thankless task that would have taxed the strength and patience of two men), he was responsible for supervising agricultural and mechanical experiments in each county, providing

Matthias Lane Dunlap, left, and Willard Cutting Flagg, right, members of the first Board of Trustees.

"needful materials" for these experiments, collating the county reports, and issuing 5,000 copies of an annual report on the progress of the University.[23] Flagg also initiated the annual series of agricultural lectures at the University (the forerunner of the extension short course), and as early as 1869, he was proposing the establishment of agricultural experiment stations at various places in the state.

Flagg's close cooperation with Gregory helped to vitiate the force of Dunlap's repeated assertions that the farmers' interests were being betrayed by the Board. Unfortunately, enough people shared Dunlap's views to prove a constant source of harassment and embarrassment to Gregory, and the regent's health, never robust, almost broke under the strain. The situation reached a climax during the Board of Trustees' meetings held at the University building in March, 1868. At one of these sessions General Brayman offered a preamble and resolutions proposing "to inquire, by committee or otherwise" into Dunlap's conduct. Brayman was appointed chairman of the investigating committee, and when the Board reconvened after the inaugural ceremonies on March eleventh, he presented his report.

This report was both extensive and damning. "The committee," it stated, "deem it unfortunate that Mr. Dunlap, while sitting as a member of this Board and sharing its deliberations, should have felt at liberty, not only to act as a newspaper correspondent, but should, in violation of propriety and fairness, indulge in palpable misrepresentations, too often accompanied by ungenerous imputations and abusive epithets, when speaking of the Regent, the Board, its committees, and of measures adopted for the management of our affairs." Brayman concluded his report with a plea that the citizens of Urbana "be relieved from the imputation . . . that they in any manner share or approve the attacks complained of,"[24] and a proposal for the adoption of the following resolutions:

---

[23] Before the University opened, Flagg sent out a circular letter asking "practical farmers" for the results of their experience with soils, crop and fruit varieties, timber, livestock, manures, and deep plowing. Flagg's questions and the farmers' answers are printed in the *First Annual Report*, pp. 216–292.

[24] At a mass meeting held in the courthouse on March 10, 1868, the citizens of

Resolved, that this Board of Trustees have undiminished confidence in the integrity, ability and fitness of the Regent, and pledge him a firm support in the performance of his duties.

Resolved, that public criticism and full investigation of the acts of this Board is invited, and that the Board will at all times give respectful consideration to measures proposed in a proper manner by its members in any matter seeming to require its action.

Resolved, that this board regard with disapprobation the conduct of M. L. Dunlap, Esq. . . . and consider the practices complained of a departure from the courtesy of official intercourse, a dereliction of duty, offensive to this board, injurious to the University, and not proper in one holding a seat as a member of the Board.

Resolved, that His Excellency, the Governor of this State, be furnished with a copy of the record made in this case.[25]

Following Brayman's presentation of the report, "a very frank discussion" took place in which Dunlap tried to justify his conduct. The investigating committee then demanded his dismissal from the Board of Trustees. At this point, John C. Burroughs, a close friend of Dunlap's on the Board but not a member of the investigating committee, appealed to Dunlap to give the regent a chance to prove himself.[26] Dunlap finally yielded and promised "not to pursue such a course in the future." He crossed the room and shook Gregory's hand "in token of reconciliation." The Board then decided not to publish the committee's report in its official minutes, and the trustees voted unanimously for the resolution pledging firm support of the regent.[27] And there, at least for the moment, the matter rested.

Urbana adopted resolutions condemning Dunlap's actions and offering Gregory their complete support.

[25] Gregory Papers. The complete report of the investigating committee is printed in Powell, pp. 579–583.

[26] Burroughs (1818–1875) was president of the old Chicago University. He was a trustee of the Illinois Industrial University from 1867 to 1870.

[27] This resolution appears on page 132 of the *First Annual Report*, along with the information that "The vote was unanimous."

THREE

Defeat of the Narrow-Gaugers

THE WORKING MASSES of mankind are waking to their needs . . . ," John Gregory said. "The thunder of machinery by the side of which they toil, and the magic power of the new processes of arts which they daily employ, have roused the long slumbering power of thought. Brains are coming into use and honor in all the fields of human labor, and brains will speedily demand light. . . ."[1] But the light the University was able to provide that first semester was not — at least for the aspiring agriculturist or "mechanician" — a very bright one. The institution designed "to promote the liberal and practical education of the industrial classes" in the State of Illinois was not able to offer a single course in agriculture or the mechanic arts.[2] It found itself in the position of a salesman who has finally persuaded a reluctant customer to buy a certain product and then discovers that he has no product to sell.

As a part of its successful bid to obtain the location of the University, Champaign County had donated three farms to the new

---

[1] *First Annual Report*, p. 63.

[2] The academic year was divided into three twelve-week terms — fall, winter, and spring. These ended in early December, March, and June, respectively. According to Gregory's plan, the most important courses were to be offered during the fall and winter semesters because so many students were needed on the home farm in the spring. The first term in which the University was open was the spring term — the last one-third of the academic year. The only courses offered during that term were mathematics, natural philosophy, history, rhetoric, and Latin.

31

institution. These were the 410-acre "stock farm" located slightly over a mile south of the Institute grounds, the 160-acre "experimental farm" adjoining the campus, and the 400-acre Griggs farm two and one-half miles to the southeast.[3] According to Gregory's original plan of organization, the professor of agriculture was to manage the farms — "these being his laboratory and apparatus of instruction." Since there was no professor of agriculture, however, this responsibility fell upon the shoulders of Jonathan Periam, the head farmer. Periam, later to become editor of *Prairie Farmer*, was appointed by the Board on November 27, 1867, and started work the following January first. In addition to his salary of $1,500 per year, he was given the use of the house on the stock farm. Upon inspecting this farm, Periam "found the fences . . . broken down, and in some instances carried away — stock of all

---

[3] The experimental farm, which Champaign County had described as "adjacent" to the campus, was in fact over one-half mile away. The University purchased the intervening forty-acre tract during the spring of 1867, bringing the size of the farm up to 200 acres.

Jonathan Periam, head farmer at the University from 1868 to 1869, and later editor of *Prairie Farmer*.

kinds running at will over the fields . . . ranging from sucking pigs to droves of cattle and horses, some of them . . . owned by persons who ought to have felt above allowing their stock to pasture in the road."[4]

To make matters worse, the spring of 1868 was exceptionally rainy, and much of the first planting was washed out. The rain was succeeded by a prolonged drouth, and the soil became so hard that the "parsnips, onions, swedes, salsify, and other roots were an entire failure. . . ." The rhubarb was nearly killed and had to be removed to better soil, and three acres of potatoes, although "faithfully plowed, and also hoed by hand twice," yielded only ninety-five bushels.[5] And the few crops that managed to survive the depredations of the weather were subject to the equally severe depredations of humans, who looked upon the University's sweet corn and tomatoes as community property. Despite these setbacks, Periam managed to grow sixty-one varieties of vegetables that were exhibited at the Champaign County Fair, "receiving, as a whole, a complimentary premium, besides notices upon specialities."[6] But Periam was not happy with his situation. As acting "superintendent of practical agriculture," he was required to submit "his plans for the treatment of each field and crop, and for the several experiments to be tried"[7] to the regent and the committee on agriculture. Thoroughly disgusted with what he termed the "bigotry and mismanagement" of the committee on agriculture, Periam resigned as head farmer at the March 10, 1869, meeting of the Board of Trustees.

"The Faculty," Gregory proudly proclaimed at this meeting, "without exception, came from the laboring classes. They were all trained in boyhood to hard labor and, by their own industry, won and paid for the education which now enables them to teach others. Becoming educated men, they have not ceased to be practical men — farmers and mechanics."[8] But Gregory was wrong. There was one man on the faculty to whom this descrip-

---

[4] *Second Annual Report* (1869), p. 43.
[5] *Second Annual Report*, p. 43.
[6] *Second Annual Report*, p. 47.
[7] *First Annual Report*, p. 62.
[8] *Second Annual Report*, p. 63.

tion did not apply, and ironically, he was the very man who might have been most expected to fit it — Willard Flagg Bliss. Bliss was appointed professor of agriculture on March 11, 1868 (at the same trustees' meeting that witnessed Dunlap's discomfiture), and he started work the following fall, along with three other new instructors.[9] Although Bliss was a practicing farmer, he was not a member of — nor did he come from — the laboring classes. A native of Essex, Vermont, Bliss was graduated from Phillips Exeter Academy and Harvard with a sound knowledge of Greek, Latin, and French. After teaching Latin at Washington University in St. Louis from 1856 to 1860 (with a year out for study and travel in Europe), he bought a large farm near Nokomis, Illinois. He had been farming for eight years when he came to Urbana as professor of agriculture. Perhaps more than any other man on the faculty, Bliss possessed the "high-toned, gentlemanly character and culture" that Gregory cited as one of the three requirements for "a good college professor."[10]

After Periam's resignation, Bliss assumed the duties of superintending the University farms. Unfortunately, more than "high-toned, gentlemanly character and conduct" were necessary to cope with the problems of the stock farm. "The Board of Trustees should understand," Bliss said on March 8, 1870, ". . . that when this farm came into the hands of the University it was very much run down, and . . . a great deal of labor and . . . money must be expended on it before it can be brought even into as good condition as a common, well-ordered farm."[11] In addition to managing the farms, Bliss taught all the courses in agriculture [12] and

---

[9] These were Lieutenant Colonel S. W. Shattuck, assistant professor of mathematics and instructor in military tactics; A. P. S. Stuart, professor of chemistry; and Captain Edward Snyder, instructor in German and bookkeeping.

[10] *First Annual Report*, p. 61. The other two were "eminent and extensive scholarship, at least in his department," and "thoroughly tested ability to teach."

[11] This was precisely the reason, in fact, that the former owner had sold it. Since the farm had "reached that point of exhaustion where no further profits could be expected," he considered it "a fair subject for the application of agricultural science." *Third Annual Report* (1870), p. 60.

[12] Bliss taught "two classes in Agriculture, numbering 5 in the Advanced Class, upon Soils their origin and properties, and 15 in Elementary Study." *Third Annual Report*, p. 79.

a course in French, and was responsible for carrying out the plans of the committee on horticulture — literally the work of three men. He asked the Board to be relieved "from the charge of the Horticultural Department and from the active superintendence of the farms," and this request was granted. But three months later, on June 7, 1870, Bliss resigned his position — "compelled," as he said, "by the requirements of my own business."[13] His resignation became effective on September first, and once again the Illinois Industrial University was without a professor of agriculture.

But the loss of Willard Bliss was more than offset by the gain of Thomas Jonathan Burrill as professor of botany and horticulture. Burrill was born in Pittsfield, Massachusetts in 1839, the son of a weaver. His father, John Burrill, was not able to earn enough by his trade to support a wife and seven children, and in 1848,

---

[13] *Third Annual Report*, p. 125. After his resignation, Bliss farmed in Illinois until 1906, when he bought a farm near Sterling, Virginia. He died at Leesburg, Virginia, in 1915 at the age of eighty-six.

Willard Flagg Bliss, Professor of Agriculture, 1868–1870.

he moved his family to northern Illinois. The family traveled by train to Albany, New York, by boat through the Erie Canal to Buffalo, and again by boat from Buffalo to Chicago. At Chicago, they hired teams of horses to take them to what Burrill later described as "our particular portion of the promised land." The area in which the Burrill family settled was known as "Irish Grove" — a farming community located between the towns of Freeport and Rockford in Stephenson County. The Burrill house, the first frame house in the area, was built from lumber hauled overland from Chicago. Thomas helped his father on the farm, attended the country school for a few months each winter, and, by teaching in both private and district schools, earned enough money to go to high school in Freeport. "For this purpose," Burrill said,

> I had been provided with a new suit of home-made all wool cloth, but which had been cut out by a tailor, since I was to wear it in town. The other work upon the important suit (frock coat, etc.) was done at home. My fine gray suit contrasted too conspicuously with the 'store clothes' worn by the Freeport school children. I suddenly grew larger in stature, with bigger feet and hands than had previously been recognized. Some of the boys were kind to me and evidently tried to make the stranger forget his shyness, but it would not do. Homesickness overtook me and after three weeks of the struggle, I started one afternoon afoot and alone for a tramp of 13 miles, back to my own people. . . .

The following fall, when Burrill was twenty years old, he decided to try high school again — this time at Rockford.

> After the corn had been gathered, I started on horseback to Rockford with the idea of making arrangements for entering the high school and for a boarding place, not quite daring to face again my acquaintances in Freeport. Strangers would not know of my former failure. I remember my hands were rough and begrimed from the corn husking and I wore a pair of gray lisle thread gloves while calling on the school principal. But adjustments were satisfactorily made at the school and for choring for board. I rode home again the next day, a distance of 18 miles, and soon afterward packed up for a second venture away from home at school. I went with less confidence than upon the former occasion, but

with determination the need for which had been recognized. And the country boy did not again lose out.[14]

Three years later, in 1862, Burrill entered Illinois State Normal University (now Illinois State University). A young man with a love for natural science, especially botany, could not have asked for a more congenial environment. Dr. J. A. Sewall, Burrill's botany teacher, was curator of the museum of the State Natural History Society. At the Society's meetings held in nearby Bloomington, Burrill became acquainted with Dr. D. B. Walsh, the state entomologist, Professor Jonathan Baldwin Turner, and Dr. George W. Vasey, later botanist of the United States Department of Agriculture.[15] After graduating from Normal in 1865, Burrill became principal of the Urbana public schools. His interest in botany had been stimulated by Dr. Sewall and the other men he had known in the State Natural History Society, and during the two years that he served as principal, he made a comprehensive collection of the flora of Champaign County. In the summer of 1867, Burrill joined Major John Powell's first expedition to Colorado as a botanist.[16]

The Illinois Industrial University opened the following spring. A few days after classes started, Judge Cunningham, one of the local trustees, walked into the room in which Gregory was teaching algebra. Gregory said that he did not have time to teach the class because of his many administrative duties, and he asked

---

[14] Thomas J. Burrill Papers, Record Series 15/4/20, Box 1.

[15] During his college vacations, Burrill also received practical experience in horticulture through selling trees for a Bloomington nursery. He was reportedly "an excellent salesman, his bearing and address giving everyone confidence . . . in the exact truth of everything he said." Eugene Davenport, "Dr. Thomas Jonathan Burrill Memorial Address," Illinois State Horticultural Society, *Transactions for 1916*. n.s., L (n.p., 1917): 69. Hereafter cited as *Transactions*.

[16] Most of the botanical specimens that Burrill collected on this expedition were lost when the burro carrying them was drowned in a swollen mountain stream. The few specimens that Burrill was able to save, together with his collection of local flora, became the nucleus of the University's herbarium. Powell, the celebrated explorer of the Grand Canyon and later director of the United States Geological Survey, was appointed professor of natural history and geology on March 11, 1868. But Powell never actually served on the University staff. He was detained on a second expedition to Colorado, and submitted his resignation to the Board of Trustees in March, 1869.

Cunningham if he could recommend another instructor. Cunningham replied that the Urbana public schools had recently closed because of lack of funds, and that "perhaps the principal, Mr. Burrill, will take the place." [17] And so, on April 20, 1868, Thomas Burrill joined the staff of the institution that he was to serve for nearly half a century. [18]

When Burrill first came to the University (he was hired as an instructor of algebra but was quickly promoted to assistant professor of natural history), he "taught most of the day, . . . planted with his own hands, or saw to the planting of most of the trees on the campus, after he had laid it out for treatment, wrote reports, lectured here and there, served on innumerable committees, collected specimens up and down the state, and, lest some remnant of his time should be unoccupied, was charged by the Board with the sale of a pair of mules, whose labors on the south farm showed that they were not so able to stand the strenuous life as he was." [19]

Burrill was appointed professor of botany and horticulture on March 9, 1870, the day after Willard Bliss asked to be relieved of the burden of the "horticultural department." [20] His duties roughly paralleled those of the professor of agriculture. He was responsible for all instruction in horticulture, and, as "superintendent of the gardens and ornamental grounds," was required to "present to the Faculty for their discussion and approval, his plans for the management of such grounds and gardens." [21] "The horticultural

---

[17] Nevins, *Illinois*, pp. 58–59.

[18] During his long career with the University (from 1868 to 1912), Burrill served as dean of the College of Science, General Faculty, and Graduate School, as vice-president (from 1879 to 1912), and as acting president four times. But the administrative aspects of Burrill's career, except to the extent that they bear directly upon the College of Agriculture, are beyond the scope of this history.

[19] *Alumni Quarterly* II (1908): 136.

[20] The 1868 University catalog described the "Agricultural Department" as including "the course in Agriculture proper" and "the course in Horticulture and Landscape Gardening." These courses, or "schools," as they were called in the 1869 catalog, were designed "to fit students to manage successfully, for themselves or others, agricultural and horticultural estates and enterprises." In 1870, the various departments of the University were renamed "colleges," and the newly christened College of Agriculture embraced the School of Agriculture Proper and the School of Horticulture and Fruit Growing.

[21] *First Annual Report*, p. 62.

38

duties," Burrill later wrote, "were addenda. After the class-room exercises were over for the day, drains could be located, grounds laid out, trees planted, fruits gathered, plant diseases studied, etc. It is almost certain no man could have long sustained himself in these practical affairs taken by themselves." In horticulture, as in agriculture itself, no scientific, thoroughly defined body of knowledge existed, and Burrill attributed his own long career as professor of botany and horticulture to his "connections with the first subject in the title."[22]

Burrill was not the only man on the faculty with more than one "subject" in his title. In an attempt to give each college the ap-

---

[22] Thomas J. Burrill, "Some Early Inside History and Its Lessons," *Dedication Agricultural Building University of Illinois, May 21, 1901* (printed pamphlet). Copy in College of Agriculture files. Burrill was professor of botany and horticulture from 1870 to 1903, and professor of botany only from 1903 until his retirement in 1912.

Thomas Jonathan Burrill about the time he joined the University staff.

pearance of solidity, John Gregory listed nearly all of the University faculty as staff members of at least two colleges.[23] This subterfuge was fairly transparent, and it probably fooled no one. The fact remains that Gregory had succeeded in placing the University on a broad enough base so that it could develop into a true institution of higher learning. He had also — temporarily, at least — successfully withstood all efforts to narrow that base. But Gregory's troubles were far from over. M. L. Dunlap, despite his promises to the Board of Trustees at the March, 1868, meeting, continued to attack the University in his "Rural" column in the *Chicago Tribune*, and "his course on the street and . . . his intercourse with citizens from other parts of the state were scarcely less objectionable than previous to that meeting."[24] Gregory wrote General Brayman on December 21, 1868, that "Rural . . . has thrown off all masks and is fighting . . . to prevent my reelection in the spring. As far as I am personally concerned, it will give me no grief. Pleasanter fields beckon me where no vulgar falsehood and abuse will assail me. But a change in the administration of the University at this juncture would be dangerous if not fatally disastrous."[25]

It was in this kind of atmosphere that the University presented its first annual course of agricultural lectures and discussions the following month.[26] This course, which followed the precedent set

---

[23] For example, the faculty of the College of Agriculture, as shown in the University catalog for 1870–1871, includes Gregory himself as Professor of Political Economy; A. P. S. Stuart, Professor of Chemistry; Edward Snyder, Professor of Agricultural Bookkeeping; S. W. Robinson, Professor of Agricultural Machinery; S. W. Shattuck, Professor of Agricultural Engineering; and D. C. Taft, Professor, *pro tempore*, of Geology of Soils. None of these men had anything directly to do with agriculture.

[24] J. O. Cunningham to Mason Brayman, November 23, 1868, Gregory Papers, Box 2.

[25] John M. Gregory to Mason Brayman, December 21, 1868, Gregory Papers, Box 2.

[26] This course was proposed by Willard Flagg, the corresponding secretary of the University, in a letter to Newton Bateman dated November 21, 1867. One month earlier, at a meeting of the Executive Committee of the Board of Trustees, M. L. Dunlap had made essentially the same proposal. "But this wise committee," Dunlap wrote in the *Chicago Tribune* of December 18, 1867, ". . . said no. The people must wait, for if it should not prove a success, it will damage the institution;

by the Yale lectures of 1860, was held at Champaign during two weeks of January, 1869. Although the University advertised the lectures in *Prairie Farmer, Western Rural,* and other farm papers and distributed circulars throughout the state, attendance was disappointingly small. A substantial part of the audience was made up of University students and citizens from the Twin Cities. The speakers included Willard Flagg, Jonathan Periam, H. C. Freeman of the State Geological Survey, Dr. John A. Warder, the well-known pomologist (who had delivered a course of twelve lectures to the agricultural students earlier in the month), M. L. Dunlap, and John Gregory. "The university," Gregory said in his welcoming address on January twelfth,

> . . . leaving for the moment its place near the gateways of prac-
> tical life, where it sits to train those about to enter, and to fit them
> for life's great duties, seeks to go out into the very midst of the
> busy throng of labor, and mingle its counsels and lend its light to
> the struggling, toil and thought of the practical world. Not con-
> tent to teach its sciences to the young, it also seeks to enlighten,
> with its learning, the labors and the lives of the grown men and
> women who are doing the world's great work and bearing the
> burden of its endless battles.

Gregory had worked hard to acquire this elegance of expression (the mark of an educated man in nineteenth-century America), and certainly his predilection was for the "literary" rather than the "practical." But he was himself the son of a poor farmer, and he had escaped a similar fate only through the twin accidents of possessing a good mind and bad health. Gregory had a deep interest in improving the lot of the hewers of wood and drawers of water, but he knew that agriculture could not progress until it was established on a scientific basis. "Looking at the crude and disjointed facts which agricultural writers give us," he told the assembled farmers and students, "we come to the conclusion that we have no science of agriculture. Botany is a science, because the facts which underlie it are established by fixed laws. Chemistry is a science for the same reason. But agriculture is not a science in

---

just as though any more could be done to make it unpopular with the great mass of the people."

any sense."[27] The following day, however, Gregory himself advanced a theory based upon the fact that people die when they are frozen. Why, he asked, wouldn't a tree "frozen to the heart" also die?[28] In the *Chicago Tribune* of March 2, 1869, M. L. Dunlap gleefully lamented that the advocate of such a theory should be head of the state industrial university. What the University needed, Dunlap wrote, was a good businessman, "certainly not a man who thinks that because a man dies who is frozen stiff *ergo* that a tree dies that is frozen to the heart. . . ."

On March 9, 1869, Gregory was reelected regent.[29] The Board took advantage of the occasion to pass (over Dunlap's objections) a resolution expressing to Gregory their "assurances of continued confidence and respect," and vindicating "this institution, its officers and faculty, against the charges of wresting it from its primary and normal design, and from all bitter and unfounded charges made and put in circulation against it."[30] In an attempt to allay the growing criticism, the Board also voted free tuition for all students enrolled in the agricultural, polytechnic, and military departments. Eight days later, the state legislature passed a series of resolutions condemning the University for "being diverted in its management from the 'leading objects' for which . . . [it] was . . . established." These resolutions reaffirmed that the "essential objects" of the University were "the teaching of such branches of learning as relate to agriculture, horticulture, and the mechanic arts," and directed the Board of Trustees to adopt and enforce such regulations "as will peculiarly adapt [the University] to the educational wants of students who are looking forward to the adoption of farming or mechanics. . . ."[31]

The charges made by the legislature were, as Gregory and his

---

[27] *Second Annual Report*, pp. 122–123.

[28] *Second Annual Report*, p. 164. During the 1870 course of agricultural lectures, Gregory stated that he had "known cases of typhoid fever resulting from an excess of shade." *Third Annual Report*, p. 262.

[29] The election was not unanimous. Of the twenty trustees who voted, seventeen voted for Gregory, two for Jonathan Turner, and one trustee deposited a blank ballot.

[30] *Second Annual Report*, p. 84.

[31] Powell, p. 328. The sting of this rebuke was partially allayed by the fact that this legislature appropriated $60,000 to the University, the first appropriation it received.

friends well know, grossly unfair. To prevent further "injurious misapprehensions," the University catalog issued in the spring of 1869 contained a "new and enlarged statement" of the courses in agriculture and the mechanic arts. But the criticisms persisted. At the Board of Trustees' meeting a year later, Gregory tried to answer these criticisms by pointing out that no instance was

Announcement of first course of agricultural lectures held at the University.

OFFICE CORRESPONDING SECRETARY,

BOARD OF TRUSTEES,

ILLINOIS INDUSTRIAL UNIVERSITY.

CHAMPAIGN, DECEMBER 19, 1868.

The First Annual Course of Agricultural Lectures and Discussions, instituted by the Illinois Industrial University, will be held at the University, in Champaign, commencing Tuesday, January 12th, 1869, and continuing during four days of that and the subsequent week, with three sessions in each day.

This is intended to be an annual gathering of the Farmers of the State, and of their sons and daughters, for the purpose of discussing the best methods of Agriculture; and it is earnestly hoped that all who desire to improve our tillage, our crops and our live stock, will be present and lend a helping hand.

No charge is made for admission. The University provides a hall properly warmed and lighted, and pays the expenses of the gentlemen who have kindly consented to open the discussions.

Each lecture, essay or "talk," will be followed by a discussion on the same subject, in which all are invited to participate.

Dr. John A. Warder, author of American Pomology, will lecture daily from 4 to 5 P. M., on the subject of Fruit Culture.

Good boarding places can be had convenient, and at reasonable rates.

Railroads will be solicited to return persons in attendance at reduced rates.

J. M. GREGORY, *Regent.*

W. C. FLAGG, *Corresponding Secretary.*

PROGRAMME:

Tuesday, January 12th.	Morning, 9 o'clock.	Introductory Address. Agricultural Facts and Theories.	Dr. J. M. Gregory.
	Afternoon, 2 o'clock.	The Natural Sciences and Agriculture.	Prof. W. F. Bliss.
	Evening, 7 o'clock.	Relation of Chemistry to Agriculture.	Prof. A. P. S. Stuart.
Wednesday, January 13th.	Morning, 9 o'clock.	Meteorology.	Prof W. M. Baker.
	Afternoon, 2 o'clock.	The Soils of Illinois.	H. C. Freeman, of the State Geological Survey.
	Evening, 7 o'clock.	Management of Soils.	Dr. John A. Warder.
Thursday, January 14th.	Morning, 9 o'clock.	Grass.	Dr L. D. Morse, Editor Journal of Agriculture.
	Afternoon, 2 o'clock.	Corn.	M. L. Dunlap, Agric'l. Corres't. Chicago Tribune.
	Evening, 7 o'clock.	Wheat.	W. C. Flagg.
Friday, January 15th.	Morning, 9 o'clock.	Potatoes.	Jonathan Periam, Supinten't. Practical Agriculture.
	Afternoon, 2 o'clock.	Root Crops.	Jonathan Periam.
	Evening, 7 o'clock.	Agricultural Book Keeping.	Capt. Ed. Snyder, Instructor in Book-Keeping.
Tuesday, January 19th.	Morning, 9 o'clock.	Orchard Fruits.	Dr. E. S. Hull, of Alton.
	Afternoon, 2 o'clock.	Grapes.	Hon. Geo. Husmann, of Hermann, Mo.
	Evening, 7 o'clock.	Small Fruits.	Samuel Edwards, of Lamoille.
Wednesday, January 20th.	Morning, 9 o'clock.	Breeds of Cattle.	Sanford Howard, Sec'y. Mich. State Board of Agric'e.
	Afternoon, 2 o'clock.	Horses.	Col. N. J. Colman, Editor Rural World.
	Evening, 7 o'clock.	Swine.	Hon. Elmer Baldwin.
Thursday, January 21st.	Morning, 9 o'clock.	Sheep.	A. M. Garland, Pres't. Ill. Sheep Growers' Ass'n.
	Afternoon, 2 o'clock.	Agricultural Botany.	Assistant Professor Thos. J. Burrill.
	Evening, 7 o'clock.	Vegetable Physiology and Economy.	John H. Tice, Sec. Missouri Board of Agriculture.
Friday, January 22d.	Morning, 9 o'clock.	Rural Economy and Rural Life.	Dr. J. M. Gregory.
	Afternoon, 2 o'clock.	Fences and Hedges.	Dr. John A. Warder.
	Evening, 7 o'clock.	Timber Growing.	O. B. Galusha.

[EDITORS PLEASE NOTICE.]

known of students in the industrial studies being diverted into the professions, but that several students studying for the law had decided to enter the agricultural course. "I mention these facts," Gregory said, ". . . not in reply to the senseless charges so often made against us, and which I have learned to disregard as nearly harmless ebullitions of a toothless malice or pitiable delusion, but as evidence of the success of our plans and of the brightening future before us." [32]

Meanwhile, on January 27, 1870, the Northern Illinois Horticultural Society, meeting at Dixon, Illinois, adopted resolutions expressing their thorough disapproval of the policies of the University and calling for a convention of the various agricultural societies to consider "the present state and future prospects of our Industrial Institution, and to make such indications of their wishes as will be a sure guide in attempting their reformation." [33] Among the members of the committee appointed to call a convention was Jonathan Baldwin Turner. When Champaign County was awarded the location of his beloved "industrial university," Turner was convinced that the forces of evil had finally won, and he had lapsed into a morose, unaccustomed silence. His dream had become a reality, but he was no longer a part of it. Events had passed him by, and Gregory had usurped his place as spokesman for the new education in the state. Here, at last, was an opportunity to enter the arena again. [34]

The convention was scheduled to be held at the courthouse in Bloomington on March 2, 1870. "A crisis is upon us," Gregory wrote General Brayman on February twenty-fifth. "The men, the place [Bloomington had been an unsuccessful competitor for the location of the University] and all the signs point to an unfair and hostile conclusion. We shall try to be ready for the onset." [35] On the day of the convention, Gregory, a delegation of the faculty, and a number of prominent citizens from the Twin Cities went to Bloomington. At the earliest possible moment, Gregory

---

[32] *Third Annual Report*, p. 38.
[33] Powell, p. 332.
[34] General Brayman wrote Gregory on February 24, 1870 that "Professor Turner still lives but cannot live without agitation." Gregory Papers, Box 3.
[35] *Ibid.*

obtained the floor and invited all of the delegates to adjourn to Champaign so that they could see for themselves what the University was doing. He even offered them free transportation over the new Indianapolis, Bloomington and Western Railroad.[36] This invitation "evidently disconcerted the convention," but Jonathan Baldwin Turner, never at a loss for words, had an answer. Although he was willing to concede that the delegates could not judge the actual administration of the University without making a trip to Champaign, he saw no reason why they could not discuss "the scope of the organization" as described in the annual trustees' reports. Turner then began reading aloud the list of courses in the *Second Annual Report of the Board of Trustees.* "First," he said, "we find here Chemistry. This you will say is right. Next comes Natural History. This is as it should be. Then follows Agriculture, Mechanical Philosophy, Mathematics, Civil Engineering, and so forth, and this you will say is right. And what comes last? The Languages, just as they should. All this is much better than the old system, and this institution is far in advance of others in those particulars."[37]

Turner's only real criticism of the University was that it did not "allow a boy to go there and study such agricultural or mechanical branch as he may choose without taking everything else in the curriculum. If a man has peculiar faculties for blacksmithing, in God's name, let him be a blacksmith. Metaphysics, what is it? Ten pages will contain the substance of the labors of all the metaphysical fools from Aristotle down. All the new theories are simply changes of words."[38] But the University, Turner said, was

---

[36] C. R. Griggs, the man who was instrumental in obtaining the location of the University at Champaign-Urbana, was president of this railroad.

[37] Based upon an account of the meeting in the *Champaign County Gazette,* March 9, 1870.

[38] Carriel, p. 231. If Turner had read the trustees' report more carefully, he would have discovered that the University accorded the student precisely the freedom for which he was pleading. Under the heading "Departments of Study," the report stated that "on special request, he [the student] may give his whole time to any one department, if the studies and practice in that department will afford him full employment." *Second Annual Report,* p. 4. "Without knowing it," the *Champaign County Gazette* commented, ". . . he made a most effective defense of the plans of the trustees, and we count confidently on Professor Turner as a firm supporter of those plans when he shall give them careful attention."

not entirely to blame for failing "to rise above the other colleges which follow the feudal idea and build up . . . elaborate metaphysical nonsense." The new education was immeasurably more complicated and expensive than the old. "So much so that all the cabinets and apparatus of all the colleges, and all of the high schools and academies west of the mountains, would not make even a respectable outfit for one single first-class university." [39]

Turner talked for over an hour, "much to the gratification of all parties." When he finally sat down, one of the delegates arose and read a paper purporting to prove that the study of all languages, ancient or modern, was immoral. The delegates then voted for a resolution asking the Illinois Constitutional Convention to appropriate adequate funds for industrial education, a committee was appointed to accept Gregory's invitation to visit the University, "examine into the management of the same, and make such report as circumstances shall seem to justify to a future meeting," [40] and the convention closed "in the midst of good feeling."

This committee made its report at the State Fair held in Decatur the following fall. Upon visiting Champaign-Urbana a few days earlier, the committee had found 194 young men and fourteen young women attending the University, each carrying three or more subjects. Fifty students were enrolled in agriculture, fifty-four in mechanics and civil engineering, sixty-five in chemistry, 138 in mathematics, and twenty-three in military tactics. Only twenty students were enrolled in Latin and none in Greek — exactly the number that the committee wished to find in that much-maligned subject. The report was, in effect, a complete vindication of the University. [41] M. L. Dunlap, no longer a trustee, retired in defeat to his orchards near Savoy, [42] and Jonathan

---

[39] Carriel, pp. 229, 233.

[40] Carriel, p. 230.

[41] The committee's sole criticism was that the University farms had not yet attained the "model" condition envisioned by Turner, although, "like patients recovering from smallpox," they were "doing as well as could be expected." Powell, p. 337.

[42] Matthias Dunlap died in 1875, aged sixty, and his son, Henry M. Dunlap (class of 1875) succeeded to the family orchards. As a state senator (from 1892 to 1912, and again from 1916 to 1932), Henry Dunlap assiduously promoted the interests of the University of Illinois in the legislature. In 1911 he secured the passage

Turner became an outspoken champion of the institution he had once deplored. In John Gregory, Turner recognized a kindred spirit — a fellow talker whose oratorical abilities exceeded perhaps even his own — and the two men, so much alike in everything except physical stature, became good friends.

"For the first time," Turner said at the cornerstone-laying of the new University building on September 13, 1872,[43]

> I came to this University last winter to see for myself. I did not find any one of the Professors and Teachers either omniscient or omnipotent; nor yet angels walking the earth with sublime grandeur, with wings at their shoulders, all plumed and ready for the skies. . . . But I found . . . good, honest-hearted, intelligent men, prosecuting a great, arduous, and difficult public work — new in its ends and aims, and untried in its modes and methods — with a patience, a zeal, and a self-devotion worthy of their great cause. . . . This Institution will still need, in the future as in the past, a magnanimous patience within, and a magnanimous forbearance from without its walls; our little and censorious criticisms can neither destroy nor aid it. Thank God, it has already . . . become too big for any such result.[44]

For once, Turner's rhetoric was commensurate with the reality. By ending organized opposition to the University, the report of the Bloomington committee allowed Gregory to concentrate upon the internal problems of the institution itself. The greatest of these problems was the College of Agriculture.

---

of a bill giving the University one mill for each dollar of the assessed valuation of the taxable property in the state. Henry Dunlap died at Savoy, Illinois on January 8, 1938 at the age of eighty-five.

[43] The old Institute building, which was poorly constructed, was partially destroyed by a windstorm on December 30, 1871. The new building, University Hall, was located on the present site of the Illini Union.

[44] *Fourth Annual Report* (1872), pp. 353–354.

FOUR

Manly Miles,
"The First Real Professor
of Agriculture in the Country"

From 1870 to 1875, the College of Agriculture was without a regular professor. During this period, the University resorted to makeshift measures to carry on the agricultural work. Gregory and "various members of the faculty gave assistance, such as it was, in class instruction," E. L. Lawrence, who had succeeded Periam as head farmer, managed the University farms, and Willard Flagg was in charge of crop experiments and the annual course of agricultural lectures. The lectures for 1870, instead of being held only in Champaign, as in 1869, were held for one week each at Rockford, Champaign, and Centralia. "By this change," the trustees' report for 1869–1870 announced, "the northern, central, and southern parts of the State were made more acquainted with, and interested in, the education of the farmer, and the officers and faculty of the University brought in contact with the masses of the people."[1] John Warder again delivered twelve lectures on fruit culture ("the price not to exceed $50 per lecture"), Dr. Heinrich J. Detmers spoke on veterinary science, and Willard

---

[1] *Third Annual Report*, p. 164.

Flagg discussed both rural literature and rural economy. But the "name" speaker at these lectures was Dr. Manly Miles of the Michigan Agricultural College. Often referred to as "the first real professor of agriculture in the country," Miles enjoyed a reputation as an agricultural scientist comparable to that of Lawes and Gilbert in England and Baron von Liebig in Germany.

Miles was born in Homer, New York, in 1826, the grandson of a Revolutionary War soldier and a lineal descendant of Captain Miles Standish. When he was eleven years old, his family moved to a farm near Flint, Michigan. Like Gregory and Burrill, Miles was eager for an education, and there is a story, possibly apocryphal, that he learned geometry by drawing the problems on a shingle, attaching the shingle to a plow-beam, and studying the problems as he plowed. After graduation from Rush Medical College in 1850, Miles practiced medicine for nine years. But he was more interested in the natural sciences than in the healing arts, and in 1859 he was made assistant state geologist in the Michigan department of zoology. The following year, he was appointed professor of zoology and animal physiology at the Michigan Agricultural College. In 1865, he became superintendent of the farm at Lansing and the first "professor of practical agriculture" in the United States.

After the resignation of Willard Bliss, Miles served as "non-resident professor of agriculture" at the Illinois Industrial University. He came to Urbana for the winter term, delivered lectures to the students and at the annual agricultural course,[2] and spent the remainder of the year in Lansing. But this arrangement was far from satisfactory, and since Miles could not be persuaded to give up his position at Michigan, the University decided to "create" its own professor of agriculture. The man selected for this position

---

[2] In 1871, the series of agricultural lectures was held at Champaign, Springfield, and South Pass. The following year, Dixon, Pontiac, Avon, and Pittsfield were the host towns. The lectures for 1873 (or "Farmers' Institutes," as they were called in the trustees' report of that year) were held for three days each at Peoria, Jacksonville, Pana, Greenville, Kankakee, Gilman, and Belvidere. Miles did not speak at this series, but Jonathan Turner lectured upon the "Conservation of Animal Force in Agriculture." The lectures were not held in 1874 because the Board decided "that, in the present condition of the finances of the University, it would be unwise to spend money in this direction. . . ." *Seventh Annual Report*, p. 103.

was Charles W. Silver, one of the brightest members of the class of 1872, the first class graduated from the University. Silver, an assistant in chemistry, studied for a year at the Agricultural School of Halle, Germany, and in 1874, he was appointed an instructor in agricultural chemistry. His appointment lasted only one year. The reasons for Silver's leaving are not known. The trustees' report for 1875–1876 states only that he submitted his resignation on June 9, 1875, and Burrill, with that genteel reticence about discussing unpleasant matters that characterizes the period, said that "personal reasons in this case more than in any other caused the termination of the engagement. . . ."[3]

On the same day that the Board accepted Silver's resignation, Manly Miles was made professor of agriculture. Miles played the academic game of balancing one job offer against another with great adroitness, and upon his "assurance that he was seriously considering the acceptance of offers from other State Institutions,"[4] the University agreed to pay him a double salary ($2,000 a year as professor of agriculture and $1,000 as instructor in agricultural chemistry). It seemed to Gregory and the other members of the Board that they were getting their money's worth. If any man could make the College of Agriculture a success, that man was Manly Miles. "He entered upon service here," Thomas Burrill wrote, "with anticipations . . . of great accomplishments. The perplexing, disappointing, discouraging, and disagreeing condition of things . . . was to come to an end. . . ."[5] Certainly the prospects that greeted Miles were more encouraging than those that had greeted Willard Bliss six years before. Although the University was still subject to sporadic criticism,[6] it was relatively free to pursue its own destiny, and the legislature was more kindly disposed toward it.

Under the provisions of the Morrill Act, Illinois had received land scrip for 480,000 acres (30,000 acres for each of its sixteen

[3] Burrill, "Some Early Inside History and Its Lessons."

[4] *Eighth Report*, (1877), p. 137.

[5] Burrill, "Some Early Inside History and Its Lessons."

[6] As late as 1885, *Western Rural* (in language strikingly reminiscent of M. L. Dunlap) described the University as "a shadow of the Greek and Latin mills," and other farm papers voiced similar sentiments.

members of Congress). Nearly 455,000 acres had been sold at an average price of seventy cents per acre, giving the University a permanent endowment fund of about $319,500. This fund could not be used for erecting buildings, purchasing equipment, or paying salaries, and the income from it, amounting to between $25,000 and $30,000 a year, was barely enough to meet running expenses. "It is certain," Gregory told the Board of Trustees at the November, 1868, meeting, "that the agricultural operations planned here, and expected by the Legislature and the people to be carried out, cannot be sustained by the funds of the University without seriously crippling its proper work of instruction."[7] As a result of Gregory's impassioned plea to the legislature of 1869, the agricultural and horticultural departments received appropriations of $25,000 and $20,000, respectively, for buildings, teams, tools, fencing, drainage tile, trees, seed, and livestock.

The University farms were divided into three "departments" — the stock farm, the experimental farm (including the gardens, nurseries, and orchards), and the ornamental grounds and greenhouses — with a foreman in charge of each.[8] Fences were repaired or rebuilt, two new barns and a greenhouse erected, and nearly five miles of hedges planted. The farms, despite the continued depredations of poachers, were actually showing a profit, and at least a start had been made in field and cattle-feeding experiments under Flagg, Lawrence, B. F. Johnson of Champaign, and H. K. Vickroy, the foreman of the horticultural grounds. In April, 1871, the legislature, in an unprecedented burst of generosity, appropriated $1,750 annually for two years to the horticultural department for "additional seeds, and labor for the forest plantations," and $3,000 annually for two years for agricultural experiments.

To carry on these experiments, Gregory directed the staking out of a series of plots containing one-twentieth of an acre each.

---

[7] *Second Annual Report,* p. 48.

[8] The foremen of the stock and experimental farms were given sixty dollars per month, the use of a house and one cow, and garden vegetables for their families, "provided that they . . . board hands employed on the farm . . . at reasonable rates. . . ." *Fourth Annual Report,* p. 119. Thomas Franks, the English gardener in charge of the ornamental grounds and greenhouses, received seventy-five dollars per month.

One set of plots was devoted to experiments with fertilizers, another to various methods of cultivation, a third to crop rotation, and a fourth to the testing of different varieties of the same grain. But all of these experiments, as Flagg and Lawrence knew, were concerned with the art of agriculture rather than the science.

"It can scarcely be said," Lawrence remarked in his report of his cattle-feeding experiments, "that we have any such thing as agricultural science. . . . Corn and grass fed to cattle will produce beef. Corn fed to hogs will produce pork. But how much of each, and what formula to follow, to give the best results, taking into the account climate, age, breeds, etc., is a thing in a great measure unknown. It is these variations of circumstances and conditions that seem to multiply themselves in every experiment that lie in the way of definite conclusions." [9]

Miles was well aware of "these variations of circumstances and conditions," and at a convention of the agricultural colleges held at Chicago in August, 1871, he had carefully warned would-be experimenters against trying to find out too many things at once. "In the first place," Miles said,

the experiments should be as simple as possible. A large proportion of the experiments made thus far have been of no value, for the reason that too much was attempted. For instance, a person wishing to test the real value of potatoes of different sizes for seed, plants his small potatoes in drills two feet apart, and the large potatoes in rows three feet apart. Here, you see, is a double variation. There was no condition the same, and no chance to compare such experiments, and a very large proportion of experiments have been vitiated in this way. It arises from attempting to determine two things at once, that is, the effect of variation in size of the seed, and the effect of variation in the rows. You have two elements, and you may try experiments as long as you please without any valuable results. It would be better to try one experiment and settle the matter in regard to size, having all the conditions precisely the same, and then take as a separate experiment, one in which the different distances of the rows was the object of the investigation. [10]

---

[9] *Seventh Annual Report*, p. 109.
[10] *Fourth Annual Report*, p. 227.

Miles came to Urbana on July 1, 1875, and immediately set to work. He changed the "internal arrangements" of the barns "to give increased accommodations for animals and secure a greater economy of labor in the care of them,"[11] defined the boundaries of the horticultural grounds and experimental farm, reorganized the stock farm for greater efficiency, and installed a windmill and machinery for grinding feed. "I believe the Board will be gratified with the changes introduced by Mr. Miles," Gregory said at the trustees' meeting in December, 1875. "I feel a new encouragement in my hopes for the final triumph of an elevated and systematic agricultural education."[12] There seemed ample justification for Gregory's hopes. Few men in the United States possessed a more thorough knowledge of agricultural problems than Manly Miles, and his approach to solving these problems was clear-minded and painstaking. "The leading object," Miles said in his report to the

---

[11] *Eighth Report*, p. 143.
[12] *Eighth Report*, p. 150.

Manly Miles, Professor of Agriculture, 1875–1876.

Board of Trustees on December 1, 1875, "should be to add to our knowledge of agricultural facts and principles by a system of accurately conducted experiments. From the very nature of the investigations it is desirable to make, and the precautions required to secure accuracy in the results, it will be readily seen that the necessary expenditures will largely exceed the value of the products of the farm."[13]

Six months later, Miles was no longer professor of agriculture. The reasons for the abrupt termination of his contract in June of 1876 are almost as obscure as those for Silver's departure. "Alas!" Thomas Burrill wrote. "The transplantation did not succeed. Perhaps the roots were down too deep to permit the severance; perhaps the new soil was ill suited to development of this second foot-hold."[14] Although this statement reflects Burrill's interest in horticulture, it is not very informative. The unpleasant truth is that Gregory and Miles did not get along well together. Miles, who was described by one of his contemporaries as "a bit lacking . . . in academic polish," was used to having his ideas venerated and his orders obeyed. The meager financial resources of the University, reduced even further by the panic of 1873, acted as a brake on his plans.[15] And Gregory, despite his belief in the importance of agricultural experiments, could not quite rid himself of the idea that somehow the University farms should be made to show a monetary profit. The differences between the two men reached a climax in a disagreement over the curriculum of the University as well as that of the College of Agriculture itself. The Board and faculty agreed with Gregory, and Miles left

---

[13] *Eighth Report*, p. 153.

[14] Burrill, "Some Early Inside History and Its Lessons."

[15] Miles seems to have experienced a similar difficulty with finances at the Michigan Agricultural College. In an adulatory essay printed shortly after Miles's death in 1899, the anonymous author states that "Dr. Miles was not appreciated by the politicians, or by all of the Board of Agriculture, or even by the public at large. Unkind and captious criticisms were made of his work, and it was found fault with on economical grounds, as if its prime purpose had been to make money. He therefore resigned his position in 1875, and accepted the professorship of agriculture in the Illinois State University [Illinois Industrial University]." "Sketch of Manly Miles," *Appleton's Popular Science Monthly* LIV (April, 1899): 839.

Urbana.[16] "The internal dissensions and troubles of the University," Gregory wrote in his diary, ". . . disappeared with the removal of a troublesome professor."[17]

Until the summer of 1876, the University and the College of Agriculture shared a common history and (at least in the minds of many people) a common destiny. "The Agricultural College," Gregory told the Board on June 6, 1876, "has always been placed at the front . . . in every catalogue, circular and advertisement which we have issued, from the outset. You have expended more money on this college than upon any other, more teachers have been employed in it than in any other, and every effort has been made to recommend it to the people at large, and to the students who have come here for study. The efforts made for it have been hearty, earnest and unceasing."[18] The culmination of these efforts had been the hiring of Manly Miles, the best-known professor of agriculture in the United States. When Miles failed to achieve the success expected of him, the University no longer felt the same degree of responsibility toward the College of Agriculture. Everything had been tried; everything had failed.

The "removal" of Miles marks a divergence between the histories as well as the destinies of the College of Agriculture and the University proper. Neither Gregory nor Selim Hobart Peabody,[19] his successor as regent in 1881, seems to have been aware of this divergence, and they continued to emphasize the "agricultural interests" in speeches, advertisements in farm papers, and in the University catalogs. But the divergence was nonetheless real. The University, its fate no longer inextricably bound up with

[16] The Committee on Course of Studies reported to the Board on June 6, 1876 that "After examining the courses submitted by the Regent and Professor of Agriculture and consulting the Regent and members of the Faculty, we approved and presented the course submitted by the Regent. . . ." *Eighth Report,* p. 184.

[17] Allene Gregory, *John Milton Gregory: A Biography,* p. 282.

[18] *Eighth Report,* p. 182.

[19] Peabody was born at Rockingham, Vermont, in 1829 and was graduated from the University of Vermont in 1852. After teaching high school for many years, he joined the Illinois Industrial University staff as professor of mechanical engineering and physics in 1878. Peabody served as acting regent of the University from September, 1880 to March, 1881, and as regent until September, 1891. He died in St. Louis, Missouri at the age of seventy-three.

the success or failure of the College of Agriculture, was at last free to follow a path of its own. This path was by no means a smooth one (for many years the University remained small, despised, and desperately poor), but it led inexorably — though at times almost imperceptibly — uphill, and the University enrollment increased from 274 students in 1876–1877 to more than 2,200 students at the beginning of the new century.

The path followed by the College of Agriculture during the next three decades led just as inexorably — and most perceptibly — downhill. Enrollment in agriculture decreased from an average of forty-nine students during the 1870's (with a high of seventy-nine students in 1871–1872, nearly one-fifth of the entire student body) to an average of ten students through the 1880's and 1890's. And the situation at Illinois was not essentially different from that at most of the other land-grant universities. Only three students were enrolled in agriculture at Cornell in 1874, the University of Wisconsin graduated one agricultural student before 1880, and there were no agricultural students at the University of Min-

Selim Hobart Peabody,
Regent of the University,
1880–1891.

nesota until 1899.[20] Throughout the country the dream of agricultural education — the dream that had started so bravely — had become a prolonged, vaguely shameful nightmare.

There were many reasons for deterioration of the dream. Gregory pointed out that the agricultural schools of Europe had existed for a quarter of a century before they proved their worth, and that "the entire traditional feeling of this country is in favor of the old classical college education."[21] College was generally regarded as a means of entering the learned professions, especially law and medicine. The idea that a professor could teach agriculture was considered ridiculous, and the popular conception of the professor of agriculture as a kind of maladroit mountebank persisted throughout the century. To a large extent this conception was justified. It was an accepted fact that chemistry and physics laboratories required extensive apparatus and materials, but no one, not even the professor of agriculture himself, seemed to realize that agricultural education required equivalent facilities. The professor of agriculture's equipment consisted of a lecture room with a desk, several chairs or settees, and a few charts or pictures upon the walls; his laboratory was the barn and the fields.

"There was," as Thomas Burrill wrote, "woeful want of understanding in regard to what one man could and could not do."[22] Agriculture was conceived of as a single department, and the professor of agriculture had to develop and teach all of the subjects suggested by his title. In the absence of a science of agriculture, his teaching was necessarily empirical. He could teach only the art of agriculture — the "how" rather than the "why" of farming. Since the art varied with the locality, soil, and climate, the professor and his students disagreed as to what constituted proper practice. After the first flush of enthusiasm, disillusionment set in. One can imagine the reactions of a student, fresh from courses in chemistry and physics with well-equipped laboratories and well-prepared professors, to the following classroom "lecture" on corn culture:

---

[20] Edward Danforth Eddy, Jr., *Colleges For Our Land and Time* (New York, 1957), p. 67.

[21] *Eighth Report*, p. 182.

[22] Burrill, "Some Early Inside History and Its Lessons."

" 'Now, we are going to raise a crop of corn on this field. Of course we will have to plow it first, and this is the way to plow it.' There wasn't much discussion . . . on this point, but when we came to cutting the corn and putting it in the shock, there was a big discussion as to whether we should tie two hills together across where four hills come, or all four of them. Here discussion waxed hot. There was some discussion about cultivation, because the people who lived on clay land had learned to cultivate the land differently than those who lived on sandy land." [23]

The public had been led to expect too much too soon. It was widely believed, for example, that chemical analysis of a soil would infallibly indicate the crops that would succeed on that soil. The so-called "agricultural scientists," like partially informed people in every field, were overconfident, and when their emphatic statements did not find support in actual practice, agricultural science itself was discredited. The few textbooks were of foreign origin or filled with material from foreign sources. There was no body of tested knowledge derived from purely American experience. And the farmer himself was not convinced of the value of an agricultural education for his son. As late as 1891, a speaker at a farmers' institute in New York assured his audience that profitable farming was the result of "natural ability rather than . . . scholarship." A well-trained agricultural chemist might fail as a farmer, he said, while a man who could not "state wherein a nitrate differs from a phosphate" might be very successful. As a final argument for the uselessness of an education, the speaker mentioned that he had known a successful dairy farmer who was illiterate. [24]

"We have often had farmers' sons sent here for the express purpose of educating them for some other calling or profession," Gregory said; "and cases have not been wanting in which parents have opposed their sons pursuing the study of Agriculture even when the boys strongly preferred it." [25] But many farmers' sons

---

[23] Eugene Davenport, address delivered at an open meeting of Phi Upsilon Omicron, April 19, 1932. Typed manuscript in College of Agriculture files.

[24] Ross, *Democracy's College*, p. 119.

[25] John M. Gregory, "Agricultural Graduates," *Illini*, March, 1875.

(and in the early days of the University they comprised about seventy-five percent of the student body) did not want to study agriculture. "Although the University has been . . . extensively advertised in the various agricultural papers of the country," the *Illini* commented in 1885, "the increase of the number of students in the college of agriculture is not what it should be. There are many persons who sneer at the idea of anyone's taking a course in agriculture."[26] Five years later, the *Illini* reproduced a hypothetical conversation between two students:

> Mr. Bullywag — "How de do."
> New Student —"How are you?"
> Mr. Bullywag — "New student, eh?"
> New Student — "Yes sir, I have just entered the University and think I shall like it."
> Mr. Bullywag — "That so? What course you takin'?"
> New Student — "I expect to take the agricultural course."
> Mr. Bullywag — (with a smile of heavenly superiority) "Oh! You takin' agriculture? I'm takin' engineering."[27]

In contrast to agriculture, engineering, or "mechanic arts," as it was first called, was an almost unqualified success from the beginning. The great development of manufacturing, railroading, mining, irrigation, and road and bridge building after the Civil War created a demand for engineers that far outran the supply. In the 1880's a graduate in engineering could command a salary between $100 and $175 a month, while the agricultural graduate was fortunate if he could obtain a position as a farmhand at $25 a month. As a result, the only young men who studied agriculture were those who planned to take over their father's farms — and there were not many of these.

Many of the courses in agriculture were "merely nominal," and to make the curriculum stretch over four years, it was necessary to add a liberal dosage of courses from the other colleges. The first year at Illinois was devoted to vegetable physiology, chemistry, elements of agriculture, and elements of horticulture; the second to soils, fertilizers, botany, and entomology; the third to

---

26 *Illini*, October 5, 1885.
27 *Illini*, October 25, 1890.

agricultural engineering and architecture, animal husbandry, and landscape gardening; the fourth to rural economy, meteorology and physical geography, the history of agriculture, and rural law. None of these courses offered practical facts about agriculture, and many Illinois farmers, even those who had been kindly disposed toward the "new education," rapidly lost interest in it. Their apathy turned into active dislike when the University was renamed the University of Illinois in 1885. The reasons for changing the name and for the farmers' hostility to that change were centered in the word "industrial." "There seems to be a common impression," the *Illini* remarked in 1881, "that the boys come here to learn to hoe corn and potatoes and cabbage, and the girls, to wash dishes and churn and make butter. Potatoes and corn are good in their places, and even cabbage heads are sometimes useful, but they are not much needed here. This is an Industrial University, but not in the above sense. It is industrial in that it teaches the application of science to the common industries of life."[28]

The original name, "Illinois Industrial University," was meant to define both the intention and scope of the new institution. But the name no longer adequately described a University designed to meet the broad educational needs of an entire state, and the word "industrial" had acquired a pejorative meaning that led to misunderstanding of and contempt for the University's work. In England, reform schools were euphemistically called "industrial schools," and this connotation of "industrial" had crossed the ocean. Many former students of the University were asked why they had been "sent up," and both Gregory and Peabody received many letters from well-meaning but badly informed people asking them to take care of orphaned or obstreperous children. The following letters are typical:

> I have a boy, I am at a loss to know the best course to pursue. I cannot see him go down to ruin and not make some effort to save him. He is not a hardened boy nor past redemption by any means, but he needs wholesome discipline just now. He is sixteen years old, a child of many prayers. I want him to learn a trade that will fit him for usefulness.

---

28 *Illini*, February 2, 1881.

.   .   .

I lately lost a wife who left me six children the eldest eleven years of age, the youngest two. As yours is an Industrial University, I desire to commit them all now into your hands, that they may be suitably trained to "Learning and Labor." [29]

The agricultural press unanimously lamented the change in name, the *Iowa Homestead* suggesting that, in deference to the sensibilities of the "dude students," the University motto should be "Lavender and Lily White" instead of "Learning and Labor." The farmers equated "industrial" with "agricultural," and they had believed that the University, for better or worse, belonged to them. Now they felt that they had been betrayed, and an old farmer and former trustee told one of the professors that he "gave the University up — the industrial classes had lost it." [30]

---

[29] *Illini*, January 28, 1884.
[30] Nevins, *Illinois*, p. 121.

FIVE

George E. Morrow, The Voice
Crying in the Wilderness

O N SEPTEMBER 13, 1876, George Espy Morrow was appointed
to succeed Manly Miles as professor of agriculture. In appointing
Morrow, the Board seemed intent upon getting a man as little like
Miles as possible. If Miles's temperament could be characterized
in medieval terms as "choleric," Morrow's was unreservedly "sanguine." No one, not even his enemies if he had had any, would
have described George Morrow as "troublesome."

Morrow was born on an Ohio farm on October 19, 1840. The
youngest of nine children, he was the family favorite, and since
he was "sprightly in manner, quick to learn, and kind and affable
in his associations with everybody, his life was pleasant to himself
and a joy to his companions." Four months after the Civil War
broke out, Morrow enlisted as a private in the Union Army. But
not even his war experiences could dampen his optimism. "I saw
much happiness and in every way fared better than I expected,"
he wrote to one of his sisters a year after his enlistment. "Today
I believe I am better physically, mentally and morally than I was
one year ago, and if it be God's will for me to spend another year
in the army, I expect to live better, more happily and more use-
fully than in the last." [1]

---

[1] Thomas J. Burrill, "George Espy Morrow," c. April, 1900, Botany Correspondence, Record Series 15/4/1, Box 1. Hereafter cited as Botany Correspondence.

Morrow was wounded in the arm at Perryville, Kentucky, in October of 1862. Six months later, he was discharged from the army because of ill health. In the fall of 1865, Morrow enrolled with his brother Josiah in the University of Michigan law school. Although George soon discovered that he was not interested in the law and did not seem to have studied much, he had little difficulty in completing the course. According to his contemporaries, Morrow had a remarkable memory, and even after a long period of time he could recite a lecture almost verbatim.

While Morrow was in law school, a new agricultural journal, *Western Rural,* began publication in Detroit. As a soldier, Morrow had written accounts of battles for the *Cincinnati Gazette* and *New York Daily Tribune,* and he contracted with the publisher of *Western Rural* to write an article each week for the sum of eight dollars. Since Morrow wrote with facility and had a deep interest in all aspects of agriculture, he found this work much more congenial than the study of law. Upon his graduation from law school in the spring of 1866, Morrow became assistant editor of *Western Rural.* The paper moved its offices to Chicago in the early winter of 1867, and the following spring, Morrow made his first trip to Champaign-Urbana to report the inaugural exercises of the University.

Late in 1868, Morrow and his eldest brother, David, purchased the *Western Farmer* of Madison, Wisconsin, and George became editor-in-chief. But the paper got into financial difficulties, partly as a result of the depression of 1873–1874. David died in 1875, and Morrow went back to work for *Western Rural,* taking with him the unexpired subscription list of *Western Farmer.* He voluntarily transferred the debts accumulated by *Western Farmer* to his own account, and worked for many years to pay off these debts.

In the spring of 1875, Regent Gregory arranged for a course of agricultural lectures to be given to the senior class of the University. This course, which was meant to partially compensate for the absence of a professor of agriculture, was presented by certain faculty members and several outside speakers. One of these outside speakers was George Morrow. During his ten years as an agricultural journalist, Morrow had established a reputation as "one of the foremost workers in the new agriculture. . . ."[2] In Wisconsin, he had been a leader in the Northwestern Dairymen's Association and Wisconsin State Horticultural Society, and secretary of the National Agricultural Congress.[3] His work with these organizations had developed his abilities as a public speaker, and he was known as one of the most effective writers and lecturers upon agricultural subjects in the United States.

In March, 1876, Morrow was appointed professor of practical agriculture at the Iowa Agricultural College (now Iowa State University). Six months later, he was offered the professorship of agriculture at the Illinois Industrial University. Morrow accepted the Illinois appointment with alacrity. Like Gregory, Morrow believed that agricultural education would thrive best in a broad intellectual environment, and during his visit the previous spring,

---

[2] *Ibid.*

[3] In recognition of his contributions to Wisconsin agriculture, the University of Wisconsin awarded Morrow an honorary Master of Arts degree in 1882.

George Espy Morrow,
Professor of Agriculture,
1876–1894, and first Dean of
the College of Agriculture,
1878–1894.

he had been impressed by the fact that Gregory had laid the foundations for a true university rather than simply an agricultural college.

Morrow arrived at Urbana in early December of 1876 "with high expectations of worthy achievements."[4] The prospects seemed bright enough, even for a man much less sanguine than Morrow. Fourteen buildings now rose from the flat prairie — the original Institute building, the large "main building" (later to be named University Hall), a combination mechanical laboratory and drill hall, two men's dormitories, an astronomical observatory, a veterinary clinic, three farmhouses, two greenhouses, and two barns. And the prairie itself was no longer barren — Thomas Burrill and his assistants had transformed it into a verdant island of orchards, gardens, nurseries, and forest plantations.

The College of Agriculture seemed to share in this general felicity. The stock barn was equipped with the latest conveniences, including a steam boiler for preparing feed and an engine to furnish power for grinding, threshing, and cutting, and the College possessed "a fine stock . . . of neat cattle, embracing Short Horns, Herefords, Devons, Ayrshires, and Jerseys,"[5] as well as several breeds of sheep and swine. Experiments were being conducted in fertilization, crop rotation, cultivation, steer-feeding, and soil treatment, and the farms, under the competent management of E. L. Lawrence, the head farmer, were showing a modest profit. But the decline of the College of Agriculture had already begun. During the previous year (from September, 1875 to September, 1876) the enrollment in agriculture had decreased nearly fifty percent — from forty-nine students to twenty-six students. In the fall of 1877, only seventeen students enrolled in the College.

Morrow was convinced that he could increase the enrollment in agriculture by making people aware of the "nature and value of the education" offered by the College. The Board of Trustees

---

[4] Burrill, "George Espy Morrow." Morrow's appointment actually started on January 1, 1877. Since the term at Iowa Agricultural College had ended, however, Morrow came to Urbana almost a month early, and was present at a faculty meeting on December 8, 1876.

[5] *Seventh Annual Report*, p. 24.

shared his conviction, and at their September, 1877, meeting, they passed two resolutions designed to make use of Morrow's talents as a writer and speaker. The first resolution authorized Morrow to prepare "a special circular in relation to the agricultural department, and to advertise the department in the leading agricultural papers of the state."[6] The second provided for the reactivation of the annual course of agricultural lectures or "Farmers' Institutes."[7] Morrow threw himself into the task of advertising the College among the farmers and their sons with a "devotion . . . limitless in time and boundless in endeavor."[8] He tramped the state from Chicago to Cairo, speaking to as many as ten farmers' meetings a month, preaching the cause of agricultural education whenever and wherever he could find an audience.

On February 18, 1878, the senior professor of each college was appointed dean of that college. As the senior — and indeed only — professor of agriculture, Morrow became the first dean of the College of Agriculture. But the honor was an empty one. Enrollment in the College remained small, and attendance at the Farmers' Institutes was almost uniformly poor. Realizing the need to improve "his instructions," Morrow obtained a leave of absence for the summer of 1879 "to make some observations . . . upon the agriculture of Great Britain and France."[9] While he was in England, he visited the famous experimental farm of John Bennet Lawes at Rothamsted, where continuous agricultural experiments had been carried on for more than forty years.

This visit made a deep impression upon Morrow, and when he returned to Urbana, he laid out a series of experimental plots modeled on the Rothamsted plan. These are the oldest experi-

---

[6] *Ninth Report* (1878), p. 44.

[7] Part of the $3,000 appropriated by the legislature of 1871 for agricultural experiments was used to defray the expenses of lecturers at the Farmers' Institutes of 1872 and 1873. This appropriation was not renewed, and no lectures were held in 1874 because of lack of money. In 1875, the Board of Trustees authorized Willard Flagg "to arrange for Farmers' Institutes, without expense to the University. . . ." The Institutes do not seem to have been held in 1876 and 1877.

[8] Burrill, "George Espy Morrow."

[9] *Tenth Report* (1881), p. 172. According to Burrill, Morrow paid all of his expenses on this trip by writing articles for the agricultural papers.

mental plots in the United States. The year for their establishment is variously given as 1876 and 1879, but there is no real discrepancy between these two dates. Although the "Morrow Plots" were started in 1879 and officially approved in 1880,[10] early bulletins of the Illinois Agricultural Experiment Station, as well as records of the Department of Agronomy, clearly indicate that three of the original ten half-acre plots were planted by Manly Miles in 1876.[11] Morrow simply incorporated Miles's plots with

---

[10] On March 9, 1880, Morrow asked the Board of Trustees for approval "of what is designed to be a long continued experiment to show the effect of rotation of crops, contrasted with continuous corn growing — with and without manuring, and also the effect of clover and grass in a rotation. A commencement was made last year (1879), and we are fortunate in having a piece of land more than usually well adapted for such a test." *Tenth Report*, p. 232.

[11] In 1903, all but three of the Morrow Plots were discontinued. The following year, each of these plots was reduced to about one-fifth of an acre and divided in half, making a total of six one-tenth-acre plots. This is the size of the plots today. The two north plots (started by Miles) have grown corn continuously since 1876, the two middle plots have been cropped to a corn-oats rotation, and the two south plots have been cropped to a corn-oats-red clover rotation since 1901. Be-

Morrow Plots, oldest continuous experimental plots in the United States, in 1897. The astronomy observatory at the upper left was completed the preceding year.

his own. It is ironic, when one considers the abilities of the two men, that Morrow, the writer and lecturer, rather than Miles, the scientist, was responsible for developing the first continuous experiment in crop rotation in this country. But the establishment of the plots that bear his name was Morrow's only significant contribution to agricultural science.

While Morrow was in Europe, Henry A. Weber and Melville A. Scovell, the professors of chemistry and agricultural chemistry, began a series of experiments on the extraction of sugar from sorghum cane. A pamphlet describing these experiments and fifty pounds of the sugar exhibited at a Chicago fair attracted a great deal of interest. Morrow considered this new method of manufacturing sugar "the most promising new branch of agriculture for our State," and at his request, the Board of Trustees appropriated money to continue the experiments. On December 14, 1880, Regent Selim Peabody reported to the trustees that the sorghum experiments "have been crowned with notable success, and they must result in great benefit to this industry, and reflect credit upon the University." [12] A year later, Peabody was dismayed to learn that Weber and Scovell had patented part or all (the records are not clear on this point) of the new processes for making sugar. He protested "kindly but earnestly" that the two professors were not entitled to the products of work carried out under the authority of the Board of Trustees, and with money appropriated from the funds of the University. But Weber and Scovell remained adamant, and the trustees first condemned them, and in June, 1882, following the recommendations of the governor and attorney general, discharged them from the University. [13]

Not all of the experiments carried on under the direction of

fore 1901, the rotation was corn-corn-oats-meadow-meadow-meadow. For detailed information, see "The Morrow Plots," University of Illinois College of Agriculture Circular 777 (rev. July, 1960). In June, 1968, the Morrow Plots were designated a National Historic Landmark by Secretary of the Interior Stewart Udall.

[12] *Eleventh Report* (1882), p. 162.

[13] Weber and Scovell set up a sugar-manufacturing plant in Champaign-Urbana, but the plant soon failed. In 1885, Scovell became director of the newly founded Kentucky Agricultural Experiment Station. He served in this position until his death in 1912.

Morrow ended so inauspiciously, but as early as 1880, he complained to the Board about "the lack of sufficient time and money at the disposal of those in charge of the work."[14] These twin lacks were to harass Morrow throughout his career with the College. Between 1877 and 1894, the year Morrow left the University, the state appropriations to the College, exclusive of salaries, totaled only $6,000. All of this money was used to construct new buildings or repair old ones, and more than a third of it was assigned to horticulture rather than to agriculture proper. No state money was appropriated for agricultural experiments from 1873 to the beginning of the new century.[15]

Although the trustees paid lip-service to the need for agricultural experimentation, most of them (W. C. Flagg was a notable exception) were primarily interested in increasing the profits from the University farms. These farms had been considered a mixed blessing almost from the beginning. "The management of the University farms and gardens will always be one of the most difficult parts of our enterprise," Gregory warned the trustees on March 8, 1870. "It will require constant vigilance from all who have the control of them to prevent their becoming a very onerous charge on the funds of the University."[16] A committee appointed to investigate the "condition and management" of these farms reported that only 600 acres (the 200-acre experimental farm and the 410-acre stock farm) would be needed for the University work, and recommended that the 400-acre Griggs farm be sold "as soon as it can be done wisely."[17] By the time Morrow came to Urbana as professor of agriculture, all but 160 acres of the Griggs farm had been sold and the remainder leased.

Shortly after Morrow's return from Europe in the fall of 1879,

---

[14] *Tenth Report*, p. 47.

[15] In 1873, the legislature appropriated $1,500 for agricultural experiments. A request for $3,000 for experiments was turned down by the legislature in 1875, and the profits from the University farms for that year (slightly over $2,000) were given to the College.

[16] *Third Annual Report*, p. 45.

[17] *First Annual Report*, p. 68. "It is believed by some," Gregory said, "that in the end the two hundred acres of the experimental farms and gardens will be as much land as the University will need to retain for its immediate use." *Third Annual Report*, p. 45.

the Board appointed a three-man Farm Committee "to super-intend all matters pertaining to the general and experimental farms . . . , and to recommend . . . such improvements as they shall deem important."[18] On December 15, 1880, the Farm Committee decided, for reasons of economy, to dispense with the services of E. L. Lawrence, the head farmer, and "place the farms of the University under the control and management of the Professor of Agriculture, to be conducted by him with the advice of the Regent and Farm Committee."[19] This decision was an unfortunate one. Although Morrow was deeply interested in agriculture, he knew little about the techniques of actual farming, and he seems to have been devoid of manual skills. One of his contemporaries said, with unnecessary bluntness, perhaps, but

---

[18] *Tenth Report*, p. 218.

[19] *Eleventh Report*, p. 171. For his services as superintendent of the farms, Morrow was allowed to live rent-free in the house formerly occupied by Lawrence, and (beginning September 1, 1881) was paid an additional $200 per year.

Thomas Forsythe Hunt, Morrow's assistant from 1881 to 1888. Hunt later became Dean of Agriculture at The Ohio State University, Pennsylvania State College, and the University of California.

with more than a modicum of truth, that Morrow "could not drive a nail, much less hang a door screen." [20]

In March, 1881, Morrow hired an agriculture student, Thomas Forsythe Hunt, "as Foreman and Assistant on the Farm, to commence work at the close of the present term." Hunt, whose father owned a tavern between Rockford and Freeport, Illinois, had grown up in the same area in which two of the University's most prominent scientists, Thomas Burrill and Stephen Forbes, spent their boyhoods. After graduation from Freeport High School, Hunt enrolled at the Illinois Industrial University in 1880. When he became Morrow's assistant, he was nineteen years old. "Mr. Hunt is young," Morrow admitted to the Board of Trustees, "but is well informed and experienced in practical farm work. As he is desirous of continuing his practical studies in general and experimental work he is well content to receive barely more than the wages of a common laborer, or $30 per month." [21]

The relationship between Morrow and Hunt was a close one, each man respecting the other for those qualities that he himself did not possess. Morrow recognized Hunt's abilities as a farmer, teacher, and scientist, and Hunt considered Morrow "one of God's noblemen, an inspiring teacher, a devoted and true friend." But his reverence for Morrow did not obscure his awareness of the latter's shortcomings. "Professor Morrow," he said, "had neither the time nor the taste for systematic detail necessary to the highest research work." [22] Morrow was well aware of his own limitations as a farmer and scientist, and whenever he could, he left the farms and his dwindling classes in the hands of his brilliant young assistant, and escaped to the only kind of work he really liked — lecturing to farmers. He was a commanding figure on the speakers' platform. The tall, lean body, the sharply regular features, the pale eyes flashing above the full beard, the strong, clear voice — all of these awakened the admiration and

---

[20] Eugene Davenport to A. S. Alexander, October 25, 1933. Typed copy of letter in College of Agriculture files.

[21] *Eleventh Report*, p. 176. This is the same T. F. Hunt who later became dean of agriculture at The Ohio State University, Pennsylvania State College, and the University of California, as well as one of the pioneers in agricultural economics.

[22] *Illinois Agriculturist* V (1901): 10, 16.

respect of his audiences. Eschewing the florid rhetoric employed with so much relish by Gregory and Turner, Morrow "spoke in simple but dignified language, which . . . while perfectly understood by the most unlettered, appealed no less strongly to the most learned."[23]

"As our agriculture advances," Morrow said, "and it becomes more difficult for those without a capital either of money or of skill and knowledge to succeed as they have succeeded in the past, . . . the money payment for thorough training will be more certain. This change is going on faster than we are apt to think. Within the next quarter of a century, there is to be a greater change in our agriculture than in any former equal time, and he is wise who prepares himself to take advantage of this."[24] Morrow had a remarkably clear — indeed almost clairvoyant — conception of the future of agriculture, but his words touched neither his listeners' minds nor their hearts. Like his celebrated antecedent, John the Baptist, Morrow was a "voice crying in the wilderness."

"Does the interest taken in the Institute warrant its continuance?" the *Illini* asked rhetorically on February 10, 1883. "If these meetings were properly appreciated the lecture room would be too small for the listeners. At the last session a majority of the audience was composed of students and city people. Farmers were a scarce article and three-fourths of the supply was furnished by this county."[25] At the Board of Trustees' meeting the following month, Morrow reluctantly admitted that the attendance of farmers "was not encouraging," and that there was not "a present large demand for the instruction we are able to give here in technical agricultural subjects."[26]

In an attempt to increase the demand for agricultural education, the College offered a one-year "Farmers' Course" and a three-week series of lectures in agriculture, horticulture, and veterinary medicine immediately preceding the Institute meetings. But the annual enrollment in agriculture averaged fewer than sixteen students during Morrow's first six years with the University. "Our

---

[23] *Ibid.*, p. 14.
[24] George E. Morrow, "Agricultural Education," *Illini*, February, 1877.
[25] *Illini*, February 10, 1883.
[26] *Twelfth Report* (1885), p. 185.

love for the farmer is unbounded," the *Illini* stated succintly,
"but we don't believe in offering him drink when he isn't
thirsty."[27] Despite these setbacks, Morrow was not discouraged.
He maintained, with dogged optimism, that the farmer was not
thirsty for agricultural knowledge because he had not been told
often enough that he should be thirsty. "Nine years' experience
and pretty wide observation," he said in 1885, "convince me that,
for some little time to come, 'Mahomet must go to the mountain.'"[28] That year the enrollment in agriculture dropped to an
unprecedented low of six students; it was not to rise above thirteen students during any of Morrow's ten remaining years as dean
of the College of Agriculture.

"It has been the habit of certain agricultural writers," Regent
Selim Peabody said in 1886, "to refer to the schools of agriculture of . . . Michigan, Kansas and Mississippi as unqualifiedly
successful, and to count those of other states, including Illinois,
as without question failures." There was, Peabody pointed out,
"a semblance of truth and a large portion of error in both these
statements." The so-called "successful" agricultural colleges were
not colleges in the true sense at all. They were simply schools of
general science that offered work of high school rather than college grade, and that reported all of their students as "agricultural."
Illinois, on the other hand, was a true university of "specialized
science." Only the students registered in the College of Agriculture were counted as "agricultural," and the curriculum contained "an amount of actual technical agriculture . . . larger than
is found in any institution in the west. . . ."[29] Peabody's arguments were generally valid, but the point is an academic one.
The failure of the colleges of agriculture during the nineteenth
century was national in scope. The relative "success" of any
particular college was comparable to George Bernard Shaw's description of the least homely sister as the family beauty. "Agricultural education . . . was poor and halting because it was
before its time," Thomas Burrill said. "The inertia of the ages

[27] *Illini*, February 24, 1883.
[28] *Illinois Agriculturist* V (1901): 9.
[29] *Thirteenth Report* (1887), p. 135.

was upon it. There was no self-generation of power. A second birth was needed . . . a birth of the spirit and of the understanding."[30]

This second birth took place on March 2, 1887, when President Grover Cleveland signed the Hatch Act into law. The Hatch Act, named for Representative William H. Hatch of Missouri, who introduced the bill in Congress, established agricultural experiment stations at each of the land-grant universities. Under the provisions of this act, the federal government appropriated $15,000 annually to each station "for the necessary expenses of conducting investigations and experiments and distributing the results." George W. Atherton, one of the members of the original faculty of the University, and president of Pennsylvania State College when the Hatch Act was passed, was one of the most active participants in the movement to establish experiment stations.[31] But neither Atherton nor any other man was primarily responsible for that movement. The Hatch Act, like the Morrill Land-Grant Act a quarter of a century earlier, was the culmination of a general desire to improve agriculture. It is perhaps worth noting, however, that Illinois, the first state to propose a national system of land-grant universities, was also the first to propose the establishment of agricultural experiment stations at these universities. This proposal was made by Willard C. Flagg, corresponding secretary of the University, at a convention of the land-grant colleges held at Chicago in August, 1871.[32]

The Illinois Agricultural Experiment Station was established in the spring of 1888 under a nine-member Board of Direction appointed by the trustees. The Board consisted of Peabody as president, Morrow as agriculturist, Burrill as botanist and horti-

---

[30] Burrill, "Some Early Inside History and Its Lessons."

[31] In his introduction to Powell's *Semi-Centennial History of the University of Illinois,* Edmund James, president of the University from 1904 to 1920, states that Atherton was "perhaps of more influence in the passage of the Hatch Act . . . than any other man." But James, who made similarly extravagant claims for Jonathan Baldwin Turner as "the father of the Land Grant Act," is open to the charge of chauvinism.

[32] *Fourth Annual Report,* p. 343. Unfortunately, Flagg, who was one of the genuine leaders in agricultural education during the nineteenth century, did not live to see the realization of his dream. He died in 1878 at the age of forty-nine.

culturist, William McMurtrie as chemist, two trustees, and representatives of the State Board of Agriculture, the State Horticultural Society, and the State Dairymen's Association. The station
was considered a department of the University and was housed
on the top floor of the chemistry building.[33] A staff and secretary
were appointed, and about $3,500 of the initial Hatch funds were
spent for "books and periodicals relating to agriculture, horticulture, botany, and chemistry."[34]

During its first two years of operation, the station carried out
over one hundred experiments in field crops, cattle feeding, dairying and horticulture, and published eleven bulletins. By the close
of Peabody's administration in 1891, experiments were being conducted at Mattoon, Odin, Flora, and Farina, Illinois, and more than
a score of bulletins had been published. These early experiments
were crude and superficial by present standards, but they captured the farmer's imagination in a way that the College of
Agriculture had never succeeded in doing. Farmers wanted immediate answers to their most pressing problems; the experiment
station did its best to provide those answers. The station had
neither the time nor the staff for conducting fundamental research, and "the emphasis was on today's best action, not tomor-
row's lasting solution."[35] The station's work in testing varieties
of wheat and corn, feeding livestock, and controlling diseases and
insects demonstrated that the application of science to agriculture could increase the farmer's income. For the first time, the
benefits of "book farming" were brought home to the farmer in
terms he could understand. Although a few farmers continued to
plant according to the phases of the moon, an increasing number
of them "began to feel that the college man must know something

<hr />

[33] The chemistry building, now named Harker Hall, was completed in 1878.
It is the second oldest building on the University campus.
[34] The experiment station staff included Thomas F. Hunt as assistant agriculturist, George W. McCluer, an 1884 graduate of the University, as assistant horticulturist, and John A. Miller as assistant chemist. William L. Pillsbury of
Springfield, a native New Englander and Harvard graduate, was appointed secretary, a position that entailed keeping the Station accounts, handling the correspondence, and supervising the editing and printing of all bulletins and reports.
In 1893, Pillsbury was made registrar of the University.
[35] Eddy, p. 95.

not generally known and had ways of finding out things not possessed by the man between the corn rows or in the feed lot." [36]

If the station seemed to be prospering, the College of Agriculture itself most emphatically was not. Only six students were registered in the College in 1889, seven in 1890, eight in 1891, and thirteen in 1892. Even these figures are misleading; most of the students originally enrolled in agriculture either quit the University after one or two terms or transferred to one of the other colleges. Between 1889 and 1892, only three students received degrees in agriculture, and during two of these years (1890 and 1892), there were no graduates from the College. "The experience here," Morrow said in September, 1892, ". . . seems to make it certain . . . that for the present it is to short courses that we must look for any considerable number of students of agriculture." [37] At Morrow's suggestion, the trustees approved a twelve-week farmers' short course during the winter term. The course was free, and the only requirement for admission was that an applicant must be at least eighteen years old. Thomas Burrill, the acting regent, said cautiously that the short course "ought to attract a good attendance, . . . but former failures of like efforts to reach considerable numbers of young farmers make it hazardous to predict great success this time." [38] Burrill's circumspection was justified. Of a total University enrollment of 709 students in March, 1893, only twenty-five students were registered in the winter short course.

The trustees, after long conditioning, had learned to accept the low enrollment in agriculture as an unpleasant fact of life; it was less easy for them to accept the steadily decreasing profits from the University farms. Under the management of E. L. Lawrence,

---

[36] Davenport, "Early Trials of the Agricultural Colleges and Experiment Stations." Thomas Burrill wrote a farmer in 1905 that "It is too late in the day to plant potatoes either in the new or the old of the moon, better plant them in the soil when that is ready. The moon has no more influence upon the crop than does a trip to Europe." Thomas J. Burrill to W. Holden, May 18, 1905, Agriculture Experiment Station, Botanist's Correspondence, 1901–1910, Record Series 8/2/11, Box 1.

[37] *Seventeenth Report* (1894), p. 22.

[38] *Seventeenth Report*, p. 59. Burrill served as acting regent from September 1, 1891, when Peabody resigned as regent, until August 1, 1894, when Andrew Sloan Draper became president of the University (the title of the head of the University was changed from regent to president in 1894).

the head farmer from 1871 to 1880, the farms had shown an average balance of about $2,000 a year. During the thirteen years that Morrow supervised the farms, the average annual balance was less than $600, and in some years, the expenditures actually exceeded the profits by several hundred dollars. The fault was not entirely Morrow's. In 1880, Morrow, with the blessings of the Farm Committee, had purchased a herd of purebred cattle for feeding experiments. The market for fine cattle fell off sharply a few years later, and it remained in a depressed state for nearly a decade.

Between December 1, 1891, and the same date the following year, the inventory of the stock farm was reduced from $13,165.00 to $9,835.00. "This remarkable reduction," Morrow explained to the Board of Trustees in December, 1892, "is due to the valuation put upon the cattle, which are now estimated at their value with-

"Mumford House." Constructed in 1870 as a model farmhouse, it is the oldest building on the University campus. The house was occupied successively by three deans of the College of Agriculture — George E. Morrow, Eugene Davenport, and Herbert W. Mumford.

out reference to their purity of breeding. . . . The 70 head of pure bred cattle, now valued at $2,450, would properly have been appraised at from $7,000 to $10,000 eight years ago." The only solution, Morrow believed, was "to reduce the herd to small proportions as rapidly as may be." [39] Three months later, Morrow reported to the Board that the cattle numbers had been "reduced somewhat," and that there was "some promise of improvement in prices." But the farm profits for the three-month period ending in March, 1893, were only $382.17.

Morrow had an evangelistic faith in the importance of agricultural education, but the discrepancy between the magnitude of his efforts and the visible results of those efforts was discouraging. "He often went from his office at the close of the day with a heavy heart," Thomas Burrill wrote. "His tired brain too frequently suggested: What is the use? Why prolong the contest?" [40] After Peabody's resignation as regent in 1891, Morrow was appointed president of the experiment station's Board of Direction. Two years later, he was made chairman of the University exhibits at the World's Columbian Exposition in Chicago, and in 1894, he served as president of the Association of American Agricultural Colleges and Experiment Stations.[41] In addition to managing the farms singlehandedly (after 1888, Thomas Hunt was largely occupied with the work of the experiment station),[42] Morrow supervised the station experiments, lectured to farm organizations, wrote for the agricultural press, and taught two classes daily. Under this regimen, Morrow's health, which had been poor since the Civil War, almost broke down completely.

"In view of the increasing pressure of other duties laid upon

---

[39] *Seventeenth Report*, p. 64.

[40] Burrill, "Some Early Inside History and Its Lessons."

[41] The Association was founded in 1887. Its name was changed to the Association of Land-Grant Colleges in 1919, and the words "and Universities" were added in 1926. In 1955 the organization became the American Association of Land-Grant Colleges and State Universities, and in January, 1965, the National Association of State Universities and Land-Grant Colleges.

[42] Hunt resigned as assistant agriculturist of the station in January, 1891, to become professor of agriculture at Pennsylvania State College. In his report to the trustees in March of that year, Regent Peabody described Hunt as "a person of unusual adaptability to the work required of him in the Station, patient, methodical, exact, and full of resources. . . ." *Sixteenth Report* (1892), p. 64.

me," he said in his report to the Board of Trustees on March 8, 1893, "I respectfully request that some changes be made in regard to the direct management, at least, of what is known as the stock farm. Especially for the present year, I shall not be able to give the attention to the care of this farm it should receive." Morrow then suggested that the stock farm be rented or put under the management of a competent foreman. He also asked that part of the livestock and equipment of the stock farm, the "hay, straw and grain in the experiment station barn," and the experimental farm itself be turned over to the experiment station. The trustees referred Morrow's report to the Farm Committee. This Committee decided to donate the experimental farm to the station and "to rent so much of the stock farm as is not needed for Experiment Station purposes and to sell off the cattle and other animals as fast as is practicable." The stock farm was rented to "a reliable farmer," part of the livestock was given to the experiment station, and the remainder was sold. On March 6, 1894, Morrow reported to the Board that "all the stock belonging to the university has been sold, with the exception of two young mares and two colts."[43] Except on paper, the College of Agriculture no longer existed. One week later, Morrow submitted his resignation as professor of agriculture, to take effect on September 1, 1894.

On March 24, 1894, Thomas Burrill wrote Jonathan Periam, then editor of *Prairie Farmer*, that Morrow "sent in his resignation because of the criticisms coming from one man. At least only one man has spoken out in such terms as to make the professor feel that in justice to himself and other members of the Board [of Direction] he must offer his resignation. . . . The charge is that the agricultural department is not sustaining itself, and especially because the farm [stock farm] has not paid much and there has not been worked up some such thing as the dairy school in Wisconsin. There is also a disposition on the part of the same party to belittle the results of the experiment station. . . ." The man referred to in Burrill's letter was Napoleon B. Morrison of Odin, Illinois, a member of the experiment station's Board of Direction

---

[43] All quotations from *Seventeenth Report*, pp. 82, 86, 223.

and chairman of the Farm Committee of the Board of Trustees. In early March, the Board of Direction decided to sell off steers used for feeding experiments and buy cows for dairy tests. Morrison made a motion that all the members of the stock-feeding and dairy committees except Morrow be appointed to carry out the change. "This was done in such a manner," Burrill told Periam, "that it was soon seen to have been an intended expression of 'want of confidence'. . . . The professor so interpreted it." [44]

At a special meeting on August 1, 1894, the Board of Trustees voted to accept Morrow's resignation. The agricultural press reacted to this news with shocked dismay. "He is a man of the people, intelligent, hard-working, and thoroughly honest," *The Breeder's Gazette* wrote of Morrow on August eighth. "His work has been of a creditable and valuable character and his influence has been distinctly felt for good. . . . He is a man of fine character, and young men studying under him could not fail to catch his spirit of earnest devotion to the cause of advanced agriculture and higher and broader life on the farm. In the agricultural development of the State his works will follow him."

On October 1, 1894, the members of the faculty unanimously adopted a series of resolutions expressing their affection for Morrow and their regret at losing his "cheering presence and able assistance." [45] Morrow replied several weeks later, thanking the faculty

---

[44] Thomas J. Burrill to Jonathan Periam, March 24, 1894, Andrew S. Draper Letterbooks, Record Series 2/4/3, Box 1. Hereafter cited as Draper Letterbooks. Although Morrison was the most vociferous of Morrow's critics, he was by no means the only one. Another trustee who strongly favored Morrow's resigning was James E. Armstrong of Chicago. "We regret spending so much of the people's money in trying to show a handful of boys what they can better learn on some good farm," Armstrong said. "In accepting Professor Morrow's resignation and electing a trained scientist, I believe we will decide the future course for the University." James E. Armstrong to Andrew Sloan Draper, April 27, 1894, Andrew S. Draper Personal Letters, 1892–1913, Record Series 2/4/5, Book 1.

[45] "Faculty Record," October 1, 1894, Record Series 4/1/1. "He has endeared himself to us all," the resolutions read in part, "by his constant, sympathetic, and intelligent consideration for those about him; by his sterling qualities of manhood; and by his high conception of all that is noblest and best in life. He has proved himself to be not only a man of unblemished and exalted character, but a professional worker of widely acknowledged ability, winning high honor and esteem among co-laborers at home and abroad, earning for himself a distinguished name

for this too generous expression of personal regard and appreciation for my work for the University. . . . Better than anyone else
those long connected with it, at least, know how far what I was
able to accomplish fell short of my hopes and wishes. Their kind
words are another evidence we may hope to be judged not by
what we accomplish, but by what we try to do. . . . More important by far than is the personal welfare of any of us, is the
prosperity of the University — great already and to be vastly
greater in the future. . . . Whatever of regret I feel at severing
my official relations with the University will be more than counterbalanced if, as I hope, one is secured who can better discharge
the duties which were laid upon me.[46]

During Morrow's tenure as dean, conditions in the College
could scarcely have been worse, and unquestionably he was in
"the wrong place at the wrong time." But the failure of the College during the 1880's and 1890's was so complete and unequivo-
cal that we must ask whether Morrow might not also have
been "the wrong man." The answer must be a qualified yes. Morrow is an oddly appealing figure in the history of the College of
Agriculture, and it is not the intention here to detract from his
considerable virtues. As a man, he was exemplary — a true "Christian gentleman" — and if he lacked the clarity of mind and indefatigable patience of Thomas Burrill, he was certainly the latter's
superior in breadth of understanding (a result, perhaps, of Morrow's Civil War experiences).

It is true that the initial enthusiasm for agricultural education
had already given way to apathy or open hostility when Morrow
arrived at the University.[47] It is equally true, as Regent Selim
Peabody pointed out in 1882, "that our Illinois farmers cultivate

---

in scientific and practical agriculture, extending the usefulness and advancing
the reputation of the University, and promoting the best interests of large classes
of our countrymen."

[46] "Faculty Record," November 6, 1894, Record Series 4/1/1.

[47] "The very men from whom we must look for opposition," Professor W. W.
Daniels of the University of Wisconsin said prophetically in 1871, ". . . are precisely those men for whom we are laboring. They are looking for some immediate
results. They expect, as I heard a farmer say, the kind of education from the agricultural colleges which will enable a man to take up a handful of soil and feel of
it, and tell you all it is composed of." *Fourth Annual Report*, p. 244.

a soil so fertile, so sure to honor their drafts, that they cannot abuse it so badly but it will give them always a support, and generally bountiful profits. These farmers cannot realize that agricultural education can increase their profits, or improve their situation."[48] But neither Peabody nor Morrow seems to have been aware that many farmers refused to drink at the fountain of agricultural knowledge simply because that fountain was too feeble to slake their thirst.

Morrow interpreted literally the statement in the Morrill Act that "the leading object shall be . . . to teach such branches of learning as are related to agriculture and the mechanic arts. . . ." He believed that "experimentation is, by law, made subordinate to teaching what is known," and that his first duty was to his classes, "however small they might be."[49] Morrow's mistake was in trying to cure the symptoms rather than the disease itself. He failed to realize that in the absence of a genuine agricultural science — of a body of proved principles from which the farmer could adjust his practice to suit the conditions on his own farm — the subject of agriculture was unteachable. Morrow's "failure," if it can be called that, was a failure of the imagination. The only hope for the future of agricultural education lay in the development of an agricultural science. During Morrow's career as dean of the College of Agriculture, the most significant contributions to that science were made by Thomas Jonathan Burrill and Stephen Alfred Forbes.[50]

---

[48] *Eleventh Report*, p. 61.

[49] *Illinois Agriculturist* III (1901): 10.

[50] Burrill held a joint appointment as professor of botany in the College of Natural Science (the name was changed to College of Science in 1892) and professor of horticulture in the College of Agriculture. Forbes was a member of the College of Science throughout his career with the University.

SIX

Thomas Burrill and Stephen Forbes, Pioneers in Agricultural Science

O N SEPTEMBER 13, 1894, Thomas Burrill succeeded Morrow as president of the Board of Direction of the agricultural experiment station. At that time, Burrill was also serving as dean of the general faculty, professor of botany and horticulture, and botanist for the State Laboratory of Natural History and the Office of the State Entomologist. He had just completed a three-year term as acting regent of the University. The contrast between the careers of Burrill and Morrow is a dramatic one. When Morrow left Urbana, the College to which he had devoted much of his adult life was an attenuated, abysmal failure. Almost from the beginning, the career of Thomas Burrill was brilliantly successful.

Burrill's academic background in science was meager even for his time (his only formal college training was as an undergraduate at Illinois State Normal, where he had one term of botany to six terms of mathematics), and he never worked in another man's laboratory or had the guidance of an experienced scientist.[1] But like Charles Darwin, whom he also resembled in physical appear-

---

[1] All of Burrill's graduate degrees were honorary. He received an M.A. degree from Northwestern University in 1876, a Ph.D. degree from the University of Chicago in 1881, and an LL.D. degree from Northwestern in 1893. The University of Illinois "set its seal of approval upon his immeasurable services" by awarding him an LL.D. upon his retirement in June, 1912.

ance (both men had similarly prominent brows and large, roughly modeled features), Burrill was a keen observer of nature and a painstaking, thorough, and infinitely patient investigator. Early in his career he became interested in cryptogamic botany (the study of plants that do not produce flowers or seeds, such as ferns and mosses), and he taught himself both French and German so that he could keep up with the latest developments in this field.

In the late 1860s, botany was taught at American universities through lectures and demonstrations. At a few universities a kind of pseudolaboratory study had sprung up, and students occasionally dissected flowers or were "accorded the high privilege of a glimpse through the treasured microscope of the professor." At the annual meeting of the Board of Trustees in March, 1869, Burrill received permission to take five of his students on a "botanical excursion" of Illinois during six weeks of the summer vacation. The group traveled the length of the state collecting specimens, and they returned to Champaign with a large number of plants (both named and unnamed), birds, reptiles, insects, mammals, fossils, fresh-water shells, and minerals.[2] The following semester, Burrill initiated genuine laboratory work in botany by furnishing his students with actual specimens of healthy and diseased plants. By 1874, Burrill was teaching plant pathology in his botany and horticulture courses (probably the first formal instruction in this subject in the United States), and by 1877, he had provided his students with microscopes.

During his forty-four years with the University, Burrill published over 200 papers. These papers cover an amazingly broad range of subjects, including bitter rot of apples, ear rot of corn, blackberry and raspberry rust, potato scab, peach "yellows," fermentation of silage, river pollution, microorganisms of soil, parasitic fungi (the first complete treatise on this subject in English), orchard cultivation, and forest plantations.[3] But Burrill's most im-

---

[2] The Board of Trustees appropriated $300 for the expenses of this trip (the vote was seventeen members for the appropriation and three against). Burrill spent $200 of this money, and Gregory placated the trustees by telling them that "much of the expense incurred was for outfit, which will be valuable for future service." *Third Annual Report*, p. 40.

[3] Between 1870 and 1915, Burrill contributed eighty-two papers to the Illinois

portant scientific work was with the fire blight of pear trees. In the 1860s and 1870s, fire blight was taking a terrible toll of American orchards. Many theories were advanced as to the cause of blight, including thunder, electricity, climate, soil, insects, and fungi, but none of these was substantiated by satisfactory proof. It is not known exactly when Burrill began his investigations of fire blight, but he first reported on the subject to the Board of Trustees on September 13, 1876.

> Some investigations were made during the summer upon the so-called "fire blight," revealing, perhaps, nothing new, but enough to stimulate further labor. The sap of the newly blighted limbs, especially in the young cells between the wood and bark swarms with minute living particles, visible only with high powers of the microscope. . . . The motion of these particles is a sort of uneasy vibration, as if they were attached by a short thread and were endeavoring to escape. . . . No indications are yet observed as to the origin of the . . . vibrating particles. When this is determined, something definite, and it may be, very important, will be accomplished.[4]

At a meeting of the Illinois State Horticultural Society held at Ipava in December, 1877, Burrill reported that "a thickish, brownish, sticky matter exudes from affected limbs, sometimes so abundant as to run down the surface or drop from the tree. . . . The sticky, half-fluid substance thus exuding is entirely made up of . . . minute oscillating particles. The origin of these has not yet been certainly traced. . . ."[5] The following year, at a meeting of the Horticultural Society held in Springfield, Burrill tentatively identified these moving particles as bacteria. "If we remove the bark of a newly-affected limb and place a little of the mucilaginous fluid from the browned tissue under our microscope, the field is seen to be alive with moving atoms known in a general way

State Horticultural Society, missing only the years 1891 and 1893. For a complete listing of these papers and of Burrill's circulars and bulletins printed by the University of Illinois Agricultural Experiment Station, see *Transactions* n.s., L (1917): 85–97.

[4] *Eighth Report*, pp. 199–200.
[5] *Transactions* XI (1877): 114.

as *bacteria*. Sometimes a thick, brownish fluid oozes from the bark of dying limbs and spreads over the outside or falls in drops. This is apparently made up of the living things, myriads of them to be seen at once. A particle of this viscous fluid introduced upon the point of a knife into the bark of a healthy tree is in many cases followed by blight of the part. . . ." But Burrill was cautious about stating unequivocally that the disease was caused by bacteria.

> If we look once more to the affected branch, we find the disease spreads more or less rapidly from the point of origin, and upon examination the moving microscopic things are discovered in advance of the discolored portions of the tissues. . . . Does it not seem plausible that they cause the subsequently-apparent change? It does to me, but this is the extent of my own faith; we should not say the conclusion is reached and the cause of the difficulty definitely ascertained. So far as I know the idea is an entirely new one — that *bacteria* cause disease in plants — though abundantly proved in the case of animals.[6]

For the next two years, Burrill's investigations of fire blight came to a virtual standstill. "Other interests . . . so engaged my

---

[6] *Transactions* XII (1878): 80.

Thomas Burrill in his laboratory about 1882.

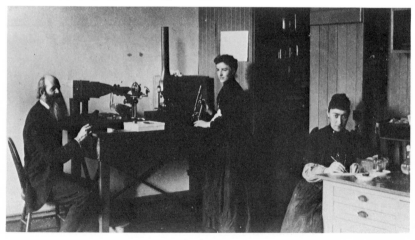

attention and time," he said, "that this was not so fully done as I heartily wished it had been. . . ."[7] These "other interests" included teaching all of the courses in botany and horticulture, supervising the 130-acre horticultural grounds,[8] and serving as dean of the College of Natural Science, vice-president, and (while Gregory was in Europe during the summer and fall of 1879) acting regent of the University. But in June, 1880, a particularly destructive outbreak of fire blight in Urbana again focused Burrill's attention on the disease. "After establishing, by thorough researches, the presence of *bacteria* in the tissues of dying limbs and the scarred blotches upon the trunks of apple and pear trees," he said in his report to the Horticultural Society in December, 1880, "I began . . . a series of experiments with the view of determining whether these organisms were really active agents in the observed changes, or simply accompanying other causes of destruction."[9]

During July and August of 1880, Burrill performed sixty-nine precise experiments on pear, quince, and apple trees. Using a sharp-pointed knife or needle, he inserted tiny pieces of bark or minute doses of the fluid from blight-infected trees beneath the bark of healthy trees. Sixty-three percent of the inoculated pear trees contracted fire blight, while less than three percent of

[7] *Transactions* XIV (1880): 157.

[8] The horticultural grounds comprised an orchard planted in 1869 containing over 1,000 varieties of apple trees as well as many varieties of pear trees, grapes, and small fruits; vegetable gardens; nurseries; an aboretum "in which all hardy, indigenous and exotic trees are planted as fast as they can be secured"; a thirteen-acre forest plantation (now "Illini Grove") planted in the spring of 1871; and the "ornamental grounds" — twenty acres of flower beds and lawn surrounding the University buildings. Burrill's love for trees was almost mystical. "Were I a heathen," he said, "not knowing the true God, I would not worship the sun, as did the Peruvians, nor the stars, as did the nations of the East, but would bow in adoration to the trees and herbs of the field." *Second Annual Report*, p. 320.

[9] *Transactions* XIV (1880): 157. Burrill presented the results of these experiments at the American Association for the Advancement of Science meeting in Boston on August 25, 1880, in his report to the regent of the University on August 30, 1880, and at the Warsaw, Illinois, meeting of the State Horticultural Society on December 16, 1880. See *American Association for the Advancement of Science Proceedings*, Section B, XXIX (1880): 583–597; *Tenth Report*, pp. 62–84; and *Transactions* XIV (1880): 157–167. All of these papers contain essentially the same information.

the trees that were not inoculated (one out of thirty-seven) became diseased.

> When it is remembered, that these trees were as nearly identical in kind and condition as it was, or ever is, possible to select, growing very near each other in the same soil, subject to the same treatment except in regard to the inoculations, the case seems to be settled, and an answer to our question obtained. The slight wounds made by the process of inoculation cannot be charged with the results, for similar wounds were made with a clean needle, and these rapidly healed without further injury. *The introduction of the virus introduced the cause of the disease, and the potency of the virus was quite positively due to the living bacteria.*[10]

Most American botanists accepted Burrill's findings, but the Europeans, especially the Germans (who claimed that bacteria could not live in the acid sap of plants) strongly doubted the validity of his work. On December 18, 1883, three years after he had first described his experiments, Burrill pointed out to the State Horticultural Society at a meeting in Bloomington that no one had disproved his conclusions or produced evidence that anything besides bacteria caused fire blight. "Still," he said, "there are many who doubt the 'bacteria theory,' as they choose to call it, and others, some of whom ought to know better, still openly assert that nothing is known of the cause of this disease." Despite the disbelief of the European botanists, Burrill refused to qualify his original conclusions. "The direct or immediate cause of the disease," he told the Society, ". . . is a specific, named, and described, living organism belonging among the bacteria, and which can be invariably found in the blighting tissues as surely as bees can be found in hives containing honeycomb. . . ."[11]

Since the pure-culture medium had not yet been discovered, Burrill was unable to furnish final proof of his findings. But this proof was to arrive two years later. In 1885, J. C. Arthur isolated

---

[10] *Tenth Report*, p. 69. Burrill used the word "virus" in a general sense to indicate the infective agent. This meaning of virus is to be differentiated from its more restricted contemporary meaning.

[11] *Transactions* XVII (1883): 46–47.

the bacterium (which Burrill had named *Micrococcus amylovorus*) in a pure culture, injected this culture into healthy trees, and produced fire blight. Burrill's vindication was complete. Working alone between teaching and administrative chores in "this field of darkness, or at best of dim half-lights and perplexed gropings," [12] Burrill had succeeded where scores of more highly educated men had failed. And he had done much more than discover the cause of fire blight. By demonstrating that living organisms cause disease in plants as well as in animals, he had created the wholly new science of bacterial plant pathology.

When a man dies, especially if he has made a positive contribution to the world, his friends invariably invest him with many virtues that he simply did not possess; Thomas Burrill was no exception to this rule. But the force and unanimity of the praise for Burrill, not only at the time of his death but throughout his long life, indicate that he was an extraordinarily good man. He was not, of course, the paragon of virtue described by his friends, [13] and to pretend that he had no faults is to do a disservice to his true character and achievements. Burrill was narrowly moral (often interrupting classroom lectures to inveigh against the evils of alcohol); he conducted his business affairs with a penuriousness oddly at variance with his professed Christianity; and he was not above condemning a man on merely hearsay evidence. [14] But these fail-

---

[12] Erwin F. Smith, "In Memoriam Thomas J. Burrill," *Journal of Bacteriology* I (May, 1916): 269. The darkness was literal as well as figurative. Burrill worked by kerosene lamp (Edison developed the incandescent electric light in 1879) during most of these experiments, and he invented a heliostat for his microscope to give him a stronger source of light.

[13] One of these friends said that Burrill was "the greatest interpreter of the character of Christ." Another rather ineptly described him as "biologically speaking. . . . a monster of goodness." Rev. James C. Baker, "The Funeral Sermon," *Alumni Quarterly and Fortnightly Notes* I (May 1, 1916): 334.

[14] In January of 1900, Burrill wrote letters to President Draper and to several faculty members protesting the possible rehiring of a football coach because the man had reportedly frequented Champaign saloons. "His history here was enough to condemn him for all time," Burrill wrote. "To win on the athletic field by such a compromise with immorality would be worse than a thousand failures in honorable contest." A few weeks later, Burrill wrote George Huff, the University athletic director, that he had made "a mistake *as to the man*. . . . The error came about in misplacing the date in connection with other occurrences here." January 2 and 27, 1900, Botany Correspondence.

ings were largely the failings of his time, and the narrowness of Burrill's beliefs was counterbalanced by a liberality of spirit that inspired the affection of everyone who knew the man. Burrill loaned money to students from his own meager savings, often without expectation of repayment; he was willing to talk to students or to his fellow faculty members at any hour of the day or night and for almost any length of time; and he protested what he termed the "striking down" of George Morrow when it was certainly impolitic to rise to the latter's defense.

Shortly after Burrill's death on April 14, 1916, Edmund Janes James, president of the University from 1904 to 1920, said that "in the quality of his work he ranks with the great scientists of his generation, and if it had not been for his devotion to his teaching, to his administrative work, to his duties as a citzen, he would doubtless have been distinguished for the quantity of his work as well as the quality." [15] It is fruitless, however, to speculate about what Burrill might have done if he had been an entirely different kind of man. The great scientist, like the great artist, is obsessed with his work. He will sacrifice his leisure, his secondary pleasures, even his family and friends to its demands, and he is ruthless in dealing with anyone or anything that interferes with it. But Thomas Burrill devoted most of his life to teaching and university administration, turning aside, as his friend Stephen Alfred Forbes said, "into what seemed to him the path of his duty, with no shadow of hesitation or appearance of regret. . . ." [16]

Burrill and Forbes came from strikingly similar backgrounds. Both men were sons of poverty-stricken farmers, both grew up in Stephenson County, and both received only fragmentary formal training in science. Forbes, five years Burrill's junior, was born near Silver Creek, Illinois, on May 29, 1844. He went to the district school until he was fourteen, studied at home for two years under an older brother (who taught him both French and Ital-

---

[15] Edmund J. James, "The President's Tribute," *Alumni Quarterly and Fortnightly Notes* I (May 1, 1916): 337. Burrill died of a microbial infection — pneumonia — eleven days before his seventy-seventh birthday. He was buried in Woodlawn Cemetery at Urbana, Illinois.

[16] Stephen A. Forbes, "An Appreciation," *Ibid.*, p. 337.

ian), and attended Beloit Academy briefly in 1860. When the Civil War broke out the following year, Stephen enlisted as a private in the Seventh Illinois Cavalry. He rose rapidly through the ranks, becoming an orderly sergeant at eighteen, a lieutenant at nineteen, and a captain when he was twenty years old. In 1862, Forbes was captured near Corinth, Mississippi, and spent four months in Confederate prisons before he was exchanged. During his imprisonment, he learned Greek from a grammar that his captors permitted him to buy at Mobile, Alabama. Later, between battles, he taught himself Spanish.

Forbes participated in twenty-two military engagements, including Colonel Benjamin Grierson's daring raid into Mississippi

Stephen Alfred Forbes as a Civil War soldier.

in 1863.[17] Except for scurvy and malaria contracted when he was a prisoner, however, he came out of the war unscathed. Speaking of his war experiences many years later, Forbes said, "Those of us who survived the Civil War in good health and strength, with morals unstained and minds still alert, have had no final cause to regret what seemed at the time the complete wreckage of our plans of life. To us war was not hell, but at worst a kind of purgatory, from whose flames we emerged with much of the dross burned out of our characters and a fair chance still left to each of us to win our proper place in the life of the world."[18]

After his discharge from the army in 1865, Forbes entered Rush Medical College in Chicago, but because of lack of money and "certain psychological difficulties revolving around surgery without anaesthesia," he never finished the course. While teaching school in southern Illinois, he became interested in natural history, especially botany, and in the fall of 1870, he published two papers dealing with the plant life and topography of Union and Jackson Counties in the *American Entomologist and Botanist*. These papers, like the hundreds of others Forbes was to publish during the succeeding sixty years, were written with a felicity of style rare in scientific literature, and they led directly to his appointment as curator of the Museum of the Natural History Society at Normal, Illinois, in 1872.

As curator, Forbes greatly increased the Museum collections, especially in zoology and cryptogamic botany, and introduced the natural sciences into the curriculum of the Illinois public schools. He sent duplicate specimens to the schools, organized high school and college associations of natural history, and wrote articles about the study and teaching of the biological sciences. To stimulate public interest in these sciences, Forbes accepted an appointment as instructor of zoology at Illinois State Normal in 1875. The following year, he founded the Museum *Bulletin* [19]

---

[17] See D. Alexander Brown, *Grierson's Raid* (Urbana, 1954) for a detailed account of this raid and Forbes's part in it.

[18] Stephen A. Forbes, "War as an Education, *The Illinois* III (October, 1911): 9–10.

[19] The *Bulletin of the Illinois Museum of Natural History* became the *Bulletin of the State Laboratory of Natural History* in 1877, and the *Bulletin of the Illinois*

and published his "List of Illinois Crustacea" in its first issue. This paper, still the most comprehensive work on the lower crustacea of the state, established Forbes as one of the leading students of aquatic biology. When the Museum was reorganized as the State Laboratory of Natural History in 1877, Forbes was made its director, and that year he brought out another important pioneer study — "The Food of Birds." In 1878, he published papers on "The Food of Illinois Fishes" and "The Breeding Habits of Corixa" (an aquatic insect).

Forbes did little further work with insects until his appointment as state entomologist in 1882, but during his first year in this position, he published two papers on chinch bugs and a paper on "The Regulative Actions of Birds Upon Insect Oscillations." In 1884, Indiana University awarded Forbes a Ph.D. "by thesis and examination" even though he did not have a bachelor's degree.[20] On January 1, 1885, Forbes came to the University of Illinois as professor of zoology and entomology, bringing with him the Office of State Entomologist. Shortly afterwards, by action of the legislature, the State Laboratory of Natural History was also transferred to the University.[21]

When Forbes joined the University staff, he had already established a reputation as a naturalist that extended far beyond the borders of Illinois, and in 1886, he was elected president of the Entomological Club of Harvard College and received a first-class medal from the *Societé d'Acclimatation de France* for his scientific publications. That year, Forbes brought out the first volume

---

Natural History Survey in July, 1917. Since late 1932 it has been known as the *Illinois Natural History Survey Bulletin.*

[20] Forbes's paper on "The Regulative Actions of Birds Upon Insect Oscillations" served as his Ph.D. thesis.

[21] Forbes was professor of zoology and entomology from 1885 to 1909 and professor of entomology only from 1909 until his retirement from the University in 1921. The acquisitions of the State Laboratory of Natural History brought to the University about 75,000 specimens, including 13,500 fungi, 300 bird skins, 11,700 fishes, 1,400 reptiles and amphibians 3,700 mollusks, and 42,000 mounted insects. The State Laboratory occupied three rooms in the basement of University Hall, and the Entomologist's Office was located in a room on the first floor of the building. In the spring of 1893, the State Laboratory was moved to the new Natural History Building, where it occupied five rooms on the first floor and two in the basement.

of the natural history survey of the state, covering ornithology as far as the water birds, and the first volume of the *Bulletin* to be published after the State Laboratory was transferred to the University. This volume contained papers by Forbes on fishes and contagious diseases of insects and a 115-page treatise on Illinois fungus by Thomas Burrill.

Although Forbes and Burrill shared similar backgrounds and a mutual interest in cryptogamic botany, they differed widely in temperament and character. As a teacher and as a writer, Forbes expressed himself with facility and precision, and his descriptions of new species of insects, fishes, and crustaceans are marvelously exact. Burrill spoke slowly and hesitantly, with more concern for the details of the science he was teaching than for the larger implications of that science, and in writing scientific papers, he often paced his office for as long as an hour, searching (sometimes vainly) for the precise word to describe a disease or fungus.

Forbes himself suggested the essential difference between the two men when he said of Burrill that "it took something of a gale to blow his inner fires up into full flame."[22] Forbes's own inner fires were always burning brightly. Tall and muscular, with an erect carriage, bristling moustache, and fierce eyebrows, Forbes was above all a man of action, and "at the height of his powers his course through the Natural History Building could be traced by the slamming of the doors behind him."[23] Although Forbes hated manual labor (he once said that, for him, it would be like "hitching a race-horse to a dump cart"), he loved physical exercise, and he walked, ran, rowed, swam, golfed, roller-skated, swung Indian clubs, rode horseback, and bicycled with ferocious zest.[24] Since Forbes required only about five hours' sleep, he spent

---

[22] Stephen A. Forbes, "Thomas Jonathan Burrill," *Alumni Quarterly and Fortnightly Notes* I (July 15, 1916): 410.

[23] Ernest Browning Forbes, "Stephen Alfred Forbes — His Ancestry, Education and Character," *In Memoriam Stephen Alfred Forbes, 1844–1930* (Urbana, 1930), p. 11. Ernest Forbes's remarkably objective account of his father's life and character was a valuable source of information.

[24] Forbes was introduced to the automobile late in life, and, according to his son, "he drove to the accompaniment of his intensely concentrated thinking, without knowing that he failed to give the job his full attention." *Ibid.*, p. 12. Anna C. Glover, publications editor of the College of Agriculture from 1915 to 1954, was

most of the night reading in bed. His reading tastes were broad, embracing philosophy, psychology, pedagogy, genetics, and scientific theory and method. For relaxation, he "devoured quantities of French fiction," and he loved the poetry of Robert Browning. He was also fond of the theater and music, and enjoyed playing the organ.

Forbes never lost the habit of command he had acquired during the Civil War, and he expected his orders to be carried out with military precision. To those who did not know him well, he seemed aloof and even brusque, but his reserve masked an inherent shyness and a deep interest in his fellowmen. A self-proclaimed agnostic,[25] Forbes believed that man was the victim

---

once a reluctant passenger in Forbes's automobile. When she protested about his fast driving, Forbes proudly announced that he had been the hardest rider in his cavalry company during the Civil War.

[25] In 1923, Forbes wrote "I was, and still am, a rationalist and an agnostic, for whom what is known as faith is merely assumption, often practically necessary, since in active life one must very often act as if he believed what he does not and cannot really know, but unexcusable in purely theoretical matters." He later drew

Stephen Forbes about 1920.

95

of forces beyond his control. This naturalistic view of life, which he shared with his contemporaries Clarence Darrow and Theodore Dreiser, was compassionate. Since man was the product of his heredity and environment and could not do otherwise than he did, Forbes pitied and forgave him.

During his more than half a century of service to his native state and its university, Forbes achieved an international reputation as a scientist. His published papers, numbering over 400, deal with aquatic biology, ornithology, insect pathology (he seems to have been the first man to propose controlling insects by means of their contagious diseases), and economic entomology. The statistical methods Forbes devised for determining the distribution of bird species are still used today, and his studies of the food of birds and fishes have become classics in biological literature. Despite its amazing diversity, all of Forbes's scientific work reflects his intense interest in what has become known as the science of ecology (the relations between organisms and their environment). Forbes himself seemed largely unconscious of this interest in his early papers, but in an address given before the Peoria Scientific Association in 1887 (subsequently printed under the title "The Lake as a Microcosm"), he spoke of "the impossibility of studying completely any form out of relation to the other forms; the necessity for taking a comprehensive survey of the whole as a condition to a satisfactory understanding of any part."[26]

This ecological point of view, which Forbes developed two decades before ecology was conceived of as an offspring of the biological sciences, dominated his work on insects, as well as his investigations of birds and fishes. "Economic entomology is, in fact," he said, "a special division of ecology. It has to do with the relations of insects to the welfare of man. It is the science of the

---

a line through the words "and still am," and wrote above them "as a younger man." Ernest Forbes said that "this change was dictated by a growing hope that there is more to life than a scientist knows, or can know. At this time he [i.e., Stephen Forbes] was much attracted by the beauty and comfort of the orthodox beliefs of his childhood, which he had lost during his scientific career." Ibid., pp. 10–11. The Unitarian Church of Urbana was organized in Forbes's home.

[26] Stephen A. Forbes, "The Lake as a Microcosm," Bulletin of the Natural History Survey XV (November, 1925): 537.

interactions, direct and indirect, between man on the one hand and insects on the other, in so far as these interactions affect human welfare. The welfare of man is the primary study, and entomology comes into the field only in a secondary way."[27] As state entomologist, Forbes published eighteen biennial reports dealing with Illinois insects and methods of combating their attacks.[28] These reports are distinguished for their combination of sound scientific research and the application of this research to the problems of the farmer and horticulturist. Forbes believed that entomology should be used to improve the lives of the people, and he had little patience with "pure" scientists. "There are entomologists," he said, "whom any trace of humanistic values in their entomology seemingly repels almost like a taint of disease or decay. They remind one of the famous English mathematician who is reported to have said that he thanked his God every day on his bended knees that he had never discovered anything useful."[29]

Forbes's Civil War experiences left a lasting mark on his character and habits of thought, and he saw himself as a general of science engaged in an unremitting war against an implacable and resourceful enemy. "The struggle between man and insects," he told a joint meeting of farmers and teachers at Normal, Illinois, on December 13, 1910, "began long before the dawn of civilization, has continued without cessation to the present time, and will continue, no doubt, as long as the human race endures. . . . Here and there a truce has been declared, a treaty made, and even a partnership established, advantageous to both parties to the contract — as with the bees and silk-worms, for example; but wherever their interests and ours are diametrically opposed, the war still goes on and neither side can claim a final victory."[30]

---

[27] Stephen A. Forbes, "Aspects of Progress in Economic Entomology," *Journal of Economic Entomology* II (February, 1909): 28.

[28] Forbes was responsible for four series of publications: the state zoological reports and *Bulletin of the Laboratory of Natural History*, and the biennial reports and bulletins of the Entomologist's Office.

[29] Stephen A. Forbes, "The Ecological Foundations of Applied Entomology," *Annals of the Entomological Society of America* VIII (March, 1915): 6.

[30] Stephen A. Forbes, "The Insect, the Farmer, the Teacher, the Citizen, and the State," Illinois State Laboratory of Natural History pamphlet (1915), p. 2.

In his role of a general of science, Forbes wanted to know everything possible about his enemies before ordering an attack, and his extensive studies of the San Jose scale, chinch bug, Hessian fly, army worm, corn root louse, white grub, wireworm, swamp bill bug, and many other insects may properly be considered "intelligence" reports. For example, in one experiment Forbes studied the complete life histories of tens of thousands of codling moths so that he could tell apple orchardists exactly when to spray to destroy the young caterpillars. But Forbes knew that the war could not be won simply by providing the farmer with suitable weapons. "It is not the facts of entomology we discover," he said, "but those which we persuade the farmer . . . to use diligently for the protection or the preservation of his crops, which make our entomology economic. To publish valuable results without making sure of their appreciation and appropriation by our constituents, is to fail of real usefulness. To bring a result to bear on the practice of one man only when a thousand are suffering for the want of it, is to fail in 99.0 per cent of our proper undertaking." [31]

On December 9, 1890, despite his manifold duties as professor of zoology and entomology, chief of the State Laboratory, state entomologist, and dean of the College of Science, [32] Forbes volunteered to serve (without pay) as consulting entomologist to the agricultural experiment station. To convince his "fighting squads" of farmers that they must use the weapons he had placed in their hands, he lectured to farmers' organizations throughout the state, often appearing on the same program with the ubiquitous George Morrow. In 1893, Forbes was made director of the Aquarium of the United States Fish Commission at the World's Columbian Exposition held in Chicago. He was also in charge of the exhibits of the State Laboratory and Entomologist's Office, and served as chairman of the International Congress of Zoologists

---

[31] Stephen A. Forbes, "The Kind of Economic Entomology Which the Farmer Ought to Know," Illinois State Entomologist's Office pamphlet (1904), p. 4.

[32] Forbes was dean of the College of Natural Science from 1888 to 1892 and dean of the College of Science from 1892 to 1905. In 1913, the College of Science and the College of Literature and Arts were combined to form the College of Liberal Arts and Sciences.

held in conjunction with the Exposition. On April 1, 1894, Forbes established a biological experiment station at Havana to study "the entire system of life in the Illinois River and connected lakes and other adjacent waters." During the following five years, Forbes and his staff conducted a series of scientific investigations that were to make the biology of this river better known than that of any other river in the world.[33]

When the State Laboratory and the Entomologist's Office were combined as the Illinois Natural History Survey in 1917, Forbes became first chief of the new organization. The following year, he was elected to membership in the National Academy of Sciences.[34] Although Forbes retired from the University as professor emeritus in 1921, he continued to serve as chief of the Survey until his death on March 13, 1930, when he was nearly eighty-six years old.[35] He was mentally alert throughout his life, and worked until nine days before the end. Shortly after Forbes's death, the following lines, written in pencil and signed with his initials, were found among his papers:

> He is not old who loves the young,
> Whom the young love is young himself;
> The full heart is the happy one,

[33] *Seventeenth Report*, pp. 311–312. Two of the most important products of this work were Charles A. Kofoid's extensive studies of the plankton (minute plant and animal life) of the Illinois River and *The Fishes of Illinois* by Forbes and R. E. Richardson. Kofoid's studies appeared in volumes 5, 6, and 8 of the *State Laboratory Bulletin*. *The Fishes of Illinois* was first published in 1908 and reprinted in 1920. For more than forty years, this handsome book was the definitive state publication on fresh-water fishes.

[34] Forbes was also a member of many other scientific organizations, and he served at various times as president of the American Association of Economic Entomologists, the National Society of Horticultural Inspectors, the Illinois Academy of Science, and the Entomological Society of America. He was awarded the LL.D. degree from the University of Illinois in 1905.

[35] Forbes was buried at Roselawn Cemetery in Champaign. Theodore Henry Frison became acting chief of the Survey upon Forbes's death, and served as chief from 1931 to 1945. Leo Roy Tehon was acting chief from 1945 to 1947, and Dr. Harlow B. Mills was chief from 1947 to 1966. Since October 1, 1966, Dr. George Sprugel, Jr. has been chief of the Survey. In 1940, the Illinois Geological Survey and the Natural History Survey moved to the new Natural Resources Building on the University of Illinois campus. The staff of the Natural History Survey has increased from sixteen members in 1930 to eighty-five members in 1969.

The empty dish goes on the shelf.
May the full heart, the curious mind,
Be yours until your latest day;
Then shall your age be fresh as youth,
And late December bloom like May.[36]

---

[36] *In Memoriam Stephen Alfred Forbes*, p. 20.

SEVEN

Enter Mr. Draper
and Mr. Davenport

URING THE SEVENTEEN YEARS that George Morrow served as
professor of agriculture, the University slowly developed into a
true institution of higher learning. This development was marked
by the granting of degrees beginning in 1878 (before that time
only "certificates" were awarded), changing the name of the University in 1885, the popular election of trustees in 1888, and passage of the Morrill Supplementary Act in 1890. Under the provisions of this act (the so-called "Second Morrill Act"), each of the
land-grant colleges received an additional endowment of $15,000.
This sum was to be increased $1,000 a year until the permanent
annual payment reached $25,000.[1] But the Illinois legislature was
reluctant to appropriate the necessary funds to meet the growing
needs of the University. During the eleven years of Selim Peabody's administration (1880–1891), state appropriations totaled
only $272,450. Nearly one-third of this amount was appropriated
for a drill hall and the Natural History Building, leaving an average of slightly over $19,000 a year to meet all other expenses of
the University.[2]

---

[1] The money was "to be applied only to instruction in agriculture, the mechanic
arts, the English language, and the various branches of mathematical, physical, natural, and economic science, with special reference to their application in the industries of life, and to the facilities for such instruction."

[2] The legislature appropriated $10,000 for a drill hall in 1889. This was the

Thomas Burrill, who became acting regent on September 1, 1891, believed that it was the business of the University administration to ask for the money actually needed to carry on its work, and it was the business of the legislature to say how much money would be granted. The final responsibility for the welfare of the University rested upon those who held the purse strings — the members of the state legislature — and Burrill did not propose to relieve them of that responsibility. Acting upon this principle, he was able to wrest over $295,000 from the legislature for the 1893–1895 biennium.[3] With this money, Burrill enlarged the faculty, increased salaries, and established the graduate school, summer session, extension teaching, the department of municipal and sanitary engineering, and courses in architectural engineering. Student life, which had been straitened and repressed under both Peabody and John Gregory, also flourished. The first junior prom was held; fraternities, which Gregory had roundly condemned as leading to "forbidden dissipations," were reinstated; and art, chemistry, glee, and mandolin clubs appeared on campus. The three years of Burrill's acting regency were, as Allan Nevins said, "years of unprecedented growth in every direction."[4]

On August 1, 1894, Andrew Sloan Draper became president (a title he insisted upon) of the University of Illinois. Although born on a farm in western New York, Draper had spent nearly all of

---

first money provided for a large building since the appropriation of $40,000 for the chemistry building (now Harker Hall) in 1877. The Natural History Building was erected in 1892 at a cost of $70,000, but it was not completely furnished until the following year.

[3] Although more than half of the appropriation was for an engineering building, the $120,000 for instruction was more than twice the amount appropriated for this purpose in any previous biennium. The legislative appropriations for 1891–1893 and 1893–1895 totaled $430,900 — only $120,450 less than the entire appropriations for the preceding twenty-three years.

[4] Nevins, *Illinois*, p. 141. During Burrill's interregnum, the University enrollment increased from 420 to 552 students and the faculty from forty-three to sixty-seven members. The Board of Trustees named a campus street in Burrill's honor on December 12, 1895. This street, Burrill Avenue, formerly extended the length of the University campus, but it is now bounded by Springfield Avenue on the north and Green Street on the south. See *Eighteenth Report* (1896), p. 209. Burrill Hall, dedicated in 1959, houses the departments of Physiology and Microbiology of the University of Illinois.

his life in cities, and he had little appreciation of the value of agricultural education. In fact, one of his conditions for accepting the presidency was that he would not be held responsible for any lack of progress in the College of Agriculture. A self-made man in the Horatio Alger tradition, he had begun his working life as a newsboy in Albany, New York, at wages of $2.50 per week.[5] Draper attended the Albany Academy for three years and the Albany Law School for one year. At eighteen he became a teacher, and was principal of a graded school at twenty. In 1871, at the age of twenty-three, he was admitted to the bar. Before he was thirty, Draper had established a substantial law practice, become active in politics, and been president of the Independent Order of Good Templars of New York State.[6] After serving on the Albany Board of Public Instruction and in the state legislature, he was appointed a judge on the Federal Court of Alabama Claims. In 1886, Draper was elected State Superintendent of Public Instruction by the New York legislature. Six years later, he was appointed superintendent of schools at Cleveland, Ohio. From this position, he came to the University of Illinois. He was then forty-six years old.

Since Draper did not have a university education, he accepted the presidency with certain misgivings. "My limitations in training and my total inexperience in administering the affairs of a

---

[5] In later years, Draper was inordinately proud of the fact that his wages as a newsboy were raised to $3.00 per week. It is in keeping with the Horatio Alger elements in Draper's life that the State Education Building in Albany, for which he was largely responsible, occupied the site of the former newsboy's humble home. *Alumni Quarterly* VII (July, 1913): 164.

[6] Draper's political career actually started before he was old enough to vote. In 1868, when he was twenty years old, he stumped his native county for General Ulysses S. Grant in the latter's campaign for the presidency of the United States. As president of the Templars, Draper often appeared on the same platform with such noted temperance speakers as Horace Greeley, Neal Dow, and John B. Gough. But Draper was not always a teetotaler. In a letter to his cousin Alden Chester dated January 2, 1863, Draper wrote "I celebrated New Years most to [sic] much yesterday and the effect is that I have a sore throat and do not feel very nice but I did not get quite tipsy for I used to be a 'Band of Hope' member." Harlan Hoyt Horner, *The Life and Work of Andrew Sloan Draper* (Urbana, 1934), p. 20. Horner, a 1901 graduate of the University, served as Draper's secretary for six years. His biography of Draper, although undiscriminating and adulatory, contains useful facts about the latter's life.

university," he told the trustees, "have combined to arouse serious apprehensions in my mind as to the wisdom of your choice."[7] Certainly Draper was not a scholar. Although he had selected and guided teachers for many years, he had scant sympathy for pure pedagogy, and was not himself capable of planning a detailed course of study. He was not versed in languages, he had little interest in poetry, and he reportedly read only one novel in his life — *David Harum*.[8] He had not thoroughly explored any broad field of knowledge, and he sometimes blundered in discussing the classics.[9] But whatever his cultural deficiencies, Draper possessed

[7] *Seventeenth Report*, p. 264.

[8] Draper, a horse lover, was so fond of this novel about harness racing that he read it again on an ocean voyage. *Alumni Quarterly* VII (July, 1913): 164.

[9] According to the late Charles F. Hottes, professor of plant pathology, emeritus, the German Department asked Draper to secure copies of *Faust* for the library. Whereupon Draper ordered "all the books [by] Faust" placed on the library list. Charles F. Hottes Papers, Record Series 15/4/21, tape recording 1964, reel 2: 147–175.

Andrew Sloan Draper,
President of the University,
1894–1904.

two qualifications that the trustees wanted and the University needed. These were political acumen and administrative skill.

Four months after Draper became president, Eugene Davenport was appointed to succeed George Morrow as dean of the College of Agriculture.[10] Davenport arrived in Urbana on January 1, 1895. "I found," he said, "that everything salable in the way of equipment had been sold and the farm rented. . . . Fences were dilapidated, gates askew, and the few animals so plastered with mud that the colors were barely discernible. In defense the hostler argued that he was waiting for a curry comb. The house in which the Dean was supposed to live was in a sad state of disrepair. The sum of $60.00 was provided for the operation of the College till the end of the year. . . ."[11] Of over 800 students in the University, only nine were enrolled in agriculture, and the single course offered in the College was a twelve-week "Winter School" that met in the basement of the Natural History Building. From his office on the third floor of that building, Davenport made out his first inventory of the College equipment. The inventory consisted of an outmoded wooden model of tile drains valued at six dollars. "I raised the window," Davenport said, "hove the model out onto the rubbish pile below, marked off the item, and began at scratch."[12]

---

[10] Davenport was not among the original candidates for dean of the College. The position was offered successively to Thomas F. Hunt (then at The Ohio State University), Melville A. Scovell, director of the Kentucky Agricultural Experiment Station (see Chapter Five, p. 68), H. J. Waters of the Pennsylvania Agricultural College, and Clinton D. Smith of the Michigan Agricultural College. After Smith refused to leave Michigan, Davenport offered himself as a candidate. He was appointed dean at a meeting of the Board of Trustees held on December 5, 1894. See *Eighteenth Report*, pp. 33, 40, 42; Draper Letterbooks, Box 1; Andrew S. Draper General Correspondence, Record Series 2/4/1, Box 7 (hereafter cited as Draper Correspondence); and Andrew S. Draper Faculty Correspondence, Record Series 2/4/2, Box 1. Hereafter cited as Draper Faculty Correspondence.

[11] Eugene Davenport to Dr. A. S. Alexander, October 25, 1933. In addition to his salary of $2,000, Davenport was given free use of the house formerly occupied by Morrow. This house (now known as "Mumford House") was built in 1870 at a cost of about $2,500, including all furnishings and inside and outside paint. Morrow lived in the house for several years between 1877 and 1894, Davenport from 1895 to 1904, and Dean Herbert W. Mumford from 1904 to 1938.

[12] Eugene Davenport, "Rejuvenation of the College of Agriculture of the Uni-

The first order of business, Davenport decided, was to clean up the College grounds. But George Morrow was still living in Urbana, and Davenport did not want to embarrass him by "working havoc in situations of long standing." He went to Thomas Burrill with his problem, and Burrill assured him that nothing would make Morrow happier than an improvement in the "physical affairs" of the College. Davenport set to work with "repair tools, wrecking bar, and matches," and, as Burrill had predicted, Morrow was among the first to congratulate him upon his efforts. The two men became, in fact, close friends, and Morrow made it a point to introduce Davenport to the members of the local farmers' organization. "He was much in demand that winter at farmers' meetings," Davenport said,

> and everywhere I went I heard of the good things he said of me. I remarked to him one day, as we were riding in his carriage to meet a friend of his on a nearby farm: "Professor Morrow, why do you go out of your way to introduce me to your best friends always in such cordial terms, and why do you say so many things in my favor out over the state? You do not know me well, and I may be the worst failure on record." With that quizzical smile of his and the kindly eye that cannot be described, he replied: "But Professor Davenport, I am not altogether an idiot. I want my successor to succeed." [13]

Success seemed very far away. Davenport's job "was none other than to attempt the transfusion of blood into an extremely docile

---

versity of Illinois," November, 1933. Typed manuscript in College of Agriculture files.

[13] *Ibid.* In August, 1895, Morrow became president of the Oklahoma Agricultural and Mechanical College at Stillwater, Oklahoma. He served in this position until 1899, when failing health compelled him to retire to his farm at Paxton, Illinois. Morrow died on March 26, 1900 (apparently from cancer of the throat), and was buried at Mount Hope Cemetery in Urbana. Davenport was one of the pall bearers at Morrow's funeral. "The question arose," Davenport said, "whether to drive the hearse through the campus, there being a rule against it. I said: 'This is Prof. Morrow's last chance to be on the University grounds where he put in many years of his life, and he is going through the campus drive. I will settle with the authorities.' It was the least I could do, for it had never been possible to repay in any kind the debt of gratitude I owed him.'" "What One Life Has Seen," Davenport manuscript autobiography, 1936, Record Series 8/1/21, Box 4.

corpse." [14] The farmers were still angry over the change in name of the University. As far as they were concerned, the College was dead, and when they wanted help with their agricultural problems, they turned to the experiment station. The station chemist, Edward H. Farrington, had been popular with the dairymen (perhaps the most influential agricultural group in the state) because of his dairy experiments, but Farrington had resigned the previous summer for a better-paying position at the University of Wisconsin. The trustees, probably to placate the dairymen, asked the 1895 legislature for a dairy building costing $40,000, but the appropriation was refused. [15] At this session, the legislature appropriated $150,000 for a library building, $30,000 for equipping the new $160,000 engineering building, and $15,000 for an astronomy observatory. "Clearly the University was to live," Davenport remarked. "Was the College of Agriculture to live with it?" [16]

But the situation was not as bad as it seemed. "I believe," Thomas Burrill had written to Jonathan Periam the previous March, "the chance is better now than it has ever been to arouse an interest at large in the agricultural side of the institution. . . ." [17] Despite external appearances, Burrill was right, and he himself was primarily responsible for providing this "chance." By basing his requests for appropriations on need rather than on what the legislature might be willing to give, Burrill had succeeded in creating a rapidly growing, diversified University. The College of Agriculture was a part of that University, and would inevitably share in its benefits. Illinois was one of the richest agricultural states in the Union, and its people were progressive. Public opinion, which had been actively opposed to the College during Morrow's time, was slowly swinging the other way. Even the agricultural press had exchanged its attitude of hostility for one

---

[14] *Annual Report of the Illinois Farmers' Institute* XIX (Springfield, 1914): 89. Subsequent citations of the Institute reports will contain only an abbreviated title, volume number, and year of publication.

[15] *Eighteenth Report*, pp. 51, 66.

[16] Eugene Davenport, "Genesis of the Illinois Agricultural Experiment Station," March, 1938. Typed manuscript in College of Agriculture files.

[17] Thomas J. Burrill to Jonathan Periam, March 24, 1894, Draper Letterbooks, Box 1. This is the same letter in which Burrill outlined the reasons for Morrow's resignation as professor of agriculture.

of cooperation. The time was propitious. "Opportunity was ready for Ability," Burrill said.[18] What the College of Agriculture needed at this point in its history was a genuine leader — a man who could, in the words of Governor John Tanner, "chase the members of the legislature over a stake and rider fence."[19] The College found this leader in Eugene Davenport.

Davenport was born amid pioneer conditions at Woodland, Michigan, on June 20, 1856. He attended the district school and a local private school, and was graduated from the Michigan Agricultural College in 1878. After working with his father for several years, he went back to the College for a master of science degree in 1884, and then returned to the family farm.[20] In 1888, Davenport was appointed assistant to William James Beal, professor of botany and horticulture in the College and botanist of the Michigan experiment station. The following year, he was made professor of agriculture and superintendent of the farm at Lansing. But Davenport does not seem to have been entirely happy in this position. Although the Michigan Agricultural College did a competent job of turning out "practical agriculturists," it was not — nor did it pretend to be — much more than a trade school. And Davenport, who believed that a young man or woman should be educated for life as well as for a vocation, felt constrained by the narrowness of this environment. Deliverance came in the person of Louiz Queroz, a wealthy Brazilian planter who wanted to establish an agricultural college — "a leetle Lansing," as he described it — in his own country. Queroz offered Davenport $6,000 (a sum large enough to cause considerable comment in the

---

[18] Thomas J. Burrill, "Eugene Davenport," *Illinois Agriculturist* XIX, (June, 1915): 737.

[19] *Ibid.*, p. 738.

[20] Davenport also received two honorary degrees from the Michigan Agricultural College — a Master of Agriculture degree in 1895 and an LL.D. in 1907. "Those ten years on the farm," he said, "were notable not so much for their events, which were quite commonplace, as for the background they afforded for an understanding of agriculture and its people. . . . The background upon which I learned to rely for guidance in shaping policies touching education for farmers was laid in the commonplace activities of the day-by-day routine of the farm and in the lives of those who live by the land." Eugene Davenport, "A Son of the Timberlands," *The Country Gentleman* XC (December, 1925): 30.

agricultural papers) to serve as president of the projected college for one year. Davenport asked for a year's leave of absence from his position at Michigan. When his request was denied, he resigned.[21]

On October 7, 1891, Davenport, accompanied by his wife and parents, sailed from New York City for Rio de Janeiro. The voyage lasted a month. When the ship finally landed at Piracicaba, where the "Collegio Agronomica" was to be located, a revolution was raging. The government proved too unstable for establishing the college, and in April, 1892, the Davenports sailed for the United States by way of England.[22] After they returned to Michigan, Davenport built a house for himself and his wife across the road from the family homestead. They had lived in this house for over a year when Davenport was appointed dean of the University of Illinois College of Agriculture.[23]

Like other universities in which agriculture was merely a department or college, the University of Illinois deferred all agriculture courses until the junior or even senior year. Davenport claimed that the strictly agricultural colleges, such as those in Michigan, Kansas, and Mississippi, had been successful because they offered courses in agriculture throughout a student's academic career. "I think it is a wrong policy with four-year students to give them two or three years of pure science before it is applied," he said. "When a student enters the agricultural course he ought immediately to be given work in purely agricultural lines and continue at intervals until graduation. . . ."[24] With

---

21 "The request was received rather coldly, it seemed to me," Davenport said. "Anyhow, the answer was negative with the intimation that if I was to go I might as well sever all connections at once — which I did with a feeling that so narrow a policy would prove a perpetual handicap upon any institution." *Ibid.*, p. 129.

22 In England, Davenport and his wife visited Rothamsted, where Sir Henry Gilbert showed them the original clover plants used to prove that nitrogen is "fixed" by bacteria living on the roots of legumes. Davenport later described this visit as his "most interesting agricultural experience."

23 After his retirement in 1922, Davenport remodeled and enlarged the house, which he had christened "The Maples." He lived in it until his death on March 31, 1941. The house is presently occupied by his son-in-law, Harold B. Tukey, formerly head of the Department of Horticulture at Michigan State University.

24 Eugene Davenport to Andrew Sloan Draper, November 26, 1894, Draper Faculty Correspondence, Box 1.

the cooperation of the faculty, Davenport completely reorganized the College curriculum so that a student began the study of agriculture as a freshman. "When a boy came from the farm to college," he said, "I did not wish him ever to see his father again at vacation time . . . until he had learned some thing about farming that his father did not know."[25] But this reshuffling of the existing agriculture courses was only a beginning. Davenport knew from his experience at the Michigan Agricultural College that the subject of agriculture was too broad to be encompassed by one man, and he had refused to come to the University as professor of agriculture.[26]

"In these days the instruction of specialists only is considered valuable," he wrote President Draper on March 4, 1895. "Live stock breeding and feeding is itself a broad subject and as distinct from the agriculture of the field as is Botany from Chemistry. . . ." Davenport proposed that the work in agriculture be divided into animal husbandry, agriculture proper (soils and crops), and dairy manufactures. He asked that he himself be assigned to the first of these subdivisions with the title of professor of animal husbandry and that a "competent man" be placed at the head of each of the other two. "In each of these lines," he said, "there is enough of instruction and investigation to fully engage both the intellect and the time of any man, and without such subdivision it will be necessary either to restrict the work of the institution to the capacity of an individual, or be forced by very extenson to do superficial work which will never redound to the credit of the University."[27]

Davenport was made professor of animal husbandry on March 13, 1895. But Draper and the trustees were reluctant to invest more money in an institution that had proved an unmitigated failure for nearly three decades, and they postponed consideration of Davenport's other proposals for the College from one

[25] Davenport, "Rejuvenation of the College of Agriculture."

[26] Davenport was appointed dean of the College of Agriculture and agriculturist of the experiment station, but the exact title of his professorship was left open.

[27] Eugene Davenport to Andrew Sloan Draper, March 4, 1895, Draper Faculty Correspondence, Box 1.

Board meeting to the next. Impatient over the repeated delays, Davenport went to see Draper. "When I called for room, equipment and an adequate faculty," Davenport said, "the answer was, 'Go out and get your students and then we'll take care of them.'" Davenport protested that the University was putting the cart before the horse.

> Suppose I could get a hundred students on faith. Would they stand around with their hands in their pockets while we were getting ready to take care of them? Besides, that's not the way things are done. The downtown merchant does not advertise that when the community will promise to trade with him he will put in the finest stock in town. On the contrary, he tears out the old weather-beaten sash, puts in a plate-glass front, fills his shelves with goods which the public wants, and trust to his wares to draw customers. And we must do the same. Adequate equipment with attractive courses and nothing else will draw students.[28]

But Davenport's protestations fell upon deaf ears. Draper was determined to maintain the College within the annual $15,000 federal allotment to the experiment station. "The experiment station funds must pay the professors' salaries," he said, "and the students must do the experimenting."[29] This conversation convinced Davenport that the only hope for the resurrection of the College lay outside the University itself. He asked the advice of E. E. Chester, the representative from the State Board of Agriculture on the Board of Direction of the experiment station, and Chester told him to "go down to Springfield and talk with Charlie Mills."[30]

Colonel Charles F. Mills was secretary of the State Board of Agriculture and publisher of *The Farm Home*, a small agricultural paper in Springfield.[31] Chester had described him to Davenport

---

[28] Eugene Davenport, "A Son of the Timberlands," *The Country Gentleman* XCI (April, 1926): 38.

[29] Eugene Davenport, "A Son of the Timberlands," *The Country Gentleman* XCI (February, 1926): 156. Davenport was "dumfounded" by this statement, and he asked Draper whether he had read the Hatch Act. "He seemed not to know precisely what that was," Davenport said, "and made some equivocal answer."

[30] Davenport, "Genesis of the Illinois Agricultural Experiment Station."

[31] Mills left Shurtleff College during his senior year to join the Union Army, and served throughout the Civil War with the 124th Illinois Volunteers. After the

as a man "as full of ideas as an egg is of meat," and this description proved to be an accurate one. "The Colonel amazed me at
once," Davenport said, "by saying that if the State of Illinois
could be waked up we should soon have a thousand students in
agriculture." Mills proposed "to organize a statewide Farmers' Institute with an appropriation from the legislature for the purpose
of holding farmers' meetings in every county of the state. . . ."[32]
This organization would be known as the Illinois Farmers' Institute, and its primary function would be to promote "among the
people . . . and before the legislature" the interests of the
farmers and of the College of Agriculture. The Institute would

war, he became a farmer and livestock breeder. Mills was head of the livestock
exhibits at the Columbian Exposition in 1893 and the Louisiana Purchase Exposition in 1904, and chairman of the livestock advisory board of the Panama-Pacific
Exposition in 1915. He served as secretary of many agricultural organizations, including the Sangamon County Fair Association, American Berkshire Association,
Clydesdale Association, and the Illinois Farmers' Institute.

[32] Davenport, "Genesis of the Illinois Agricultural Experiment Station."

Colonel Charles F. Mills,
one of the organizers of the
Illinois Farmers' Institute,
and a leader in the
"rejuvenation" of the
College of Agriculture.

consist of three delegates from each county (elected annually at the county Institute meetings) and a board of directors consisting of the superintendent of public instruction, the dean of the College of Agriculture, the presidents of the State Board of Agriculture, the State Horticultural Society, and the State Dairymen's Association, and one member from each congressional district of Illinois, to be selected by the delegates from that district at the annual state meeting.

The Illinois Farmers' Institute was created by an act passed by the state legislature on June 24, 1895. "The machinery existed for renovating the College of Agriculture," Davenport said. "The question now was how would it work in an emergency?"[33] He was determined to set this machinery in motion as quickly as possible, and at the first state meeting of the Institute held in Springfield in January, 1896, he asked the farmers for their help in developing a genuine College of Agriculture at the University of Illinois. "We need many things," Davenport said.

> We need equipment; material for illustration. . . . We need a building for offices, laboratories and class rooms. At present we have nothing except as we are accommodated in other buildings at the disadvantage both of other departments and of ourselves. Will you by your sympathy and influence help us to get these things? . . . The College of Agriculture will be what you of the State make it. . . . I beg of you see to it that your college is developed till it occupies a position which is second to none other. No other kind of college can adequately serve the needs and represent the interests of this the greatest agricultural state of the Union, and the greatest agricultural area the sun shines upon.[34]

Although the farmers liked the new dean (whom they knew to be a farmer as well as a "perfesser"), their distrust of the University

---

[33] Davenport, "Rejuvenation of the College of Agriculture."

[34] *Farmers' Institute* I (1896): 102. Davenport had made the same request of the Board of Trustees at their September 4, 1895 meeting. "If I were to say what we need most," Davenport said at that meeting, "I should say an Agricultural Hall, costing for building and equipment not less than $100,000.00." *Eighteenth Report*, p. 160.

was too deep-seated to be overcome by oratory alone, and they did not actively support Davenport's plans for the College until nearly two years later. Meanwhile, Davenport received help from an unexpected source — President Andrew Draper himself.

A man with a keen sense of neatness and order, Draper had been appalled by the appearance of the farm when Morrow was dean, and he had welcomed Davenport's efforts to clean up the College grounds.[35] Largely through Draper's influence, the trustees had appropriated a total of $3,000 at the June and September, 1895 meetings for a small horse barn and tool shed and a few good sheep, cattle, and horses. "The situation at the farm has been somewhat improved," Draper told the trustees on June 9, 1896, "and yet it is far from satisfactory." He particularly objected to the fact that the agricultural experiment station was completely independent of the College and University. "When I have advised with the Dean of the College of Agriculture about matters which I supposed were wholly subject to his direction," Draper said, "he has claimed that these matters were in charge of the Agricultural Experiment Station, and . . . that he had no more to do with them than have professors in other departments of the University who have no relation whatever to the work of the Station." Draper then proposed a "somewhat radical modification of the plan of organization" of both the College and the agricultural experiment station. His recommendations (which the trustees adopted the same day) included creating the position of director of the experiment station, to be filled by the dean *ex officio*; changing the station's Board of Direction in both name and function to merely an Advisory Board that would "recognize the Director . . . as the executive officer of all Station affairs"; and establishing the division of instruction that Davenport had originally proposed more than a year earlier.[36] These changes were to have far-reaching effects upon the College of Agriculture. The

---

[35] Draper described the farm under Morrow as "one poor barn where the farm horses and a poor lot of mongrel cattle kept company with unconscionable pigs that made the place a nuisance." Nevins, *Illinois*, p. 175.

[36] Quotations from *Eighteenth Report*, pp. 249–250.

transfer of executive power from the Board of Direction to the dean permitted a much closer relationship between the experimental work and instruction in agriculture, and the addition of two academic positions in the College paved the way for the development of a genuine agricultural faculty.

On June 26, 1896, Perry Greeley Holden (who had been one of Davenport's assistants at Michigan) was appointed assistant professor of agricultural physics (soils and crops), and Wilber Fraser, an 1893 graduate of the College, was made instructor in dairying.[37] Both men started work on September first, and the College curriculum for the 1896–1897 academic year included courses in crop production, fertility, and soils under Holden, dairying and butter making under Fraser, and stock breeding and comparative agriculture under Davenport. But the College was still "housed about in basements and garrets and in old rooms wherever a foothold could be found. . . ."[38] Ever since his arrival at the University, Davenport had stressed the need for a separate agriculture building. Now, emboldened by his new authority as official representative of both the College and the experiment station, he renewed his campaign. On September 15, 1896, the Advisory Board of the experiment station (at Davenport's instigation) recommended that the University provide a "building . . . devoted to the needs of instruction and experimentation in agri-

---

[37] Holden received Bachelor and Master of Science degrees from the Michigan Agricultural College in 1889 and 1895, and Bachelor and Master of Pedagogy degrees from Michigan State Normal School at Ypsilanti in 1894 and 1912. After serving as an assistant at the Michigan Agricultural College for three and one-half years, he became a science teacher at Benzonia College and superintendent of schools in Benzie County, Michigan. Holden was paid $1,200 and Fraser $800 per year at the University of Illinois. Their salaries were divided equally between experiment-station and University funds.

[38] *Farmers' Institute* VIII (1903): 85. "The only buildings devoted to agriculture," Davenport said, "were the Farm House . . . [i.e., Mumford House], a combined horse and cattle barn across Burrill Avenue from the Farm House [near the present site of the Animal Genetics Building], a little brick residence for the herdsman. . . , an old brick piggery filled with rats, a barn-like building known as the Warehouse, a kind of Experiment Station headquarters for the men, and a little old residence building in the grove where Lincoln Hall now stands used as a veterinary headquarters." "Genesis of the Agricultural Experiment Station."

culture . . . at the earliest practicable date."[39] Three months later, the trustees voted to ask the 1897 legislature for an agriculture building costing $80,000. "Just how much power was added to the asking I never knew," Davenport said, "though I did know that many farmers and not a few institutes [i.e., county Farmers' Institutes] strongly opposed it."[40] At any rate, the legislature refused to make the appropriation.

Davenport was not discouraged. "While I stay at the University," he said, "I shall leave no stone unturned to push our interests."[41] Although Davenport's metaphors were mixed, his intentions were clear enough. He was determined, at all costs, to put the College of Agriculture "on a sound basis." The two previous requests for an agriculture building had failed because neither Draper nor the trustees believed that there was sufficient demand for agricultural education to justify large appropriations to the College. The University refused to provide proper facilities (or, more accurately, insist that the legislature provide them) until more students enrolled in agriculture, and students refused to enroll in agriculture until the University provided proper facilities. Davenport realized that this impasse could only be broken by the farmers themselves. The farmers must be persuaded to overcome their prejudices against the University and be made to look upon their interests and those of the College of Agriculture as the same.

In February, 1898, the annual state meeting of the Farmers' Institute was held at the University. "What Illinois shall do for agricultural education depends entirely upon your opinions and what you are willing to do," Davenport told the delegates to this

---

[39] *Nineteenth Report* (1898), p. 24.

[40] Davenport, "Rejuvenation of the College of Agriculture." The trustees' committee on legislative appropriations had recommended that "a separate building . . . be erected with an attached or adjacent structure in which may be carried on a school, teaching by practical demonstration all of the various processes of dairying." *Nineteenth Report*, p. 53. The members of this committee included Draper, James E. Armstrong of Chicago, and Morrow's nemesis, Napoleon B. Morrison of Odin, Illinois.

[41] Eugene Davenport to C. A. Shamel, June 7, 1897, Eugene Davenport Letterbook 11, p. 88, Record Series 8/1/1. Hereafter cited as Davenport Letterbooks.

meeting. "Twice the people of Illinois have been asked to provide special apparatus and buildings devoted to agriculture. Twice they have said 'No.' I do not know why. I do not believe they meant 'No' any more than does the maiden in her first answer. We shall ask again, and I have faith enough in the people of this great State, and in the righteousness of our cause, to believe that Illinois will yet do even better than so many of her sister states have already done." [42] On this occasion, Davenport had more than oratory on his side. The Institute program included a tour of the College grounds, and for the first time the farmers saw what the state had "provided for the enhancement of their own interests." The sight shocked them as much (although for somewhat different reasons) as it had shocked Andrew Draper. [43] As a result of this tour, the Institute voted to petition the 1899 legislature "to carefully investigate the needs of the agricultural department of our University and furnish this department with such buildings and equipments as are commensurate with the dignity of the University . . . and . . . with the exacting demands of both practical and scientific farming." [44]

Davenport was well aware that a petition alone would have little effect upon the legislature, but it was a genuine beginning — the first gentle nudge in arousing Illinois agriculture from its long "sleep of apathy." After passage of the Hatch and Second Morrill Acts, many of the land-grant universities had provided buildings, equipment, and funds for instruction in agriculture; as a result, an alarming number of young men from Illinois were attending colleges of agriculture in other states. [45] Davenport's

---

[42] *Farmers' Institute* III (1898): 132. Between October, 1897 and February, 1898, Davenport spoke before at least twelve county Institute meetings.

[43] "Shades of the founders!" one of the delegates exclaimed. "Excuse us farmers for what we could not help and forgive us for what we could have helped and did not." L. H. Kerrick, "Address," *Dedication Agricultural Building University of Illinois.*

[44] *Farmers' Institute* III (1898): 172.

[45] In a letter to Charles F. Mills dated October 21, 1898, Davenport listed the names and addresses of seventeen agricultural students from Illinois who were attending the University of Wisconsin and four who were attending The Ohio State University. E. Davenport to Col. C. F. Mills, October 21, 1898, Davenport Letter-

plans were based upon a comparison of the agricultural facilities furnished by these states with those furnished by the state of Illinois. The discrepancies were appalling. "They have more money invested in pumps in Wisconsin," Davenport said, "than we have for teaching all of agriculture, aside from live stock."[46]

In the fall of 1898, Davenport launched a concentrated, closely coordinated campaign to awaken the people of Illinois to the needs of the College of Agriculture. Through hundreds of letters and scores of speeches and interviews, he enlisted the support of influential farmers (both inside and outside the Institute), the agricultural press, and key members of the Board of Trustees, including Mary Turner Carriel, daughter of Jonathan Baldwin Turner, and James E. Armstrong of Chicago. "I take it for granted the Trustees will ask again for an agricultural building," Davenport wrote Armstrong on October 20, 1898, "and I hope they will not only ask, but push the thing along. We should ask as before for $80,000 for a building, and besides this $20,000 for heating and equipping it, for the development of the past two years has made our needs greater now than then."[47] Between the date of this letter and the meeting of the Association of American Agricultural Colleges and Experiment Stations held in Washington, D.C. the following month, the estimated cost of the building was increased to $135,000. Davenport and Isaac Raymond, a member

book 14, p. 474. Ten days later, Davenport wrote Frederic L. Hatch of Spring Grove, then president of the Alumni Association, that "a good many Illinois boys are going to other states. . . . Out of the 127 in agriculture in New York [i.e., Cornell University], seven are from Illinois. Out of the 277 in Wisconsin seventeen are from Illinois." E. Davenport to Frederick [sic] L. Hatch, October 31, 1898, Davenport Letterbook 15, p. 17. The following month, Hatch was elected to the University Board of Trustees.

46 Ibid., Davenport to Hatch. Davenport prepared a list of the amounts of money spent for buildings "by neighboring states for instruction or investigation in technical agriculture only." The states and amounts listed were New York, $257,200; Ohio, $236,000; Minnesota, $146,700; Wisconsin, $113,000; Iowa, $97,500; and Illinois, $6,200 ($3,000 for a cattle barn, $1,800 for a horse barn, and $1,400 for a carriage and tool barn). Davenport sent copies of this list to everyone who could conceivably help him to obtain an agriculture building.

47 E. Davenport to J. E. Armstrong, October 20, 1898, Davenport Letterbook 14, p. 450.

College of Agriculture
faculty, 1898. Left, top
to bottom: Thomas J.
Burrill, Professor of
Botany and
Horticulture; Donald
McIntosh, Professor of
Veterinary Science;
Joseph C. Blair,
Instructor in
Horticulture. Right, top
to bottom: Eugene
Davenport, Dean of
the College and
Professor of Animal
Husbandry; Perry G.
Holden, Assistant
Professor of
Agricultural Physics;
Wilber J. Fraser,
Instructor in Dairying.

of both the Advisory Board of the experiment station and the Agriculture Committee of the Board of Trustees, attended this meeting. On their way back to Urbana, the two men visited the new agriculture building at The Ohio State University. Upon leaving Columbus, Raymond told Davenport "that he was satisfied that we would need all of the $135,000 estimate to provide the building that we stand so much in need of."[48] Shortly afterward, probably at the request of the Illinois Farmers' Institute, the estimate for the building was increased to $150,000.

The directors of the Farmers' Institute had been solidly behind Davenport since the February, 1898, meeting, and they appointed a four-man committee to work with the county Institutes in pushing through his plans for the College.[49] "It is in the power of your committee to do a great work this winter," Davenport wrote Amos F. Moore, president of the Institute. "There is much work to be done, and I cannot do it alone. It will rest with the people of the State to say to what extent agricultural interests are to go forward. The administration must have pressure brought to bear, before it will feel like putting large expenditure into this matter."[50] The Institute committee did its work well. When its members attended a trustees' meeting at the University in December, they "were told that the Board . . . had already decided to ask the Legislature to appropriate $150,000 for said building and fittings and furnishings." And at the Board meeting held in Chicago the following month, Governor John Tanner, himself a

---

[48] E. Davenport to Mr. Fred Rankin, November 21, 1898, Davenport Letterbook 15, p. 155.

[49] *Farmers' Institute* IV (1899): 226. The members of this committee were S. Noble King of Bloomington, a prominent farmer and cattle breeder; A. P. Grout of Winchester, president of the State Live Stock Breeders' Association; Amos F. Moore of Polo, president of the Illinois Farmers' Institute; and the indefatigable Charles Mills.

[50] E. Davenport to Hon. A. F. Moore, October 29, 1898, Davenport Letterbook 15, p. 22. Davenport closed this letter by stating that "If it [i.e., the Farmers' Institute] succeeds in putting Illinois where it belongs in matters agricultural it will have done the greatest work ever done by any Agricultural Association in the world. If you can lead it you will have done a service to Illinois agriculture such as no other man has ever rendered. I will be only too glad to help you do so."

farmer, spoke of "the great desirability of strengthening in every way the agricultural department of the University."[51]

Davenport realized, of course, that more than a building was needed to bring the University of Illinois College of Agriculture on a level with the colleges in neighboring states. "The building will provide us the opportunity for installing a real College of Agriculture," he wrote S. Noble King, a member of the Institute committee, "but work will be done not by the building, but by men. . . . Our force at present is entirely insufficient and the money devoted to providing apparatus is altogether inadequate for the work we have to do."[52] Under the terms of the Land-Grant Act of 1862 and the Second Morrill Act, the University received about $56,000 per year, but only $7,000 of this money was given to the College of Agriculture. With the backing of the Farmers' Institute, Davenport drafted a bill stipulating that one-third of the total federal funds be "set apart for instruction in technical agriculture," the remaining two-thirds to be divided equally between the College of Engineering and the teaching of such "non-technical" subjects as English and chemistry.[53]

"It was at this time," Davenport said,

> that the President of the Institute, Amos Moore of Polo, came to my house at four o'clock one morning to say that it had been agreed to take the College away from the University, set it up as an independent institution and give it the appropriation asked. Under the circumstances Mrs. Davenport and I were obliged to meet the situation alone and on the spot. We argued that such a move would injure both the College and the University besides being on the face of it a concession of defeat. We insisted that the only solution was a college of agriculture as a part of a real Uni-

---

[51] Quotations from *Twentieth Report* (1901), pp. 32, 50.

[52] E. Davenport to S. Noble King, March 18, 1899, Davenport Letterbook 15, p. 798.

[53] "The Institute officials tried their hand at drafting a bill. . . ," Davenport said, "but it was easy to see, in every draft suggested, how the intent of the bill could be thwarted if the Trustees felt so disposed, and so I drafted a form of expression that confined the use of the funds to instruction in the details of technical agriculture. . . ." "Rejuvenation of the College of Agriculture."

versity. But our friend remained obdurate, saying it had all been arranged, leaving nothing more for us than to say when it happened we should have to head for Michigan. That was the last we heard about a plan for separation.[54]

Davenport's bill was introduced in the legislature by Representative Duncan M. Funk of Bloomington on March 2, 1899.[55] "In the hearing before the Appropriations Committee of the Senate," Davenport said, "I was asked how many states could fairly be called ahead of Illinois in respect to the outfit for agricultural education. For reply I said that the only way to tell was to count them up and if the clerk would keep tally I would name them. The tally showed *nineteen* and I added that I had been exceedingly liberal in my judgments for there were a number of others that would be quick to claim superiority over Illinois."[56] The members of the legislature, subjected to pressure from the agricultural press, the governor, the Farmer's Institute, and the University Trustees,[57] were finally in a mood to do something for agriculture, and they proposed that the College be given one-half rather than one-third of the money arising from the two Morrill Acts. When Davenport objected that this division did not allow for the teaching of nontechnical subjects, the legislature

[54] Davenport, "Genesis of the Illinois Agricultural Experiment Station." Six years after this incident, Davenport wrote Liberty Hyde Bailey of Cornell University that "last week I spent a day at Ann Arbor, and also at M. A. C. [Michigan Agricultural College]. I was confirmed again in my feeling that an agricultural college connected with a university is vastly better off than when standing alone." E. Davenport to L. H. Bailey, July 21, 1905, Davenport Letterbook 40, p. 272.

[55] *Illinois House Journal*, Forty-First General Assembly, 1899, p. 292. Funk was the brother-in-law of L. H. Kerrick. Kerrick, a breeder of Angus cattle, was president of the Illinois Cattle Feeders' Association and one of the most active members of the Farmers' Institute.

[56] Davenport, "Rejuvenation of the College of Agriculture." In a pamphlet printed for the use of the Farmers' Institute, Davenport listed eighteen states as possessing "better buildings and equipment for instruction and investigation in agriculture" than Illinois. These states were Colorado, Connecticut, Indiana, Iowa, Kansas, Maine, Massachusetts, Michigan, Minnesota, Missouri, Nebraska, New Jersey, New York, North Dakota, Ohio, South Dakota, Texas, and Wisconsin.

[57] Davenport's staunchest allies among the trustees were Isaac S. Raymond, James E. Armstrong, Napoleon B. Morrison, Mary Turner Carriel, Frederic L. Hatch, and Colonel William H. Fulkerson, president of the State Board of Agriculture.

agreed to add an amount equal to that set apart for the College (approximately $28,000) to the University appropriations. "The tide has surely turned," Davenport jubilantly wrote Mrs. Carriel on March 11, 1899; "the craft will go ahead. . . ."[58] But at this point, Andrew Sloan Draper unexpectedly entered the picture.

---

[58] E. Davenport to Mrs. Mary T. Carriel, March 11, 1899, Davenport Letterbook 15, p. 713. The previous month, at the annual state meeting of the Farmers' Institute held at Princeton, Illinois, Mrs. Carriel had delivered an address entitled "Our University" that was strongly reminiscent of her father's speeches half-a-century earlier. "There have been many complaints by the agricultural students, for they have been in the attics and basements," she said in this address. "Where would you have them be? Out in the barnyard or up in the tree tops with the birds and chickens? They must go somewhere. How many students can you win to a university, when they are obliged to put up with the old furniture of the attics and basements, and are only allowed there through the generosity of the departments they are crowding into. Now, why is it? . . . I think the fault is this. When all those battles were fought and the strife was over, the farmers thought the battles were all ended, and that it belonged to them for all time, and would always be theirs without their care and protection, forgetting that ever since the world began the battle has always been against the farmer. Forgetting that it is like the battle with sin, it would last through all generations. It must be fought over and over again. They must look after their own needs and necessities. Nobody else will do it for them." *Farmers' Institute* IV (1899): 61.

EIGHT

The Dream Vindicated

BOTH BEFORE AND AFTER his retirement in 1922, Davenport wrote many accounts of his experiences as dean of the College of Agriculture. These accounts vary greatly in details (Davenport was not a systematic thinker, and he often telescoped the events of several years into one year or even a few months), but they agree on one important point: the "bitter opposition" of Andrew Draper to the development of the College. "He liked horses," Davenport said of Draper, "and there is about where his interest in matters agricultural began and ended."[1] But on September 26, 1898, Draper wrote Colonel Charles Mills that "it would doubtless require $80,000 to put the College of Agriculture of this University in a position where it would sustain a favorable comparison with like institutions in the states of Michigan, Wisconsin, Minnesota, Iowa, Ohio or Indiana. This state can very well afford to take the step and it is to be hoped that it will. Indeed it cannot afford not to do it. It will be much more costly not to do it than to do it." And the following month, he assured Mary Turner Carriel that he was "as much interested in an agricultural building as any one can be. . . . I think the time is ripe and the opportunity is come for us to secure a good one, and I am for it with all my heart."[2]

---

[1] Davenport, "Rejuvenation of the College of Agriculture."

[2] A. S. Draper to Colonel Charles F. Mills, September 26, 1898; A. S. Draper to Mrs. Mary Turner Carriel, November 30, 1898; Draper Letterbooks, Box 4. See

There seems to be a discrepancy between Draper's attitude toward the College as expressed in these letters and Davenport's accounts of the president's opposition. The discrepancy is more apparent than real. Like many other Easterners, Draper thought of farming as a means of making a living rather than as a business for making money, and he did not believe that the farmer either needed or could afford a college education. But regardless of his personal convictions, Draper was willing to do whatever was necessary to prevent the College from reflecting discredit upon the rest of the University. His disagreement with Davenport was not over the question of whether the College should be developed, but the *extent* of that development.

Draper and Davenport resembled each other in more ways than either cared to recognize: both were strong-willed and ambitious, with an overriding desire to succeed in their jobs; both lacked a genuine university education and felt out of place in an academic environment; both (although rather short by today's standards) were of imposing physical appearance; and both were skilled politicians and administrators. There were, however, important differences between them. Davenport believed that "the individual is the unit for effective work and the less he is hampered by arbitrary authority the better for all concerned. . . ."[3] In his dealings with his subordinates, he was courteous, patient, and tactful, and he was always willing to listen to opinions that differed from his own. But Draper regarded himself as a kind of academic Napoleon surrounded by well-trained but

---

also E. Davenport to J. M. Hollingsworth, October 29, 1898, Davenport Letterbook 15, p. 19; J. M. Hollingsworth to Andrew S. Draper, November 22, 1898, Draper Correspondence, Box 7; and A. S. Draper to J. M. Hollingsworth, November 25, 1898, Draper Letterbooks, Box 4. At Davenport's request, Hollingsworth, a prosperous farmer, wrote Draper to complain about the agricultural facilities at the University. Draper answered that he was "very anxious that the University should have a distinctive agricultural building. It will surely be asked for this year and it is hoped that a liberal appropriation can be secured. Illinois has not done what she should have done in this direction. . . . I trust you will see that the senator and representatives from your district are in full sympathy with us on this matter."

[3] E. Davenport to Col. C. F. Mills, October 4, 1905, Eugene Davenport Personal Letterbook, 1900–1911, p. 85, Record Series 8/1/21, Box 1. Hereafter cited as Davenport Personal Letterbook.

impractical junior officers. He believed that the president was the supreme authority for all University business, and that professors were incapable of acting responsibly on their own.[4]

"I have been greatly surprised that I have not been advised with more fully as to important movements in your College," Draper wrote Davenport on December 14, 1898, the day following the Institute committee's visit to the Board of Trustees. "I have been left altogether in the dark as to the details upon which the estimate of cost of a new agricultural building has been made. I know nothing of your plans, and I have some very decided opinions about the matter myself."[5] Davenport answered that "the cost of such provisions in other states was made the basis of an estimate of $135,000. . . . That is all I know about the agricultural building, except that the students took up the matter, and, as I have learned since the meeting of the Trustees, addressed a letter to each member of that body. I do not know how the estimate of $150,000 originated."[6] For what seemed to him excellent reasons, Davenport was not being entirely honest in this letter. He himself had persuaded the agriculture students to write the trustees (as well as the members of the legislature, the Farmers' Institute, and Governor Tanner) about the need for a building, and he must have known — or could easily have guessed — the source of the $150,000 estimate.

"Professor Davenport has run amuck among farmer politicians and political leaders in the State," Draper wrote Mrs. Lucy Flower, one of his strongest supporters on the Board of Trustees. "I have treated him with great consideration and leniency, because he means well, but the people who mean well and do ill

---

[4] "He had the military attitude toward all members of the faculty, whom he regarded not as associates in doing the work of the University but as inferiors whom he could command even as to details . . . in their own field," Davenport said of Draper. "I have seen him call members of the faculty, even Dr. Burrill, the Vice-President, to his office for no obvious reason but to humiliate him, of whose personality and influence he was extremely jealous." "People I Have Known," appendix to "What One Life Has Seen," Davenport manuscript autobiography.

[5] Andrew S. Draper to Professor Eugene Davenport, December 4, 1898, Draper Letterbooks, Box 4.

[6] E. Davenport to A. S. Draper, December 17, 1898, Davenport Letterbook 15, p. 318.

continuously are the most trying ones. It is very hard to know where we should draw the line between freedom of action on the part of the people connected with the University and the official regulation of them. I think in this case we must begin at once to draw it much nearer to the one who is acting recklessly. . . ."[7] It is not clear exactly how Draper tried to "draw the line" nearer to Davenport. Draper's correspondence offers no definite clues, and Davenport's various accounts of the president's actions are conflicting. In two of these accounts ("Rejuvenation of the College of Agriculture" and "Genesis of the Illinois Agricultural Experiment Station"), Davenport claims that Draper made a trip to Springfield to persuade the legislature not to pass the appropriation for an agriculture building. But in a letter to Edmund James, Draper's successor as president of the University, Davenport says that Draper "opposed the bill to provide funds for agriculture [i.e., the so-called "Funk Bill"] and went to Springfield to kill it."[8]

For several reasons, it seems more likely that Draper attempted to block passage of the Funk Bill rather than the appropriation for the building. Unquestionably Draper was unhappy at the asking of $150,000 for the building (all available accounts and his correspondence attest to this fact),[9] but the governor, the legislature, and his own Board of Trustees were committed to the appropriation. It is doubtful whether Draper, as an experienced politician, would have opposed their wishes. The Funk

---

[7] A. S. Draper to Mrs. Lucy L. Flower, January 27, 1899, Draper Letterbooks, Box 4.

[8] E. Davenport to Edmund J. James, March 4, 1907, College of Agriculture files. On April 14, 1899, Davenport also wrote identical letters to Frederic Hatch and Mrs. Carriel indicating clearly his belief that Draper went to Springfield to kill the Funk Bill. E. Davenport to Mrs. Mary T. Carriel; E. Davenport to Mr. Fred L. Hatch, Davenport Letterbook 15, pp. 963–964.

[9] "President Draper called me into his office to discuss the proposed bill which was to be introduced into the legislature. . . ," Senator Henry M. Dunlap said. "On this occasion I found him considerably 'put out' about the asking of the College of Agriculture for $150,000 for an agricultural building. 'We have only about a dozen students taking agriculture,' he said, 'and I think it outrageous to ask for any such sum of money, when we need so much for other departments where there are so many more students.'" Henry M. Dunlap, "A Legislative History of the University of Illinois, 1851–1939," Record Series 2/9/10.

Bill was another matter. When the members of the Farmers' Institute committee visited the Board of Trustees in December, 1898, they presented Davenport's resolution for dividing the money arising from the two Morrill Acts (the resolution upon which the Funk Bill was based). Although the trustees were "heartily in favor" of the appropriation for the building, they were considerably less enthusiastic about any division of the federal funds. Davenport's resolution was referred to the committee on instruction, where it seems to have been conveniently forgotten.[10]

It is also worth noting that the two accounts in which Davenport states that Draper tried to stop the building appropriation were written in the 1930s — more than three decades after the events described;[11] the letter to President James was written in 1907, when, presumably, these events were fresher in Davenport's mind. And Perry G. Holden, who worked closely with Davenport in the campaign for the College, wrote in his unpublished "Memoir" that "In regard to . . . the bill setting aside half the money for use in Agriculture the President . . . said, 'I'll have to go down and kill the damned thing.'" Holden repeated Draper's words to Senator Charles Bogardus, a prominent farmer and a member of the senate appropriations committee, at the latter's home in Paxton, Illinois. According to Holden,

> The senator took an Illinois Central train down to Springfield, but when it reached Urbana President Draper got on, to go down to Springfield, too. The President said to Senator Bogardus, "There

---

[10] *Twentieth Report*, pp. 32–33. The printed trustees' reports do not indicate that any further action was taken on the resolution. "This Committee [the Farmers' Institute committee] had never been informed as to what action, if any, was taken on their request," Davenport wrote Senator Dunlap on March 30, 1899. "Surely it would have been a courteous thing to have made some sort of reply to so important a Committee! None coming, these men were unable to assure members of the Assembly [the legislature in Illinois is known as the General Assembly] when asked as to whether agriculture would be likely to receive more liberal support in the future than it had enjoyed in the past. . . . This is what led that Committee to move in the matter [i.e., introduce the Funk Bill in the legislature independent of the University bill]. . . . I cannot but regret the whole state of affairs." E. Davenport to Hon. H. M. Dunlap, Davenport Letterbook 15, p. 877.

[11] "Rejuvenation of the College of Agriculture" was written in November, 1933, and "Genesis of the Illinois Agricultural Experiment Station" in March, 1938.

128

is a matter I want to talk over with you," and took him into an office (after they reached Springfield). He began to approach the subject by saying that it was ridiculous to set aside all that money for agriculture, that there were few students, etc. The Senator said, "President Draper, I think that you couldn't do a better job for the University than to take the next train back to Champaign. . . . There are a lot of us who think that the College of Agriculture needs that money, and I think they will get it." [12]

Aside from Holden's and Davenport's unsupported statements, however, there are no written records of the president's activities during this period. In the absence of conclusive evidence to the contrary, it is equally possible that Draper tried to kill both the Funk Bill and the building appropriation (he may have made two trips to Springfield), that he tried to kill only one, or that he did not try to kill either. Whatever Draper's actions may have been, they were patently unsuccessful: the legislature passed both the appropriation for the agriculture building and the Funk Bill. "Rejoice!" Davenport wrote a friend on April 14, 1899. "It looks as if the people had spoken and my four years' fight was nearing a finish. It has been a hard pull. Now a real College of Agriculture must be built up." [13]

To build up the College, Davenport needed more courses in agriculture, more faculty members, and, especially, more students. Since most farmers' sons did not attend high school, they were unable to meet the entrance requirements of the University. Davenport persuaded the faculty to revise these requirements so that country boys sixteen years old or older could be admitted as special students without examination (except in English) and

---

[12] "The University of Illinois (An Important Part of My Life)," Perry G. Holden Memoir, 1944, Record Series 8/6/0/20, Box 1. Hereafter referred to as Holden Memoir. Holden was not a careful reporter, and many of the statements in his "Memoir" are contrary to the known facts. Professor Jackson E. Towne of Michigan State University used Holden's account — apparently without questioning its validity — as the basis for an article entitled "President Draper Gets a College of Agriculture in Spite of Himself," *Agricultural History* XXXVI (October, 1962): 207–212.

[13] E. Davenport to W. H. Burke, April 14, 1899, Davenport Letterbook 15, p. 955. Burke was president of the Illinois Agricultural Press Association. Davenport wrote identical letters to A. H. Sanders, editor of *Breeders' Gazette*, and H. F. Thurston, editor of *Farmers' Review*, *Ibid.*, pp. 960–961.

without declaring whether they were candidates for degrees.[14] But time was getting short. Only twenty-five students were enrolled in the College, and by the opening of the fall semester, "a virtual accounting would be expected, not only by the legislators but by the farmers."[15] Again the Farmers' Institute came to Davenport's assistance. The Institute drafted a resolution, which was adopted by the Board of Trustees, stating that "the University receive into the College of Agriculture annually one student from each county, outside of Cook County, and one from each of the first seven congressional districts of the State, upon the recommendation of the executive committee of the Illinois Farmers' Institute; that matriculation and incidental fees be remitted to the holders of such scholarships; that the benefits of the same be good for two years; and that special students be eligible thereto; *provided*, that the persons so recommended shall not have been previously in the University and shall comply with all the conditions of admission to the College of Agriculture."[16]

At the trustees' meeting on April 19, 1899, President Draper, with surprising equanimity, hailed the building appropriation as "a notable event" in the history of the University. "In all the provision which has been made in many states for agricultural education," he said, "the generosity of this munificent sum given at one time, is unprecedented. . . ." But Draper's following statements showed that, although he had lost a battle, he had no intention of losing the war. He proposed that a "central building" be erected at a cost not exceeding one-half the amount of the appropriation. This building, which would be surrounded by other buildings "of more economic construction" for the various departments of the College, would house an agricultural high school.

---

[14] "I do not ask that the *grade of instruction* should be lowered," Davenport said, "or that passing any subject should be made easier than now; all I ask is that the boys from the farms of Illinois be given a chance to try it on terms they can meet." "Rejuvenation of the College of Agriculture."

[15] Eugene Davenport, "A Son of the Timberlands," *The Country Gentleman* XCI (April, 1926): 38.

[16] *Twentieth Report*, p. 140. For earlier versions of this resolution, see *Twentieth Report*, pp. 77, 109, and *Farmers' Institute* V (1900): 178–179. Each scholarship was worth a total of $58 for the two-year period.

The College of Agriculture would continue to teach courses in technical agriculture, but "all other work of college grade, which is within the scope of any one of the scientific departments already established" would be in the College of Science.[17] These proposals, if carried out, would have made the College of Agriculture little more than a secondary school. "To say that I was frightened at the new turn of affairs," Davenport said, "was . . . to put it mildly."[18] Fortunately, Thomas Burrill and several of the trustees shared Davenport's feelings, and the proposals were referred to a special committee of the Board. The special committee reported that it disapproved of Draper's plan for an agricultural high school, and that it was "earnestly of the conviction that the entire appropriation should be devoted to the establishment of an agricultural college that shall meet the demands of the best farming intelligence of the State. . . . ." It also recommended that "the Committee on Agriculture, with Professors Davenport and Holden, and two others whom they may select, . . . visit the agricultural departments of colleges of other states, study the character of their buildings and equipment, work done, and methods used, and . . . report to the Board of Trustees at the earliest practicable date."[19]

This joint committee, accompanied by Joseph C. Llewellyn, the architect for the new building, visited the University of Wisconsin, Michigan Agricultural College, the experiment station at Geneva, New York, Cornell University, and The Ohio State University.[20] Davenport shrewdly planned for the climax of the trip

---

[17] *Twentieth Report*, pp. 70–71.

[18] Davenport, "Rejuvenation of the College of Agriculture." Although Draper had not consulted with Davenport about his plans, he had given clear warning of them at the state meeting of the Illinois Farmers' Institute in February, 1898. "I have a strong impression, which has been gaining strength in my mind since I have been here," Draper said in his welcoming address at this meeting, ". . . that it would be better for the State University to make a special agricultural school of high grade, or high school, rather than a university or college grade, with a view to taking boys directly from the farm and giving them two or three years of practical work and not a university degree, but a certificate or diploma at the end of the course to show just what they have done." *Farmers' Institute* III (1898): 29.

[19] *Twentieth Report*, p. 78.

[20] The members of the committee were Samuel A. Bullard, Frederic L. Hatch, Mrs. Alice A. Abbott, and Mrs. Carriel from the Board of Trustees, and Davenport,

to be reached at Columbus, where 164 students were enrolled in the College of Agriculture and Domestic Science. Thomas F. Hunt, then dean at Ohio State, arranged for these students to enter his office through the front door, file past the visitors, and leave by the side door. "To our eyes they seemed to run into the thousands," Davenport said. "The effect was magical."[21] As a result of this demonstration, even the most recalcitrant members of the committee were won over to Davenport's side. In its report to the Board of Trustees on June 13, 1899, the committee recommended that all of the $150,000 be used for the building, and Llewellyn was instructed to begin work immediately.[22] The committee also recommended that the faculty of the College be increased in accordance with the provisions of the Funk Bill, but Frederic L. Hatch, a farmer-trustee, told Davenport "that it had been informally agreed by the majority of the Board to do nothing about the . . . Funk Bill."[23] Davenport, who had sent Draper a list of proposed faculty positions and agricultural courses late in May, was completely taken aback. "The action of the President and the Trustees in ignoring the new legislation and shelving my recommendations . . . was unpardonable," Davenport said. "I felt that I had the advantage, and if I were to come to a trial of strength, we would soon see who had the best of the argument."[24]

The next meeting of the Board of Trustees was held at the old Sherman House in Chicago on June 27, 1899. When Davenport, who had been on a well-earned vacation at his Michigan farm, arrived at the hotel, he saw "a goodly number of farmers, especially of those belonging to the Farmers' Institute . . . about the

---

Holden, and Burrill from the University staff. Llewellyn, an 1877 graduate of the University, made the trip at his own expense.

[21] Davenport, "Genesis of the Illinois Agricultural Experiment Station." "I always jokingly accused the dean of repeating," Davenport said. "But he was too honest for that." Eugene Davenport, "A Son of the Timberlands," *The Country Gentleman* XCI (April, 1926): 154. On May 25, 1899, the day Davenport returned home from the trip, he wrote Hunt that "Your bringing in the agricultural students was a fitting and most pleasing ending to the exhibition you gave our people." E. Davenport to Professor T. F. Hunt, May 25, 1899, Davenport Letterbook 16, p. 272.

[22] *Twentieth Report*, pp. 106–107.

[23] Davenport, "Genesis of the Illinois Agricultural Experiment Station."

[24] Davenport, "Rejuvenation of the College of Agriculture."

corridors."[25] Perry Holden claims in his "Memoir" that he was responsible for the presence of these farmers, and the evidence offers some basis for his claim. On June 16, 1899, the day after Davenport left Urbana for Michigan, Holden wrote A. B. Hostetter, secretary of the Illinois Farmers' Institute, that "we are feeling disappointed that the Board of Trustees failed to give us the necessary assistants and appropriations of funds for placing the College of Agriculture on a respectable basis. We know, of course, that the farmers of the State are not going to long put up with this kind of treatment. . . . We shall ask the Board to reconsider the matter at their . . . meeting June 27th in Chicago. Of course the whole matter ought to be talked over very carefully, and possibly it may seem best to the Institute people to give the Committee on Agriculture [of the Board of Trustees] their support."[26] And in a report to the Executive Committee of the Farmers' Institute, President G. A. Willmarth stated that he had "learned from several reliable sources that there was a disposition on the part of the president of the University of Illinois and some of its Board of Trustees to evade by delay the provisions of the so-called Funk Bill. . . ."[27] Presumably one of these sources was Perry Holden.

At any rate, shortly after the opening of the June twenty-seventh meeting, Colonel W. H. Fulkerson introduced a committee of prominent men representing the various agricultural interests of the state.[28] It is not known exactly what these men said

---

[25] *Ibid.*

[26] P. G. Holden to Mr. A. B. Hostetter, June 16, 1899, Davenport Letterbook 16, p. 354. See also P. G. Holden to H. Augustine, June 29, 1899, *Ibid.*, p. 388. "I wired Professor Davenport to come to Chicago to meet with the Board of Trustees, and I wrote him a letter in addition telling him about these people who were coming, and that I would meet him." Holden Memoir. In "Genesis of the Illinois Agricultural Experiment Station," Davenport says that he "had not asked" the Institute members and other agricultural representatives to attend the meeting.

[27] *Farmers' Institute* V (1900): 187.

[28] The members of this committee were W. H. Burke, president of the Illinois Agricultural Press Association, Henry Augustine, president of the Illinois State Horticultural Society, S. Noble King of the Illinois Farmers' Institute, and B. W. Snow of the *Orange Judd Farmer.* Colonel Fulkerson was president of the State Board of Agriculture and chairman of the trustees' Committee on Agriculture. In his "Memoir," Perry Holden describes Fulkerson as "very much incensed because they had not treated Agriculture right at the University."

to the Board (the trustees displayed their usual reticence about recording unpleasant incidents in their printed report of the meeting), but whatever they said must have been effective.[29] After the committee had finished speaking, Mary Turner Carriel offered a resolution, which was adopted, requiring "the Business Manager . . . to credit to the account of the Agricultural College a sum equal to one-half the amount to be received from the Morrill funds," and Davenport was asked to submit "a detailed plan of instruction" for the College. This plan (it was the same one Davenport had given to Draper a month earlier) called for a greatly increased number of courses in agriculture and the addition of four faculty members — one each in animal husbandry, soil physics, horticulture, and dairying. Thomas Burrill, who was acting president of the University while Draper was in Europe for the summer, presented Davenport's plan to the trustees. "I can not in the least be held . . . to speak for President Draper," Burrill said, ". . . and under the circumstances I should much prefer to make no recommendations . . . yet it seems to me action is required, and the responsibility of positive movement is upon all in whom authority exists. . . ." Burrill then recommended that the additional faculty positions requested by Davenport be created, and the trustees adopted Burrill's recommendation.[30] The long, bitter struggle was over at last. "The question of whether agriculture is to form any prominent part of the work of the University of Illinois," Perry Holden wrote a friend on June twenty-ninth, ". . . is forever settled, and decidedly in the affirmative."[31]

Seven weeks later, on August 16, 1899, the Board approved

---

[29] The trustees' report states merely that the committee members "were heard with reference to matters pertaining to the agricultural department of the University." *Twentieth Report,* p. 117. In "Rejuvenation of the College of Agriculture," Davenport makes himself the central figure in the confrontation with the trustees. Although Davenport's account is highly dramatic ("And now, Gentlemen, you will recognize this law and make plans for the use of these new funds as the legislature has directed, and you will do it before you leave this room."), it is not borne out by the known facts about the meeting.

[30] *Twentieth Report,* pp. 117, 119. Burrill, an ardent advocate of agricultural education, was one of Davenport's closest friends at the University.

[31] P. G. Holden to H. Augustine, June 29, 1899, Davenport Letterbook 16, p. 388.

Davenport's list of courses to be taught in the fall. In place of the fewer than twenty courses previously offered by the College, Davenport listed eighteen courses in horticulture, six in veterinary science, and eleven each in agronomy, animal husbandry, and dairying. "It will be noticed," Thomas Burrill said, "that the elective offerings are very large, much exceeding in number those heretofore published by the University, and largely exceeding, it is believed, those offered by any other college or university in America. Of course this list could not be offered except with the understanding that the number of instructors employed should be as you have already arranged. With these instructors and with this liberal amount of required and elective instruction, the College must take very high rank." [32] At this meeting, the trustees also made Perry Holden (who had been promoted from assistant professor to full professor at the June thirteenth meeting) head of the Department of Agronomy. [33]

When Draper returned from Europe at the end of the summer, his "amazement knew no bounds," and he reportedly told Dr. Burrill that "the damage done in his absence was well nigh irreparable." [34] Draper was too good a politician, however, to oppose a situation that could not be changed. "He called me into his office and said in substance that I was 'all wrong' (a favorite expression of his)," Davenport said, "but that from then on he would approve every recommendation I might make if only it did not injure the rest of the university. He proposed, in other words, to give me rope enough to hang myself, an event he freely predicted." [35] Nor was Draper alone in his belief that the College

---

[32] *Twentieth Report*, pp. 128–133.

[33] *Twentieth Report*, p. 140. The trustees adopted the recommendation of the Committee on Agriculture "that the departments of the College . . . be known as those of Agronomy, Animal Husbandry, Dairy Husbandry, Veterinary Science, and Horticulture," but only the Department of Agronomy was actually established at this meeting. The Department of Farm Mechanics (now Agricultural Engineering) was originally a division in the Department of Agronomy. Veterinary science never became a department in the College of Agriculture. Detailed accounts of the various college departments are located in the University Archives. Some of the major developments within each department are described in Chapter Eleven.

[34] Holden Memoir.

[35] "People I Have Known," appendix to "What One Life Has Seen," Davenport manuscript autobiography.

would fail. William Pillsbury, the University registrar, told Davenport that "when the excitement is over you will have no more students than in the past," and many of Pillsbury's less outspoken colleagues were equally pessimistic.[36] But the Institute's scholarship plan was an unqualified success. "We have already registered forty-two new students in Agriculture," Davenport wrote Mrs. Alice Abbott, a member of the Board of Trustees, on September 20, 1899, "and . . . there are twenty-five scholarships already awarded that have not yet appeared for registration. . . . I think we are good for seventy-five new students before the year is out and would not be surprised if we ran up to a hundred, all told."[37] Davenport's prediction proved to be an accurate one. During the 1899–1900 academic year, ninety students (nearly four times the previous year's enrollment) were registered in the College of Agriculture. By the following year, the enrollment had increased to 159 students.[38] "It began to look," Davenport said, "as though Mr. Mills' prediction [of a thousand students in agriculture] was likely to come true."[39]

The agriculture building was completed in the fall of 1900. A handsome structure of brick and stone enclosing nearly two acres of floor space, it consisted of a main building and three wings connected by corridors around an open court.[40] Each wing was 116 feet long, forty-five feet deep, and two stories high. One wing was used for dairy manufactures and household science, another for farm and horticultural machinery, and the third for veterinary science and stock judging. The main building, three stories high, about 250 feet long, and varying in depth from fifty to 100 feet, contained offices, classrooms, and laboratories for the College

[36] Davenport, "Rejuvenation of the College of Agriculture." "The fact is," Perry Holden said, "that some of the people have been here so long and have seen so little come of the various efforts . . . to build up the College of Agriculture that they have come to see nothing in agriculture except the money which comes from the Government." P. G. Holden to Professor W. D. Gibbs, July 11, 1899, Davenport Letterbook 16, p. 440.

[37] E. Davenport to Alice A. Abbott, September 20, 1899, Davenport Letterbook 16, p. 808. William G. Eckhardt of Buffalo Prairie, Illinois, later one of the first two farm advisers in the state, was one of these scholarship students.

[38] See Appendix E.

[39] Davenport, "Rejuvenation of the College of Agriculture."

[40] This court was enclosed in 1912.

departments, offices for the State Entomologist and the agricultural experiment station, and a 500-seat assembly room.[41] On the cornice at the front of the main building were two inscriptions: "Industrial education prepares the way for a millennium of labor" by Jonathan Baldwin Turner, and "The wealth of Illinois is in her soil and her strength lies in its intelligent development" by Andrew Sloan Draper.[42] Whether the latter inscription reflected Draper's true feelings about Illinois agriculture is debatable, but it unquestionably reflected those of Eugene Davenport. "The purpose of agricultural education and research," Davenport said, "is not to benefit the farmer as an individual or even farmers as a favored class. Its primary purpose is the development of agriculture from the public standpoint as a productive occupation and incidentally and necessarily of the people who live by farming."[43]

But the College and agricultural experiment station were subsisting entirely on money from the federal government. Although enrollment increased more than seventy-five per cent between 1900 and 1901, only one instructor was added to the College staff, and the experiment station, already committed to the full extent of the Hatch Act funds, was besieged with requests for investigations of soils, crops, and livestock. "Not only is no further improvement possible under present funds," Davenport said, "but we

---

[41] On December 11, 1900, the Board of Trustees named this assembly room "Morrow Hall" in honor of George E. Morrow. *Twenty-first Report* (1902), p. 33. Fifteen months later, at the request of the Champaign County Farmers' Institute, the trustees agreed to hang "a portrait of this man whom the farmers of Illinois remember with profound respect" in the room bearing his name. *Twenty-first Report*, p. 229. The space formerly occupied by Morrow Hall is now used for offices of the Department of Geography.

[42] "These sentiments," Davenport said of the two inscriptions at the dedication of the building, "mean that no people can become great without regard to the fruits of labor. They mean, too, that labor can not be effective until it is trained; that no laborer can develop and use the resources of a country as they should be developed and used until he is intelligent. . . ." Eugene Davenport, "Address," *Dedication Agricultural Building University of Illinois*. Other speakers at the dedication were S. Noble King and A. P. Grout from the Farmers' Institute, Thomas Burrill, Senator Henry M. Dunlap, L. H. Kerrick, president of the Illinois Cattle Feeders' Association, and Thomas F. Hunt, then dean of the College of Agriculture and Domestic Science at The Ohio State University.

[43] Eugene Davenport, *Education for Efficiency* (New York, 1909), pp. 150–151.

could not run the next two years without sacrificing the best of what has already been gained, because we could not retain our best men and could not take care of larger numbers of students even as well as we are doing now."[44] The only solution was for Illinois to "put some of her own money" into the development of agriculture, as the other major states were doing. On October 19, 1900, Davenport wrote Colonel Mills that he would "shortly need $100,000.00 a year to do the work which ought to be done . . . for Illinois agriculture."[45] The federal government was providing $43,000 annually ($28,000 from the two Morrill Acts and $15,000 from the Hatch Act) to the College and station. To increase the

---

[44] *Reasons for Equipment and Increased Instruction at the Agricultural College and for Extending the Work of the Experiment Station* (printed pamphlet, February, 1901). Copy in College of Agriculture files.

[45] E. Davenport to Col. C. F. Mills, October 19, 1900, Davenport Letterbook 20, p. 227.

Old agriculture building (facing south) shortly after its completion in 1900. The Forestry (now Illini Grove), planted by Thomas Burrill in 1871, is at upper left, and the Morrow Plots are behind the astronomy observatory at right.

total funds to $100,000 per year, the state would have to appropriate $120,000 for the 1901–1903 biennium. "This is certainly not an unreasonable amount," Davenport told Mills, "when we remember that New York is devoting over $130,000.00 of state money for agricultural purposes, besides what is received through the government channels." [46]

Although $120,000 may not have been "an unreasonable amount," Davenport knew that he could not hope to obtain all of it from a president and Board of Trustees who had ignored the Funk Bill until forced to recognize its provisions. "My plan," Davenport wrote Mills, "is . . . to say frankly to the Trustees that we need $10,000.00 a year above present revenue for running

---

[46] *Ibid.* "Other states, having seen and felt the advantage of college and station work, have added largely to the original government funds until, for example, Wisconsin is using for these purposes a total fund of something over $80,000 annually, or twice that of Illinois, and Minnesota approximately $100,000 a year, or two and one-half times that of Illinois." *Reasons for Equipment and Increased Instruction.*

Old agriculture building (facing north). The building was named Davenport Hall on May 21, 1947, in honor of Dean Eugene Davenport.

expenses of the College of Agriculture in order to take care of the natural and normal growth already well under way, and a single appropriation of $10,000.00 for furnishing the building. . . . I feel that I can make excellent arguments showing why the Trustees should put this amount at least in their budget of askings. . . ."[47] Working through Mary Turner Carriel, Colonel Fulkerson, and his other friends on the Board, Davenport persuaded the trustees to ask the legislature for $10,000 annually for instruction in the College and $15,000 ($10,000 the first year and $5,000 the second) for equipping and furnishing the agriculture building.[48] For the remaining $50,000 per year that he needed to reach his goal, Davenport once again turned to the farmers. On November 23, 1900, he wrote Mrs. Carriel that

> The Trustees should lead in the expansion of the college, which corresponds to other university interests, but . . . the people should lead in the extension of the Station work, which aims at the development of the agriculture of the State outside of the line of ordinary teaching. . . . The people are anxious to help and are asking what they can do. I rather want to give them definite jobs and make them see that "there is beautiful fighting all along the line" in the battle of agricultural development. . . . Not that we shall ask the less of the Trustees, but more of the people, and so fix things that neither party would ever be likely to see its way clear to stop doing things for agriculture.[49]

With the cooperation of the Farmers' Institute, State Dairymen's Association, State Horticultural Society, and Illinois Stock Breeders' Association, as well as several agricultural organizations created specifically for his purposes, Davenport prepared a bill — known as "Bill 315" from its House number in the legislature — "to provide for the maintenance of live stock at the College of Agriculture and to extend the work of the Experiment Station."[50]

---

[47] Ibid.

[48] Twenty-first Report, pp. 30, 31, 47.

[49] E. Davenport to Mrs. Mary T. Carriel, November 23, 1900, Davenport Letterbook 20, p. 439.

[50] The complete text of Bill 315 is printed in Reasons for Equipment and Increased Instruction. The bill was introduced in the legislature by George C. Rankin of Monmouth, Illinois.

Bill 315 was divided into sections representing separate agricultural interests of the state, and each section was sponsored by one or more farm organizations. Section one provided $25,000 annually for the maintenance of livestock by the College and for feeding experiments by the station; section two, $10,000 for corn production; section three, $10,000 for chemical and physical examinations of soils; section four, $10,000 for orchard management; section five, $10,000 "to discover and demonstrate improved methods of producing and marketing wholesome milk and other dairy products"; and section six, $5,000 for investigations of sugar beets.[51] The research described in each section of the bill was to be "carried out on lines to be agreed upon by the Dean of the College of Agriculture" and a five-man "advisory committee" appointed by the agricultural organization or organizations sponsoring that particular section. "The advisory committees," Davenport said, "proved a tower of strength before the legislature, arguing that the farmer pays his full proportion of taxes and these askings were in the form of a petition for authority, as one man put it, 'to put our own hands into our own pockets for some of our own money with which to develop our own business.'" Davenport himself "took the position that it was . . . a leap in the dark in the sense that one never knows what is to be the result of research any more than of any other excursion into unknown territory." But he pointed out to the legislature that if the experiment station solved only one of the many problems then plaguing Illinois farmers it "would certainly repay the cost and possibly might recoup the state for all of the appropriations to the University."[52]

The arguments of Davenport and the advisory committees proved effective. Bill 315, carrying an annual appropriation of $54,000 (the livestock section was reduced to $16,000, the dairy section to $5,000, and the sugar-beet section to $3,000), was

---

[51] Section one of the bill was sponsored by the Illinois Live Stock Breeders' Association; section two by the Illinois Corn Growers', Illinois Corn Breeders', and Illinois Grain Dealers' Associations; section three by the Illinois Farmers' Institute; section four by the State Horticultural Society; section five by the State Dairymen's Association; and section six by the Illinois Sugar Beet Growers' Association.

[52] Davenport, "Rejuvenation of the College of Agriculture."

passed unanimously by the legislature. "Nothing like this has ever been done before in the history of agriculture," Davenport wrote Mills on May 3, 1901. "The present legislative year will leave us with a larger revenue for technical agriculture than any other single institution in the world. . . . These are great days . . . and we ourselves scarcely realize the history that is being made. . . ."[53] The College now had a building of its own ("the largest building devoted to agriculture on the continent"), $15,000 for furnishings and equipment, and federal and state funds totaling $210,000 for the 1901–1903 biennium.[54] And most importantly, the passage of Bill 315 gave Davenport the precedent he needed for obtaining future appropriations. In the spring of 1903, true to his promise to the legislature that he "would be

---

[53] E. Davenport to Col. C. F. Mills, May 3, 1901, Davenport Letterbook 23, p. 6. Davenport, a modest man, did not mention his own contributions to that history, but Mary Turner Carriel was less reticent. "I believe in every great work of life there is always someone prepared to take up the duties should anyone fail or be stricken down while in the harness," she said at the 1901 meeting of the Illinois Farmers' Institute. "But I confess to you that my faith would be sorely tried should Dean Davenport fail. A man who could lift the college from the waters of oblivion that were just ready to engulf it, and in four short years place it in the front rank of the colleges of the land . . . is a very difficult man to duplicate." *Farmers' Institute* VI (1901): 119.

[54] These were $28,000 annually from the Funk Bill, $15,000 from the Hatch Act, $54,000 from Bill 315, and $8,000 (reduced from the $10,000 requested) for operating expenses of the College — a total of $105,000 per year.

Horse-judging class in east wing of Davenport Hall, early 1900s.

back after more of the same kind two years later," Davenport received $292,000 of state funds ($122,000 for the College and $170,000 for the experiment station) for the 1903–1905 biennium.[55]

The following spring, on March 9, 1904, Andrew Draper resigned as president of the University of Illinois.[56] The public reasons Draper gave for his resignation were that he had been offered the Commissionership of Education of New York and "could not refuse the call to duty in his native state," and that the University now needed a president of a more scholarly character. But there was at least a third reason — one so personal that he confided it only to close friends. On April 6, 1902, while driving a spirited team of horses on campus, Draper was thrown from the carriage and injured his right leg. The leg was amputated three days later.[57] Although Draper returned to work the following fall, he suffered periodic pains in the stump of the amputated leg. And quite as severe as the physical pain was his sensitivity over the

---

[55] Bill 315 served as the model for all future "Association Bills." The Illinois State Florists' Association was formed in 1907, and a floricultural section was added to subsequent askings. The bill Davenport presented to the legislature for the 1903–1905 biennium called for $95,000 annually for the experiment station and $50,000 for the College. The legislature appropriated $61,000 per year to the College ($56,000 for instruction, buildings, and equipment and $5,000 for fences, drainage, and repairs), but deleted $10,000 ($5,000 each for poultry and sugar-beet investigations) from the experiment-station askings. The station appropriation was divided as follows: livestock, $25,000; corn, $10,000; soil, $25,000; horticulture, $10,000; and dairy, $15,000.

[56] Draper asked that his resignation become effective on April first, but the trustees voted that it "take final effect July 1, 1904." They granted Draper a leave of absence from April first to July first "with the understanding that he will return to perform the function of his office as President incidental to the closing work of the present year." *Twenty-second Report* (1904), p. 274. Thomas Burrill was appointed acting president on June 2, 1904.

[57] "The memory of his father's experience in having his arm amputated without anaesthetic, many years before, sustained Dr. Draper in his own trouble. 'It seemed to me,' he said afterward, 'that if I could not sustain myself through such a trial with the help of all that modern science could bring to me, I would be a very weak son of a very strong father.' It was perhaps with this memory before him that he insisted that his own son, Edwin Lyon Draper, then a senior in the University, who expected to study medicine, should witness the operation." Horner, pp. 157–158. Draper never completely recovered from this accident, and Horner believed that it shortened his life by at least ten years. Draper died at Albany, New York, on April 27, 1913.

fact that he was no longer a whole man. "I could not escape the feeling," he wrote his friend Samuel Bullard, "that it would be better for the University to have a president who was without a physical disability."[58]

On March 21, 1904, the deans of the various colleges sent the Board of Trustees a joint letter requesting that Draper's successor "be a man of broad and substantial scholarship, qualified by temperament and experience to comprehend and appreciate university standards, and to deal justly and intelligently with university men; and that he should have had actual and successful experence with university administration under conditions not far different from those existing here, to the end that his policies regarding internal interests may be foretold with reasonable certainty."[59] But the implicit criticism of Draper (he is not mentioned by name) in this letter was not entirely justified. Although frequently tactless and domineering in dealing with his staff, Draper was in many ways an excellent administrator. When he arrived in Urbana in 1894, there were six principal buildings on campus; when he left ten years later, there were nineteen.[60] During Draper's tenure as president, six new schools or colleges (law, medicine, dentistry, pharmacy, music, and library science) were added to the University, and enrollment increased from 663 to

---

[58] Samuel A. Bullard, "Makers of the University, IV, Andrew Sloan Draper," *Alumni Quarterly* IV (April, 1910): 101. Bullard, a prominent Springfield architect and 1878 graduate of the University, served as a member of the Board of Trustees from 1889 to 1907.

[59] Draft letter to the trustees of the University of Illinois, March 21, 1904, Edmund J. James Faculty Correspondence, Record Series 2/5/6, Box 1. Hereafter cited as James Faculty Correspondence. Although this letter was signed by the deans of all the colleges in Urbana (Davenport, Agriculture; Stephen Forbes; Science; Nathan A. Ricker, Engineering; David Kinley, Literature and Arts; and Oliver A. Harker, Law), the writing style suggests strongly that Forbes was the author.

[60] The buildings already in existence when Draper became president were the mechanical building, drill hall, chemistry building (now Harker Hall), University Hall, Natural History Building, and Engineering Hall. The following buildings were erected during Draper's presidency: metal shops, president's house, large observatory, library (Altgeld Hall), greenhouse, electrical engineering laboratory, power plant, agriculture building, men's gymnasium, theoretics and applied mechanics laboratory, wood shop, and chemistry laboratory (Noyes Laboratory). The Woman's Building (now the English Building), one of his pet projects, was being constructed when Draper left office.

3,335 students, the faculty from eighty to 351 members, and state biennial appropriations from less than $300,000 to more than one million dollars.[61]

The new president, Edmund Janes James, was indubitably a man of broader education and vision than Draper, and the University was fortunate to obtain him. The son of a pioneer Methodist minister, James was born in Jacksonville, Illinois, on May 2, 1855. He was graduated from the high school department of Illinois State Normal in 1873, attended Northwestern and Harvard, and received his Ph.D. degree in economics from the University of Halle, Germany, in 1877. After working as a high school teacher and principal in Illinois, James was appointed professor of public finance at the University of Pennsylvania in 1883, and later served as director of its Wharton School of Finance. He went to the University of Chicago as professor of public administration and director of extension in 1896, and became president of Northwestern University in 1902. On August 26, 1904, he accepted the presidency of the University of Illinois.[62]

At the end of James's first year in office, 406 students were enrolled in eighty-four courses in agriculture, the staff numbered

---

[61] The exact amounts were $295,000 for 1893–1895 (appropriated shortly before Draper became president) and $1,152,400 for 1903–1905. "Some years after he was no longer president," Davenport wrote of Draper, "he made a visit back to the University and came to my office, I called in the faculty of agriculture, grown then to a large body, to meet him. He evidently enjoyed the thing for he said: 'The most significant thing that happened here during my administration was the development of the College of Agriculture and I did all I could to prevent it.'" "People I Have Known," appendix to "What One Life Has Seen," Davenport manuscript autobiography.

[62] James served as president until September 1, 1920. During his administration, the University of Illinois became one of the major educational centers in the United States. More than 1,300 acres of land were added to the University holdings, fifty buildings were erected on campus, and enrollment increased to 9,208 students, the faculty to 943 members, and state biennial appropriations to $5,348,000. James died at Covina, California, on June 17, 1925, and was buried beside his wife at Mount Hope Cemetery in Urbana. He was succeeded as president by David Kinley (1920–1930), Harry Woodburn Chase (1930–1933), Arthur Hill Daniels (1933–1934), Arthur Cutts Willard (1934–1946), George Dinsmore Stoddard (1946–1954), Lloyd Morey (1954–1955), and David Dodds Henry (1955—). The most complete account of James's career is Richard A. Swanson's "Edmund Janes James" (doctoral dissertation, University of Illinois, 1966).

thirty-seven members, and appropriations to the College and experiment station totaled $312,000 for the 1905–1907 biennium. "The rapid growth of the agricultural interests of the University in recent years is unprecedented in educational history," Davenport said in his report to the Board of Trustees on June 23, 1905. "These are the largest numbers in men and money involved in this work at any single point in the world."[63]

During the following five years, however, the experiment station was developed at the expense of the College. State appropriations for the station alone totaled $671,000 between 1905 and 1910, while those for the College totaled only $374,000.[64] Meanwhile, enrollment had increased to 660 students and the staff to seventy-four members. Something had to be done and done quickly. "A new institution, like a tree, cannot stand still: it must grow or it must decay and die," Davenport told the delegates to the state meeting of the Illinois Farmers' Institute on February 22, 1910. "When we cease to give it pruning and care and fertilizer, it will begin to go back. Such is the condition that threatens the college now. . . . We need a renaissance *now* as badly as we needed a new birth in the early nineties."[65] Six months later, the Institute held a special summer meeting at the University, and Davenport took advantage of the occasion to call a conference of the experiment station advisory committees.[66] During the confer-

---

[63] *Twenty-third Report* (1906), p. 108. The following year, Congress passed the Adams Act. Under the provisions of this act, each agricultural experiment station in the United States received $5,000 for the year ending June 30, 1906, and an increase of $2,000 over the amount of the preceding year for each of the next five years until the annual appropriation reached $15,000. The Purnell Act, approved by Congress on February 24, 1925, provided an additional $60,000 annually to each experiment station. The Research and Marketing Act of 1946 removed the statutory limitation on federal funds for experiment stations.

[64] The station received $190,000 for 1905–1907, $205,000 for 1907–1909, and $276,000 for 1909–1911. The College received $122,000 for 1905–1907 and $142,000 for 1907–1909. But in the spring of 1909, when 531 students were enrolled in agriculture and the staff numbered sixty-three members, the College received only $110,000 for the 1909–1911 biennium — $12,000 less than it had received four years earlier, when there were 406 students and thirty-seven staff members.

[65] *Farmers' Institute* XV (1910): 132.

[66] On September 28, 1901, the Advisory Board (formerly Board of Direction) of the agricultural experiment station was discontinued, and its duties assumed

ence, a "General Agricultural Committee" was formed to investigate conditions in the College. This committee was too large to be effective, however, and it appointed a subcommittee "of representative men who would be able and willing to give the necessary time to a thorough and extensive investigation" of the College of Agriculture.[67]

by the various advisory committees that sponsored Bill 315. *Twenty-first Report*, p. 186. These advisory committees and the organizations that appointed them were as follows: Crops: Illinois Grain Dealers' and Illinois Corn Growers' Associations; Animal Husbandry: Illinois Live Stock Breeders' Association; Soils: Illinois State Farmers' Institute; Orchards: Illinois State Horticultural Society; Dairying: Illinois Dairymen's Association; Floriculture: Illinois State Florists' Association.

[67] *Report of the Agricultural Committee on the Needs of the College of Agriculture of the University of Illinois* (printed pamphlet, December, 1910), p. 2. Copy in College of Agriculture files. The General Agricultural Committee included all members of the advisory committees and the officers of the various agricultural associations sponsoring these advisory committees. The members of the subcommittee were Frank I. Mann of Gilman, Ralph Allen of Delavan, H. J. Sconce of Sidell, C. A. Ewing of Decatur, and W. N. Rudd of Blue Island, Illinois. Mann, Allen, Sconce, and Ewing were among the most successful farmers in the state.

Edmund Janes James, President of the University, 1904–1920.

147

Working behind the scenes as usual, Davenport suggested to Frank I. Mann, the chairman, that the subcommittee visit leading colleges of agriculture in other states. "The information gained thereby," Davenport said, "would be worth thousands of dollars to Illinois, and to the College, and would be the most forceful background upon which to rest your investigation and your argument of what is needed here." [68] In late October and early November of 1910, the subcommittee, accompanied by Davenport and two trustees (Frederic L. Hatch and A. P. Grout) visited the agricultural colleges in Iowa, Nebraska, Minnesota, Wisconsin, Michigan, Ohio and New York.[69] When the General Agricultural Committee met again at Urbana in December, the subcommittee presented its report:

> The people of our state may take just pride in their Agricultural College, . . . but we must not be blinded by the fact that we now face the greatest crisis in its history. . . . Other colleges and private commercial interests are making such inroads on our . . . corps of men that additional funds must be made available in order to maintain the present efficiency. Additional instructors must be provided to care for the more than doubled number of students for the new lines of instruction demanded. More men must be had for research. The demand for extension work from almost every township in the state must be met by an additional force. New buildings and new equipment must be provided.[70]

Rudd was a floriculturist and president of the Mount Greenwood Cemetery Association of Chicago.

[68] E. Davenport to Mr. F. I. Mann, September 8, 1910, Davenport Letterbook 60, p. 24.

[69] The subcommittee visited Cornell University at Ithaca, New York, and the agricultural experiment station at Geneva. Grout, who was alo treasurer of the Farmers' Institute, did not visit the Michigan Agricultural College at Lansing.

[70] *Report of the Agricultural Committee*, pp. 8–9. With part of the $122,000 appropriated to the College for the 1903–1905 biennium, Davenport had erected a beef cattle barn and field laboratories for agronomy and horticulture. Two years later, the College again received $122,000 for the biennium. In the meantime, however, enrollment had increased from 284 to 406 students and the staff from twenty-seven to thirty-seven members, and there were only enough funds for a farm mechanics building. The beef cattle barn cost $28,000, and the agronomy and horticultural field laboratories cost $17,000 and $18,000, respectively. The farm mechanics (now agricultural engineering) building was completed in 1907 at a cost of $33,000. An addition was constructed in 1911, a tractor laboratory and garage in 1924, and a second garage in 1928.

As a result of the subcommittee's report, the General Agricultural Committee drafted a bill calling for $574,000 for operating expenses of the College and experiment station, $326,000 to the station alone for research, and $670,750 for buildings and equipment).[71] Mann and his subcommittee were appointed members of a special committee to work for passage of this bill in the legislature. According to Davenport,

> As Mr. Mann . . . was speaking before the appropriations committee of the House, a new member not experienced in this sort of legislation thought to confuse the issue by a question tending to destroy the force of his account of the visit . . . to the various colleges and universities. So, interrupting at an especially significant point, he interposed the observation: "You certainly had a fine junket. Who paid the bills?" Instantly Mr. Mann replied, "We paid them ourselves" and proceeded with his discussion as though nothing had happened. . . . Without doubt that one question and the answer did more to pass the bill than all the arguments for it showed, as nothing else could, the whole-hearted and unselfish interests of the committee in the welfare of the University.[72]

Although the legislature reduced the funds for agricultural buildings and equipment to $175,500, the total appropriation to the College for the 1911–1913 biennium — $951,800 — was more than the entire University had received during the first twenty-seven years of its existence.[73]

---

[71] The bill asked $337,500 for an addition to the agriculture building, $100,000 for a stock-judging pavilion, $40,000 each for dairy cattle and horse buildings, $103,000 for miscellaneous buildings, $35,500 for equipment, and $14,750 for repairs to existing buildings.

[72] Davenport, "Genesis of the Illinois Agricultural Experiment Station." Mann's "legislative committee" also included three members of the experiment station advisory committees — J. P. Mason, J. Mack Tanner, and Joseph R. Fulkerson.

[73] Appropriations for operating expenses of the College and station were reduced to $415,300, for the stock pavilion to $80,000, for miscellaneous buildings to $73,000, and for equipment to $22,500, and funds were refused for an addition to the agriculture building, the dairy cattle and horse buildings, and repairs. As a partial compensation for these reductions and deletions, the legislature added $10,000 to the $326,000 requested for the experiment station (increasing the amount for soils investigations from $120,000 to $130,000) and appropriated $25,000 for two items that did not appear in the original bill — $20,000 for the purchase of forty acres of land and $5,000 for household science.

NINE

Cyril G. Hopkins, Doctor of Soils

T HIS COLLEGE is to have a glorious future," Davenport wrote Frank Mann on May 27, 1911. "A turning point in its history has been established this winter, and it is your committee that has planted the marking stone."[1] During the remaining eleven years of Davenport's administration, the College of Agriculture of the University of Illinois became one of the leading institutions of its kind in the United States. Enrollment in the College increased by seventy-five percent (from 729 students in 1911 to 1,271 in 1920), the staff doubled in size (from seventy-four to 153 members), and state biennial appropriations totaled over three and one-half million dollars between 1913 and 1921.[2] More than a dozen agricultural buildings were erected, including the stock-judging pavilion, floriculture and vegetable crops buildings, genetics building, and cattle-feeding and beef-cattle plants, and over 1,200 acres of farmland were added to the University holdings.[3] But true

---

[1] E. Davenport to Hon. F. I. Mann, May 27, 1911, Davenport Letterbook 63, p. 131.

[2] $940,980 for 1913–1915; $921,230 for 1915–1917; $845,230 for 1917–1919; and $866,080 for 1919–1921.

[3] With the sale of the last 160 acres of the 400-acre Griggs farm in 1896 (eighty acres had been sold in 1872 and 160 acres in 1878), the College lands were reduced to 566 acres. No additions to the acreage were made during Draper's administration, but between 1904 and 1920, the University acquired 589 acres of farmland near Champaign-Urbana and thirty experiment fields totaling 700 acres scattered throughout the state. The lands presently used or managed by the College total 14,670 acres in twenty-eight Illinois counties. These include the campus

achievement is not merely a matter of physical growth, and perhaps Davenport's greatest merit as an administrator lay in his ability to select the best men available to head the various College departments.[4] These men were Wilber John Fraser, Herbert Windsor Mumford, Joseph Cullen Blair, and Cyril George Hopkins.

After receiving his bachelor's degree from the University of Illinois in 1893, Wilber Fraser served as assistant in the College of Agriculture until 1896, and as instructor of dairying from 1896 to 1905.[5] When the Department of Dairy Husbandry was established the following year, Fraser became its first head. He immediately took aggressive steps to improve the dairy industry in Illinois. Through numerous publications and through speeches to farm organizations in all parts of the state, he convinced dairymen of the importance of using weighing scales and the Babcock test to determine the exact amounts of milk and butterfat produced by each cow in a herd.[6] In the spring of 1902, Fraser and Arthur J. Glover, later editor of *Hoard's Dairyman*, organized eight Illinois farmers into what was probably the first formal "cow-testing association" in the United States.[7]

---

farms (2,200 acres), outlying agricultural research centers and experimental tracts (1,502 acres), Dixon Springs Agricultural Center (5,000 acres), and endowment farms (5,968 acres). Income from the endowment farms (Allerton, Carter-Pennell, Hackett, Weber, and Wright farms) is used by the University for educational purposes, especially scholarships.

[4] In applying for the position of dean of the College, Davenport wrote Draper that "my plan with subordinates is to give them each definite lines of work and duties and to hold them strictly responsible for results. If they fail, the failure is theirs; if they succeed everybody will know it and they will be benefitted. This secures the best service, and it is just." Eugene Davenport to Andrew Sloan Draper, November 26, 1894, Draper Faculty Correspondence, Box 1. "His largest results," Thomas Burrill said of Davenport, "have been indirectly achieved through organization and direction of others, while he has been little in evidence personally." *Illinois Agriculturist* XIX (June, 1915): 738.

[5] Fraser received a Master of Science degree from the University of Illinois in 1902, and studied at Harvard University from 1915 to 1917.

[6] The Babcock Test, developed by Professor Stephen M. Babcock of the University of Wisconsin in 1890, was the first simple and practical method for measuring the butterfat content of milk.

[7] The first cow-testing association officially recognized by the U.S. Department of Agriculture was established by Helmer Rabild at Newago, Michigan, in 1905. Glover's three publications dealing with the dairy herds tested in Illinois — Univer-

Under Fraser's leadership, the Department also carried out experiments proving that good dairy cows could produce 10,000 pounds of milk annually when fed corn silage and alfalfa hay without added concentrates; that these cows could eat large amounts of silage and alfalfa daily for several lactations without suffering ill effects (it was then commonly believed that the acid content of silage caused serious digestive problems); and that corn and alfalfa provided more nutrients per acre for milk production than any other Illinois crops.[8] Realizing the need for closer cooperation in solving research problems, Fraser called a meeting of dairy department heads and investigators from the United States and Canada. This meeting, held at Morrow Hall in the agriculture building on July 17, 1906, resulted in the formation of the National Association of Dairy Instructors and Investigators (now the American Dairy Science Association).[9] In April, 1913, Dr. Harry Alexis Harding, who had served for fourteen years as bacteriologist of the agricultural experiment station at Geneva, New York, replaced Fraser as head of the Department of Dairy Husbandry.[10] Fraser remained as a professor in the Department until his retirement in 1937.

---

sity of Illinois Agricultural Experiment Station Bulletin 85, Circular 77, and Circular 84 — appeared in June, 1903, June, 1904, and December, 1904, respectively. In 1924, Professor C. S. Rhode changed the name of the Illinois cow-testing project to the "Dairy Herd Improvement Association." This name was later accepted for the national Dairy Record program.

[8] These experiments, conducted at Urbana from 1908 to 1914, comprised the so-called "Twenty-Acre Project." Fraser described this project in a series of fifteen articles for *Hoard's Dairyman* beginning with the January 19, 1923, issue.

[9] The proceedings of the meeting are given in University of Illinois Agricultural Experiment Station Circular 111 (Urbana, 1907). The National Association of Dairy Instructors and Investigators became the Official Dairy Instructors' Association in 1907 and the American Dairy Science Association in 1916. See *Journal of Dairy Science Golden Jubilee Issue* (June, 1956). On June 28, 1933, the Association presented Fraser with a citation for being "the first Professor of Dairying in America to have a clear vision of the possibilities in advancing the cause of Scientific Dairying through a closer organization of the workers in the field." The plaque bearing this citation is located in the Office of the Department of Dairy Science, 315 Animal Sciences Laboratory, Urbana.

[10] A native of Wisconsin, Harding received his bachelor's and master's degree from the University of Wisconsin and his Ph.D. from Cornell. During his seven years (1913–1920) as head of the Department, he greatly enhanced its scientific

Herbert Mumford attended Albion College for two years, and was graduated from the Michigan Agricultural College (where he studied under Davenport) in 1891.[11] After four years on the family farm in Michigan, he joined the staff of his alma mater, becoming professor of agriculture in 1899. In the fall of 1901, Davenport brought Mumford to the University of Illinois as head of the Department of Animal Husbandry.[12] Working closely with

---

standing by developing the divisions of dairy bacteriology, physiology, and chemistry.

[11] Mumford and his elder brother, Frederick Blackmar Mumford, received honorary doctor of agriculture degrees from Michigan State University in 1927. Frederick Mumford was dean of the University of Missouri College of Agriculture from 1909 to 1938.

[12] Mumford assumed Davenport's positions as professor of animal husbandry in the College and chief of animal husbandry in the experiment station. The trustees granted Davenport permission to continue teaching a course in livestock breeding (a subject in which he was particularly interested) "with the position and title of Professor of Principles of Variation and Selection in Domesticated Animals and Plants (Thremmatology)." *Twenty-first Report*, pp. 181–182. Despite Davenport's

Wilber John Fraser, Head of the Department of Dairy Husbandry, 1902–1913.

Davenport, Mumford organized the Department into divisions for each of the classes of livestock and for nutrition, genetics, and extension, a system that was later used by many other colleges of agriculture.[13]

At Michigan, Mumford had published a study of wool production, apparently the first American research bulletin on the marketing of an agricultural product. In July, 1902, he brought out another pioneer publication, "Market Classes and Grades of Cattle With Suggestions for Interpreting Market Quotations." This bulletin, the first serious attempt to divide cattle into commercial classes and grades, was largely responsible for the present system of selling livestock on the terminal market. It was followed by parallel publications dealing with market classes and grades of swine, horses and mules, sheep, and meats.[14] Although trained as a livestock man (he was considered one of the best beef-cattle judges in the United States), Mumford was especially interested in the economic aspects of agriculture, and in 1910 he initiated research in farm organization and management that led to the establishment of the Department of Agricultural Economics two decades later.[15]

A native of Nova Scotia, Joseph Blair was graduated from the Provincial College of Agriculture at Truro in 1892. For the next four years, he attended Cornell University, studying under the

---

insistence that "thremmatology" (from the Greek *thremma*, a thing bred) was a broader and more accurate term than "breeding," the new word never came into general usage. Davenport was the first and (not surprisingly, perhaps) last "Professor of Thremmatology" in the world.

[13] The horse, swine, and meats divisions were established in 1903, sheep in 1906, beef cattle in 1910, poultry and animal nutrition in 1911, animal genetics in 1912, and livestock extension in 1915.

[14] University of Illinois Agricultural Experiment Station Bulletins 78, 97, 122, 129, and 147, respectively. Louis D. Hall, the author of Bulletin 147, seems to have been the first experiment-station worker in the United States to conduct research in meats. The information reported in this bulletin served as the basis for the market classes and grades of meat used by the meat trade and the beef-grading service of the federal government. Walter C. Coffey, the author of Bulletin 129, headed the sheep division of the Department of Animal Husbandry from 1906 to 1921. He later became dean of the College of Agriculture and president of the University of Minnesota.

[15] See Chapter Eleven for some of the important contributions of the Department of Agricultural Economics.

celebrated horticulturist Liberty Hyde Bailey and under Frederick Olmstead, the designer of New York's Central Park.[16] In the summer of 1896, Blair was appointed instructor of horticulture at the University of Illinois.[17] Since his teaching assignment did not begin until fall, he set out on a horseback tour of southern Illinois to acquaint himself with its people and agriculture. When Blair reached the Ohio River, he found the site of Fort Massac, where George Rogers Clark and his "Long Knives" entered the Illinois country, and he played an important part in the purchase and restoration of this site as the first state park seven years later.[18]

In 1902, Blair was made professor of pomology (the study of fruits) and head of the newly formed Department of Horticulture, a position he held for thirty-six years. Imposing in appearance, with the physique and profile of a matinee idol, Blair proved an able department head. He organized the Department into its appropriate subject-matter divisions and established the first four-year curriculum in floriculture and one of the most advanced and complete courses in landscape architecture in the United States.[19]

Although genuine leaders in their respective fields, Fraser, Mumford, and Blair were not trained scientists; Cyril Hopkins was. Born on a farm near Chatfield, Minnesota, on July 22, 1866, Hopkins, like Davenport, spent his boyhood and early youth in a

---

[16] Blair did not receive a degree from Cornell, but he was later awarded two honorary degrees for his contributions to horticulture — an M.S.A. (Master of Science of Agriculture) from Iowa State University in 1906 and a Doctor of Science from the College of Wooster (Ohio) in 1920.

[17] *Nineteenth Report*, p. 19. Burrill wrote Bailey on May 21, 1896, asking him to recommend a horticulturist "who is either ready now to take a professorship or who will pretty certainly grow into fitness for one." Bailey recommended Blair.

[18] Blair, whose love of trees was as deep as Burrill's, planted literally thousands of trees and shrubs in the city of Urbana and on the University campus. A co-founder and first president of the Illinois Association of Park Districts, he organized the Urbana Park District (Blair Park is named in his honor) in 1907, and served as a member of the board for forty-two years.

[19] The division of vegetable crops was established in 1902, floriculture in 1908, and plant breeding and landscape gardening in 1912. The work in landscape architecture and community planning was transferred to the College of Fine and Applied Arts in 1931. The division of plant pathology, established in 1941, became a separate department in the College of Agriculture in 1955. Blair served as president of the American Society for Horticultural Science in 1922, and as president of the American Pomological Society from 1929 to 1931.

pioneer environment. In 1880, when Cyril was fourteen years old, his family moved to what was then Dakota Territory. "There," Hopkins told a group of bankers thirty years later, "I gathered the buffalo bones from before the plow that turned the rich virgin soil."[20] Through teaching in country schools, he earned enough money to attend South Dakota Agricultural College (now South Dakota State University) at Brookings, and was graduated in 1890. Four years later, Hopkins received his Master of Science degree from Cornell University. He served as assistant in chemistry at South Dakota Agricultural College from 1890 to 1892 and at Cornell from 1892 to 1893, and was acting professor of pharmacy and assistant chemist of the experiment station at Brookings from 1893 to 1894. On November 15, 1894, six weeks before Davenport came to Urbana as dean of the College of Agriculture, Hopkins was appointed chemist of the University of Illinois Agricultural Experiment Station.[21] He accepted the position with the understanding that he would be allowed to continue graduate work, and in June, 1898, he completed the requirements for the Ph.D. degree from Cornell. The following June, Hopkins received a year's leave of absence without pay (from September 1, 1899 to September 1, 1900) to study the chemistry of carbohydrates at the University of Göttingen in Germany.

While Hopkins was in Germany, an event occurred that was to change the course of his life. Early in March, 1900, Perry G. Holden resigned from the University to become superintendent of a sugar-beet refining company at Pekin, Illinois. Holden had effectively organized the Department of Agronomy into the divisions of soil physics and biology, farm management, crops, and farm mechanics, and he was an excellent teacher as well as a popular speaker at Farmers' Institutes. Davenport was genuinely fond of Holden, and was reluctant to lose him.[22] At the Board of

---

[20] Cyril G. Hopkins, "The Soil as a Bank," address delivered at the fourth annual convention of Group Four, Illinois Bankers' Association, Aurora, Illinois, June 15, 1910 (printed pamphlet). Copy in College of Agriculture files.

[21] *Eighteenth Report*, p. 40. Hopkins was selected for this position by Burrill and Draper.

[22] Holden, who was equally fond of Davenport, named his eldest son Eugene Davenport Holden in honor of his old friend and mentor. The Farmers' Institute passed a resolution expressing "deep regret" at Holden's resignation and calling

Trustees' meeting on March thirteenth, Mary Turner Carriel, at Davenport's suggestion, moved that Holden be given a leave of absence without pay until September first, and that he return to the University on that date at $2,500 per year (a salary as high as that of any professor in the University, and $800 more than Holden had been receiving). Although Mrs. Carriel's motion was adopted (by a vote of five to four), Draper reported on April eighteenth that Holden "was not ready to say what he would do, but that he did not expect to accept the proposition of the Board." Then Draper, who did not like Holden (probably because of the latter's work in securing passage of the Funk Bill), recommended that the trustees accept Holden's resignation. The Board approved Draper's recommendation.[23]

Whether Holden could have been induced to remain at the University for $1,500 less than the $4,000 salary offered by the sugar beet company is a moot question. But in asking the trustees to accept Holden's resignation, Draper unwittingly did Davenport a favor. The new prospects for the College of Agriculture opened up by passage of the Funk Bill and the appropriation for a building made it imperative that the Department of Agronomy (the only College department in existence at that time)[24] be headed by a man with a solid background in science. Perry Holden, whatever his merits as a teacher and lecturer, was not a scientist. On April 25, 1900, Davenport, with the approval of Draper, Forbes, and Burrill, wrote Cyril Hopkins at the Univer-

upon the University to offer "Professor Holden such terms as may induce him to return to his former position in which we feel he has rendered efficient service to the State." *Farmers' Institute* VI (1901): 159–160.

[23] *Twentieth Report*, pp. 274–275. Holden remained with the sugar-beet refining company only one year before becoming manager of the Funk Brothers Seed Company at Bloomington, Illinois. He was appointed professor of agronomy at Iowa State College in 1902, and served in that position for ten years. After his defeat as candidate for governor of Iowa on the Progressive ticket in 1912, Holden was made director of the Agricultural Extension Department of the International Harvester Company. He retired from this position in 1932, and died on October 8, 1959, five days before his ninety-fourth birthday.

[24] The trustees voted to establish a "department of domestic science" on March 13, 1900, but the Department of Household Science was not actually organized until the fall of 1900. The Department of Animal Husbandry was established in 1901, and the Departments of Dairy Husbandry and Horticulture the following year.

sity of Göttingen offering him the professorship in agronomy. "It is not necessary for me to say that this opportunity for work in agriculture is much broader than that of Chemist of the Station," Davenport wrote. "I believe there is no greater opportunity for work and reputation in agriculture today in this country. . . ."[25] Hopkins cabled his acceptance, and on September 1, 1900, he began work as head of the Department of Agronomy.

For the next twenty years, the careers of Cyril Hopkins and Eugene Davenport were to be closely linked. The two men had a great deal in common: both were staunch Republicans; both were God-fearing, frugal, and abstemious (Hopkins would not knowingly hire a man who used tobacco or alcohol, and Davenport once said that he would rather his daughter "marry the closest possible relative than marry any man who smokes cigarettes"),[26] and both believed in the sacred mission of agricultural education. Davenport, although not himself a scientist, also appreciated Hopkins's scientific abilities.

In the spring of 1896, Davenport and Thomas Burrill had encouraged Hopkins to undertake a series of experiments designed to change the chemical composition of the corn kernel.[27] These were not the first corn-breeding experiments to be conducted at the Illinois station: in 1889, the year after the station was established, Thomas F. Hunt crossed dent, sweet, and flint corns; George W. McCluer, assistant station horticulturist from 1888 to

[25] E. Davenport to Dr. C. G. Hopkins, April 25, 1900, Davenport Personal Letterbook, p. 14.

[26] E. Davenport to F. M. Burgess, August 15, 1910, Davenport Letterbook 59, p. 386. Hopkins eschewed the use of all "narcotics," including coffee, and ate meat only once a day; Davenport, less rigid in his personal habits, was an inveterate coffee drinker. The best insight into Hopkins's character can be gained from his *The Story of the Soil* (Boston, 1911). In this curious work, Hopkins attempted to popularize his theories of soil fertility through the medium of a sentimental love story. The hero, Percy Johnston, is obviously modeled upon the author in both physical appearance ("slightly above the average height, and solidly built") and character. Neither fiction nor nonfiction in the accepted sense, and without any redeeming literary virtues except that of honesty, *The Story of the Soil* is nevertheless interesting if one is interested in Hopkins. The entire book was serialized in *Prairie Farmer* from January 1, 1911 through February 15, 1912.

[27] Hopkins's doctoral thesis, "The Chemistry of the Corn Kernel," served as the basis for these experiments. It was published as University of Illinois Agricultural Experiment Station Bulletin 53 (Urbana, June, 1898).

1896, crossed and self-pollinated corn in 1890; and George Morrow and Frank D. Gardner, an 1891 graduate of the University, crossed corn varieties to increase yields in 1894.[28] But Hopkins's work in improving the chemistry of the corn kernel itself was without precedent in the history of plant breeding.

From the 1896 crop of Burr's White corn grown on the experiment station farm, Hopkins selected 163 "good, sound" ears. Then,

---

[28] McCluer, whose experiments were on a sizeable scale, correctly concluded that "the self-fertilized ears showed the same modification of kernels as those naturally fertilized, proving that each kernel of the crossed corn had in itself the power to produce both sweet and dent corn." University of Illinois Agricultural Experiment Station Bulletin 21 (Urbana, May, 1892), p. 95. Morrow's and Gardner's experiments essentially duplicated those performed by Dr. William Beal at the Michigan Agricultural College in 1876. The early corn-breeding work at the Illinois station, as well as that later conducted by Perry Holden (from 1896 to 1900) and Archibald Dixon Shamel (from 1898 to 1902), deserves further study. Shamel, an 1898 graduate of the University, joined the Bureau of Plant Industry of the U.S. Department of Agriculture in 1902. As principal physiologist in the U.S. Horticultural Field Laboratory at Riverside, California, Shamel did important work in improving citrus and other fruits through bud selection. He died in 1956 at the age of seventy-eight.

Cyril George Hopkins, Head of the Department of Agronomy, 1900–1919.

through chemical analyses of three rows of kernels taken length-wise from each ear, he chose seventy-two ears (twenty-four with a relatively high percentage of protein, twelve with a low per-centage of protein, twenty-four with a high percentage of fat, and twelve with a low percentage of fat) for planting. Each of these four groups of ears was planted "ear-to-row" in an isolated plot to avoid fertilization from other corn. By assigning "dam numbers" to the parent ears and corresponding "register num-bers" to their offspring, Hopkins could trace the exact pedigree of each row of corn and compare a particular row with all the other rows in the plot as well as with the ear from which the row was planted. The rows were harvested separately, and only those ears with the highest and lowest percentage of protein or oil were selected for planting the following spring.[29] In June, 1899, Hopkins reported that "it is possible to influence the composition of corn; that by proper selection of seed any of its principal con-stituents, protein, fat, or carbohydrates, may be increased or de-creased.[30] The following year, he succeeded in producing four distinct strains of corn from the parent variety.[31]

For the first few years, Hopkins carried on his corn-breeding project with only one laboratory assistant, Louie Henrie Smith.[32] But in the early summer of 1901, a young chemist named Edward Murray East was appointed to the experiment station staff to help

[29] For a detailed description of Hopkins's system of numbering ears and of the experiments themselves, see University of Illinois Agricultural Experiment Station Bulletins 55, 82, 87, 100, 119, and 128.

[30] University of Illinois Agricultural Experiment Station Bulletin 55 (Urbana, June, 1899), p. 238.

[31] The average protein content of the original Burr's White corn was 10.92 per-cent, and the average oil content was 4.7 percent. In 1900, the high protein strain averaged 12.32 percent and the high oil strain 6.12 percent. In 1968, after sixty-eight generations of selection, the high protein strain averaged 23.9 percent and the high oil strain 17.5 percent.

[32] Smith received his bachelor's and master's degrees in chemistry from the University in 1897 and 1899, and his Ph.D. from the University of Halle, Germany in 1907. He served as assistant chemist of the experiment station during Hopkins's leave in Germany, and was made chief assistant chemist in 1902, assistant chief in chemistry and plant breeding in 1903, assistant professor of plant breeding in 1905, and chief and professor of plant breeding in 1911. Smith was acting head of the Department of Agronomy in 1913–1914 and again in 1918–1919. He retired from the University in 1940, and died seven years later at the age of seventy-five.

with analyses of the ears. A native of DuQuoin, Illinois, East was graduated from the University in June, 1901, the same month he began working with Hopkins. He received his Master of Science degree in 1904 and his Ph.D. (the first awarded in agronomy by the University of Illinois) in 1907. East was employed on Hopkins's breeding project for four years before joining the staff of the Connecticut Agricultural Experiment Station, where he was to achieve fame as one of the genuine pioneers in the development of hybrid corn.[33] In *The Hybrid-Corn Makers*, A. Richard Crabb states that Hopkins ordered East to discontinue research on inbred lines of corn at the Illinois experiment station.[34] Two facts are worth noting. On December 1, 1906, Davenport wrote the Office of Experiment Stations in Washington, asking permission to inbreed corn. "When we recall Darwin's experiments with inbreeding among plants," Davenport said, "we are led to seriously doubt the soundness of the popular prejudice against inbreeding. . . . It would be our purpose to continue this experiment indefinitely."[35] And the letters Hopkins wrote East at the Connecticut station display a friendliness that would scarcely be expected if relations between the two men were as strained as Crabb implies in his book.[36] In view of these facts, the validity

---

[33] East served as agronomist of the Connecticut experiment station from 1905 to 1909, and on the faculty of Harvard University from 1909 until his death in 1938 at the age of fifty-nine.

[34] A. Richard Crabb, *The Hybrid-Corn Makers: Prophets of Plenty* (New Brunswick, 1947), p. 33. Crabb's book seems to have served as a primary source for later books dealing with the history of hybrid corn. See Grant G. Cannon, *Great Men of Modern Agriculture* (New York, 1963), p. 22; Henry A. Wallace and William L. Brown, *Corn and Its Early Fathers* (Chicago, 1956), p. 109; and the chapter on hybrid corn in Howard T. Walden's *Native Inheritance: The Story of Corn in America* (New York, 1966). Unfortunately, *The Hybrid-Corn Makers* is undocumented and inaccurate (East was not graduated from the University in 1900, Hopkins did not invent the ear-to-row planting technique). The definitive history of hybrid corn — perhaps the most important agricultural discovery of our time — has yet to be written.

[35] E. Davenport to Dr. A. C. True, December 1, 1906, Davenport Letterbook 46, p. 2.

[36] See Cyril G. Hopkins Letterbooks 17, pp. 295, 436; 19, pp. 197, 381; and 23, pp. 27, 182, Record Series 8/6/3. Hereafter cited as Hopkins Letterbooks. In recommending East for the position of agronomist of the Connecticut experiment station, Hopkins wrote E. H. Jenkins, the station director, that "Mr. East is a Christian man, an agreeable companion, and . . . both he and his excellent wife

of Crabb's statement that Hopkins ordered East to stop inbreeding corn is at least questionable. There is no question, however, that East's decision to become a plant geneticist rather than a chemist was a direct outgrowth of his work with Hopkins on the corn-breeding project.

This project attracted attention at agricultural experiment stations throughout the country, and Hopkins's "pedigree" method of numbering ears was quickly appropriated by other investigators. In choosing Hopkins to succeed Perry Holden as professor of agronomy, however, Davenport had a broader end in view than corn experiments. Like his predecessor, George Morrow, Daven-

are delightful people to know and associate with." Cyril G. Hopkins to Director E. H. Jenkins, January 28, 1905, Hopkins Letterbook 14, p. 296.

Edward Murray East, one of the genuine pioneers in the development of hybrid corn, in 1904. East received the first Ph.D. degree in agronomy from the University in 1907.

port was deeply concerned about the "wearing out" of the soil.[37] As a result of improved seed, better methods of cultivation, and the introduction of nitrogen-fixing bacteria, some of the best Illinois soils were more productive than when they were first tilled several decades earlier. "But let us not deceive ourselves," Davenport told the farmers. "If our lands do produce more than formerly it shows only that our methods are good and that the original stock of fertility was high. It does not show it to be inexhaustible." And in many areas of the state crop yields had decreased sharply. Although farmers in these areas planted clover, rotated crops, and applied so-called "complete" fertilizers, yields continued to decline. "If we have soils so unproductive as not to yield a fair return for labor and not to support a thrifty and developing population," Davenport said, "we must know the reason why."[38] As head of the Department of Agronomy, Cyril Hopkins was given the responsibility of finding out "the reason why."

In the spring of 1901, the legislature passed Bill 315. Under the "soils section" of this bill, sponsored, at Davenport's recommendation, by the Illinois Farmers' Institute, the experiment station received $20,000 ($10,000 annually for two years) for soils investigations. With this money, Cyril Hopkins began the work to which he was to devote the rest of his life: the preservation of the fertility of the soil. "The only system of maintaining soil fertility which . . . can ever safely be adopted as . . . permanent," he said, ". . . must be a system which can be applied to all of the soils of this State — not to a few farms only, or for a few years only, but to all the soils of Illinois, and for all time — yes, even more than that — it should be a system which can be applied to the soils of adjoining states — to Indiana and Ohio, to Wisconsin and Iowa — in short, to the soils of America."[39] But before Hop-

---

[37] "If I ever go insane," Davenport said, "it will be upon the subject of fertility; upon the retention of the producing power of land indefinitely." *Farmers' Institute* IX (1904): 111.

[38] *Ibid.*, pp. 109, 108.

[39] *Farmers' Institute* VIII (1903): 119–120. Hopkins seems to have been interested in soil fertility long before he became head of the Department of Agronomy. As a student at South Dakota Agricultural College, he suffered "bitter disappointment" when his chemistry professor refused to teach him how to analyze soils.

kins could develop a system of permanent agriculture, he needed definite answers to certain questions: What are the requirements of various crops? What is the total stock of plant food in the soil? How much of this plant food becomes available to the crop through conventional methods of farming? What is the most practicable and economical means of adding plant food to the soil? To answer these questions, Hopkins launched a state-wide program that included chemical and physical analyses of soils, pot-culture tests, field experiments, and, in cooperation with the United States Department of Agriculture, a comprehensive soil-survey of Illinois.[40]

Through these investigations, as well as those conducted under later legislative bills, Hopkins developed what has become known as "the Illinois System of Permanent Soil Fertility." The concept behind this system is that the farmer is a steward of the soil, and it is his duty to pass on to his descendants land that is richer, not poorer, than when he took over its management. "How shall the fertility of the soil be maintained?" Hopkins rhetorically asked the delegates to the 1903 state meeting of the Illinois Farmers' Institute.

> We hear two very common answers to this question: The grain farmer says we must grow clover. The livestock farmer says we must put the manure back on the land. But neither of these answers really answers the question. Clover will not maintain the fertility of the soil, and if all of the crops which are grown on the farm are fed on the farm and the manure all returned to the land, it will not maintain the fertility of the soil, not even if clover is

---

Ibid., p. 142. And in his first publication as experiment station chemist, a study of the composition and digestibility of various silages for livestock, Hopkins pointed out that both soybeans and cowpeas "have great value for improving the soil." University of Illinois Agricultural Experiment Station Bulletin 43 (Urbana, April, 1896), p. 201.

[40] Because of personal differences between Hopkins and Dr. Milton Whitney, chief of the Bureau of Soils, the Department of Agriculture withdrew from its agreement with the Illinois station at the end of the 1903 field season. Cooperative soil-survey work between the two organizations was not resumed until 1943. By 1969, soil maps and reports had been published for eighty-six of Illinois' 102 counties. For a detailed account of the soil-survey program in Illinois, see Herman L. Wascher, "History of the Illinois State Soil Survey," 1967 (mimeograph). Copy in College of Agriculture files.

also grown. The only way by which the livestock farmer can maintain the fertility of his soil by the use of manure is to feed, not only his own crops, but his neighbors' crops also, and then put all the manure upon his own land. This answers the question for a few farmers who are also extensive cattle feeders, but it does not answer the question for Illinois; it does not answer the question for America — we can not all feed our own crops and our neighbors' crops also. How then shall we maintain the fertility of Illinois soil? There is but one answer to this question. . . . Preserve good physical conditions and then put back upon the land all of the fertility which is taken off — not some of it, not most of it, but all of it; and not only that which is removed by cropping, but also that removed by the blowing, washing or leaching of the soil.[41]

For nearly twenty years, in literally hundreds of speeches and publications, Hopkins refined and enlarged upon the details of his system of soil fertility, but the system itself is basically simple. It rests upon three general principles: first, for profitable farming, the farmer must rely upon the cheapest possible sources of fertility; second, crop yields are limited by one of the essential elements of plant food, and a little more of the limiting element must be added to the soil than is removed by cropping and by natural causes such as drainage; and third, the acidity of the soil must be corrected by the use of finely ground limestone so that legumes can be grown. Of the ten essential elements of plant food, three — carbon, hydrogen, and oxygen — are obtained from air and water; the remaining seven are furnished by the soil. Through chemical analyses of "normal" cornbelt soils, Hopkins concluded that five of these elements — iron, sulfur, calcium, magnesium, and potassium — were present in large enough quantities to last for centuries, but the supplies of the other two, nitrogen and phosphorus, were only sufficient for the lifetime of one man.[42] "Phosphorus," he said, "is the key to permanent agriculture on these lands. To

---

[41] *Farmers' Institute* VIII (1903): 120.

[42] According to Hopkins's calculations, the typical brown silt loam of the cornbelt contained enough calcium per acre for the production of a 100-bushel crop of corn annually for 9,000 years, enough magnesium for 1,300 years, enough potassium for 1,800 years, and enough phosphorus for sixty-two years.

maintain or increase the amount of phosphorus in the soil makes possible the growth of clover (or other legumes) and the consequent addition of nitrogen from the inexhaustible supply in the air. . . ."[43]

For several years, however, most farmers were apathetic to Hopkins's teachings. "So far as I have discovered," Hopkins said in February, 1903, "in all other things Illinois farmers are intelligent, progressive, consistent, and unprejudiced; but, regarding the use and value of that element of fertility which limits the productive capacity of a large proportion of Illinois soils [i.e., phosphorus], I am compelled to say that Illinois farmers, as a rule are inconsistent, if not actually prejudiced."[44] The following fall, Hopkins suffered a further setback when the United States Department of Agriculture published the "famous" Bulletin 22 — "The Chemistry of the Soil as Related to Crop Production." This bulletin, written by Milton Whitney, chief of the Bureau of Soils, and F. K. Cameron, one of the Bureau's chemists, was a direct contradiction of Hopkins's theories of permanent soil fertility. Whitney and Cameron claimed that "practically all soils contain sufficient plant food for good crop yield, that this supply will be indefinitely maintained, and that this actual yield of plants adapted to the soil depends mainly upon favorable climatic conditions, upon the cultural methods and suitable crop rotation . . . and that a chemical analysis of a soil . . . will in itself give no indication of the fertility of this soil or of the possible yield of a crop. . . ."[45] Bulletin 22 fell upon the agricultural world like a

---

[43] Cyril G. Hopkins, *Soil Fertility and Permanent Agriculture* (Boston, 1910), p. 183.

[44] *Farmers' Institute* VIII (1903): 123. "I am neither sensational nor merely theoretical," Hopkins told the members of the Farmers' Institute. "If anything I am practical. . . . The greater part of my life I have been a practical farmer — not a 'sidewalk' farmer, but a plain, everyday farmer in plain blue overalls — with hands which are still calloused from years of farm work. . . . I do not speak of this boastingly. I speak of it because I want your confidence and the confidence of the Illinois farmers whom you represent." *Ibid.*, p. 141. But most farmers (Ralph Allen, Frank I. Mann, and A. P. Grout were conspicuous exceptions) remained unconvinced of the usefulness of Hopkins's system of permanent agriculture. Hopkins neither looked nor talked like a farmer, and he had left the farm at the earliest opportunity to become a college professor.

[45] U.S. Department of Agriculture Bureau of Soils Bulletin 22 (Washington, 1903), p. 64.

bombshell. Within a few days, experiment stations were besieged with letters from farmers and agricultural editors demanding an explanation. Although no reputable soils scientist agreed with Whitney's conclusions, Hopkins was the only man willing to challenge the authority of the head of an important government bureau. "The injury to American agriculture that may result from the wide dissemination and adoption into agricultural practice of erroneous teaching from one occupying a national position," Hopkins said, "is too vast to justify agricultural scientists and investigators in the easier and more agreeable policy of ignoring these teachings. . . ."[46]

On November 17, 1903, the Agriculture and Chemistry Section of the Association of American Agricultural Colleges and Experiment Stations held a meeting in Washington, D.C. "We have in Illinois," Hopkins said at this meeting,

an area of land whose principal type of soil contains only 600 pounds of phosphorus an acre in the plowed soil to a depth of 7 inches. A good crop of corn, such as we commonly produce on the best soils in the State, removes from the soil 23 pounds of phosphorus an acre. Twenty-five or thirty good crops would actually remove from the soil as much phosphorus as is contained in this plowed soil, and the plowed soil is considerably richer in phosphorus than the soil below it. It is mathematically impossible that the "supply will be indefinitely maintained," if good crops should be removed from this land for any considerable number of years.[47]

---

[46] University of Illinois Agricultural Experiment Station Circular 105 (Urbana, November, 1906), p. 14.

[47] University of Illinois Agricultural Experiment Stations Circular 72 (Urbana, November, 1903), p. 9. Circular 72 contains the text of Hopkins's address as chairman of the Section of Agriculture and Chemistry. "This address," Davenport explained in an introduction, "is . . . published in order to answer a mass of inquiries impossible to answer by letter, and . . . to prevent as much as possible the evil consequences to Illinois soils that would certainly follow a literal acceptance of the teachings of that bulletin [i.e., Bulletin 22]. . . . It is not a pleasant task to publish matter aiming to set aside the conclusions of any branch of government research, but the circumstances surrounding this Station and the process [progress?] of our work in soils investigations makes some general and public statement imperative. . . . This Experiment Station entertains the hope that Illinois farmers will not permit their ideas of the importance of soil fertility to be disturbed by this unfortunate incident, but that they will go on treasuring the

Hopkins realized, however, that words alone were not enough to counteract the influence of Whitney's teachings. Bulletin 22 confirmed farmers in their belief that "a simple rotation and change of cultural methods" would maintain soil fertility, and land agents welcomed this unexpected opportunity to sell worn-out farms at good prices. To refute Whitney and convince farmers of the soundness of the Illinois System of Permanent Soil Fertility, Hopkins needed to demonstrate that system on his own farm. In November, 1903, the same month in which he attacked Bulletin 22 at the Washington meeting, Hopkins purchased a 316-acre farm near Salem in southern Illinois. This farm (for which he paid an average price of $18.42 an acre) was called "Poorland Farm" because it "would raise nothing besides poverty grass and mortgages," and neighboring farmers "were inclined to question the sanity of anyone who would pay real money for such obviously poor land."[48] But it was precisely the fact that the land *was* poor that made it ideal for Hopkins's purposes. "When it was known that he had undertaken this enterprise," Davenport said, ". . . all sorts of opportunities were offered him. Admiring supporters tendered him the unlimited use of funds; fertilizers were offered free. These he declined. He even refused to buy barnyard manure from his neighbors at a nominal rate, upon the ground that he would not enrich Poorland Farm at the expense of neighboring farms, nor would he do anything upon that farm which any other farmer might not do upon his own."[49] Poorland

---

fertility in their soils for economic use and not ignore or waste the plant food required to make crops."

[48] *Farmers' Institute* XXVI (1921): 182. Hopkins acquired additional land during his lifetime, and Poorland Farm eventually comprised 573 acres. The present size of the farm is 536 acres.

[49] *Farmers' Institute* XXV (1920): 15. One of Hopkins's most "admiring supporters" was Ralph Allen of Delavan, Illinois. Allen (1854–1927) was graduated from the University of Illinois in 1876 and received his master of science degree in 1894. He served as president and as a director of the Illinois Farmers' Institute and as a member of the agricultural experiment station advisory committee on soils investigations. After Hopkins's death, Allen headed a movement to purchase Poorland Farm and maintain it as a perpetual demonstration of Hopkins's teachings. Unfortunately, "the Hopkins Memorial Association" was not able to raise sufficient money, and the project had to be abandoned. Hopkins's brother, Carl E. Hopkins, bought the farm in 1937, and it is now owned and operated by his children, Donald Wayne Hopkins and Mrs. Carl Ward.

Farm, Hopkins said, was neither an experiment station nor a "show" farm, and no commercial fertilizers would be used in its development.

To compare the effects of various soil treatments on crop yield, Hopkins reserved a check strip (six rods wide by eighty rods long) in each forty-acre field of Poorland Farm. The entire field, check strip included, received the same crop rotation and applications of manure. One-half of the check strip received limestone but no phosphate; the other half did not receive limestone or phosphate. The remaining thirty-seven acres of the field received both limestone and phosphate. "All that is needed to note the value of this soil treatment is to observe the fields," H. E. Young, secretary of the Farmers' Institute, said after a visit to Poorland Farm. "The check strips can easily be distinguished as far as the eye can see the crop. The untreated strips are devoid of clover, and continue to produce poverty grass. The grain crops are very light, and seldom pay the cost of production. The treated portion of the fields grow clover luxuriantly and produce very profitable grain crops."[50] Through the use of "natural" materials only — raw rock phosphate, organic matter (manure, clover or other legumes), and limestone — Hopkins had demonstrated that "intelligent permanent soil improvement on land that must be or will be farmed is both the safest and most profitable investment open to the farmer and the landowner."[51] By making Poorland Farm (he retained the original name) as productive as the best cornbelt farms, Hopkins proved conclusively that he was right and Whitney was wrong.

A few months after Hopkins had purchased Poorland Farm, he received a visit from M. B. Coburn, general manager and principal stockholder of a mining company that owned nearly 10,000 acres of phosphate land in western Tennessee. Coburn offered to sell the controlling interest in this company at a low

---

[50] *Farmers' Institute* XXVI (1921): 183.

[51] "Bread from Stones," University of Illinois Agricultural Experiment Station Circular 168 (Urbana, September, 1913), p. 7. This circular reports the ten-year results of practicing the Illinois System of Permanent Soil Fertility on one of the fields of Poorland Farm. The field, which had not grown crops for five years before 1904, produced 1,320 bushels of wheat in 1913.

price, and Hopkins not only bought bonds himself but persuaded his friends at the University (including Davenport and Burrill) and farmers throughout the state to do the same.[52] Hopkins's financial connection with the phosphate property became the subject of growing criticism, especially among fertilizer manufacturers, during the winter and spring of 1905. The following fall, after consultation with President James and the University trustees, Hopkins and Davenport, as well as their associates in the investigation of Illinois soils, disposed of their interests in the phosphate company.[53] One of these associates, Jeremiah G. Mosier,

---

[52] See C. G. Hopkins to Director Eugene Davenport, January 31, 1905, Hopkins Letterbook 14, pp. 322–324. Hopkins purchased $1,500 in bonds of the New York and Saint Louis Mining and Manufacturing Company, receiving as a bonus thirty shares of capital stock (with a face value of $3,000) from the company's treasury and 100 shares of Coburn's personal stock. Acting as an agent of the phosphate company, Hopkins sold $23,500 in bonds during the summer and early fall of 1904. For this service, he was given an additional 470 shares of Coburn's stock. Davenport purchased $500 in bonds, and received a bonus of ten shares of capital stock in the company.

[53] See E. Davenport to Dr. C. G. Hopkins, January 28, 1905, Davenport Letter-

Cyril Hopkins about 1910.

claimed that Hopkins's sole motive in investing in the company was to insure a sufficient supply of phosphorus to Illinois farmers. "He even went so far as to burden himself financially to accomplish this generous purpose," Mosier said, "but the selfish ones, attributing to him the same motive which they themselves possessed, caused the attempt to result in temporary failure."[54] And Davenport said that Hopkins "borrowed money to help develop a phosphate mine for service to Illinois, not for the money that might be made out of it, but to convince people that he was honest in what he said about soil treatment. . . . When it was decided that sound University policy did not permit of commercial investments in line with service, he readily understood that his motive might be misinterpreted and relinquished his interests."[55]

There is no question that Hopkins was concerned about the possibility of a phosphorus shortage in this country. Of the

---

book 38, p. 128; E. Davenport to Hon. Charles S. Deneen, January 31, 1905, *Ibid.*, p. 139; John C. Baker to Governor Deneen, February 25, 1905 (typed copy of letter in College of Agriculture files); E. Davenport to Hon. Charles S. Deneen, March 3, 1905, Davenport Personal Letterbook, p. 53; E. Davenport to Mr. John C. Baker, March 4, 1905, *Ibid.*, pp. 54–56; *Twenty-third Report*, pp. 257, 266–269.

[54] *Farmers' Institute* XXV (1920): 29. Mosier, an 1893 graduate of the University, was in charge of the field work of the Illinois Soil Survey for nearly twenty years. He resigned as professor of soil physics in August, 1922, because of ill health, and died three months later at the age of sixty.

[55] *In Memoriam Cyril George Hopkins, 1866–1919* (Urbana, 1922), p. 67. Hopkins was less reticent than Mosier and Davenport about stating his reasons for investing in the phosphate company. "My object or purpose," he told the members of the Illinois Farmers' Institute on February 23, 1905, "was three-fold; first, to secure a supply of phosphorus for my own farm; second, personal financial gain from the phosphate stock obtained; third, the desire to have Illinois farmers and land owners obtain control, if possible, of a supply of phosphorus sufficient for the needs of Illinois soils. . . . In securing an Illinois farm and in securing stock in a phosphate company, I am practicing what I preach, fully believing that the people who are interested in Illinois agriculture are not only willing that I should own stock in Illinois soil and in Tennessee phosphate, but that knowing these facts will increase your confidence in the work which we are doing in trying to discover and in helping to establish a system of farming which shall insure a profitable and a permanent agriculture in the commonwealth of Illinois." *Farmers' Institute* X (1905): 166, 168. The complete text of Hopkins's address to the Farmers' Institute was reprinted as University of Illinois Agricultural Experiment Station Circular 87 (Urbana, March, 1905).

1,600,000 tons of rock phosphate mined annually in the United States, more than a million tons were being shipped to Europe, and he protested against this exportation long before he met Mr. Coburn or knew of the existence of his company. The evidence indicates, however, that neither Hopkins nor Davenport "readily understood" that investment in the phosphate company constituted a conflict of interests, and that neither man "relinquished" his stock in that company until forced to do so by President James and the trustees. Hopkins wrote Davenport on September 9, 1905, that "while it seemed necessary and wise for me to invest in the enterprise personally in order to encourage others to do so, it is not now necessary for me to retain my financial connection with it, *although surely entitled to do so by any legal or moral standard of justice.*" [56] And Davenport's letters to James and to Samuel Bullard, president of the Board of Trustees, show a similar lack of perception of the issues involved. [57] But Bullard's condemnation of Davenport and Hopkins for not possessing "that keen moral discernment which marks the truly and highly cultured man" is unduly harsh. Both Davenport and Hopkins worshipped a nineteenth-century God who punished the weak and idle and rewarded the strong and industrious — who helped those who helped themselves. They simply could not understand why they should

---

[56] Cyril G. Hopkins to Director Eugene Davenport, September 9, 1905, Hopkins Letterbook 17, p. 160. Italics mine. Davenport transmitted this letter to President James the same day, and it was printed in the proceedings of the Board of Trustees for September 12, 1905 (*Twenty-third Report*, pp. 268–269). In a letter written to James the previous month, Hopkins defended his right to retain the phosphate stock on the grounds that "many University people have . . . investments . . . in direct line with their University work. Thus, engineers have invested in the companies manufacturing engineering supplies, chemists in applied chemistry, and literary people in publications." Hopkins also pointed out in this letter that "at least twenty-five other University employees have purchased stock in this phosphate company, in amounts ranging from $500 to $20,000. Among this number are five deans and a dozen heads of departments, and some assistants, including several in my own department." Cyril G. Hopkins to President Edmund J. James, August 14, 1905, Hopkins Letterbook 17, p. 10.

[57] See *Twenty-third Report*, p. 267; S. A. Bullard to Prof. E. Davenport, September 21, 1905 (original copy of letter in College of Agriculture files); and E. Davenport to Hon. S. A. Bullard, September 26, 1905, Davenport Personal Letterbook, pp. 68–84.

Cyril G. Hopkins

not profit financially from believing in something that was good in itself, and it can be said in extenuation that this view was probably shared by most successful business and professional men of their generation.

With the success of Poorland Farm, Hopkins's fame spread far beyond the borders of Illinois. The farm became a mecca for enterprising farmers, and Hopkins himself was regarded with that admixture of awe and affection usually reserved for great statesmen and military heroes. His more enthusiastic disciples compared him with Joseph because of his concern about "providing against the lean years," and with Saint Paul because "he gave most of his life to a work which was not of his choosing, but to which he was called. . . ."[58] But these comparisons are overdrawn. Cyril Hopkins had far more in common with a country doctor than with biblical prophets. In his diagnosis and treatment of the "ailments" of individual soils, in his strictures against the use of "complete" fertilizers, which he likened to patent medicines,[59] and even in appearance (one is reminded of Luke S. Fildes's famous painting of "The Doctor"), Hopkins resembled the typical rural physician of his time. "He was a demonstrator, to an extent, a middleman in science," Edwin W. Allen, Chief of the Office of Experiment Stations in Washington, said of Hopkins. "He was not merely a compiler, a purveyor, but a digester and interpreter of investigation. He translated the results into terms of practical farming, and he demonstrated the lessons and

[58] *In Memoriam Cyril George Hopkins*, p. 69.
[59] A "complete" fertilizer contains nitrogen, phosphorus, and potassium. One of the most common commercial fertilizers in the early 1900's was "2-8-2," containing two pounds of nitrogen, eight pounds of phosphorus pentoxide (usually described as "phosphoric acid") and two pounds of potash per 100 pounds. Hopkins pointed out that since a 100-bushel crop of corn requires about 100 pounds of nitrogen, this fertilizer could only act as a soil stimulant, and any increase in crop yield would be at the expense of the nitrogen already in the soil when the fertilizer was applied. "It is best to diagnose the case before trying a remedy," he said. "There are medicines that seem to do good for a time, but as an 'after effect' they leave the patient worse instead of better, the temporary strength being secured at the expense of his own vitality." *Farmers' Institute* XX (1915): 24. It should be explained that "complete" fertilizers have been greatly improved in the last fifty years, especially since the Second World War, and are now used profitably by farmers throughout the United States.

expounded them to wide audiences with power and far-reaching effects." [60]

By 1910, when he published his major work, *Soil Fertility and Permanent Agriculture*, Hopkins was probably the best-known soils scientist in the United States. In the fall of 1913, he received a year's leave of absence to serve as director of the Southern Settlement and Development Organization, a nonprofit association devoted to restoring the depleted soils of the Deep South.[61] Five years later, he went to Greece as a major in the American Red Cross to study the soils of that country and work out methods to increase the production of food grains. For his success in carrying out this assignment, Hopkins was decorated by the king with the rarely bestowed Order of Our Saviour. Although he had suffered a slight attack of malaria during his year in Greece, he was in apparently good health when he sailed for home on September 15, 1919. Soon after he was at sea, however, Hopkins was stricken again with malaria and quickly became delirious. He was carried from the ship to the British military hospital at Gibraltar, where, despite the efforts of a team of English and American doctors, he died on October 6, 1919.[62]

"Among his contemporaries," Frederick B. Mumford, Dean of

[60] *In Memoriam Cyril George Hopkins*, p. 58. Allen served as chief of the Office of Experiment Stations in Washington from 1915 until his death on November 11, 1929.

[61] *Twenty-seventh Report* (1914), p. 641. The Southern Settlement and Development Organization was largely supported by southern railroads and the International Harvester Company. During Hopkins's absence (from November 1, 1913 to the same date the following year), Professor L. H. Smith served as acting head of the Department of Agronomy.

[62] The cause of death was vaguely described as "congestion of the brain." Whether malaria brought on this condition or was merely incidental to it is not known. On November 7, 1919, the casket bearing Hopkins's body, "draped in the American flag and couched in a maze of ferns and flowers," rested in state for the funeral services held at the University Auditorium. Interment took place in Mount Hope Cemetery at Urbana. The body was brought back to the United States by Captain George J. Bouyoucos, a native-born Greek who had accompanied Hopkins on the mission to Greece. Bouyoucos was graduated from the University of Illinois in 1908 and received his Ph.D. from Cornell in 1911. He served on the staff of Michigan State University from 1911 until his retirement in 1958. In February, 1968, Bouyoucos received the Award of Merit from the Agriculture Alumni Association of the University of Illinois.

the University of Missouri College of Agriculture, said shortly after Hopkins's death, "Dr. Hopkins was the greatest exponent of the science and practice of soil conservation in America. His reliance upon the importance of fundamental research, his remarkable judgment in applying discoveries of science to the practice of soil improvement, is a glowing example of the opportunity which awaits every young man of imagination who devotes himself with a single-minded purpose to the development of agriculture through scientific research."[63] Most of the facts upon which Hopkins based his system of permanent agriculture had been known for many years. But as Baron von Liebig, the great German agricultural chemist, once pointed out, "facts are like grains of sand which are moved by the wind . . . principles are these same grains cemented into rocks." Cyril Hopkins's unique contribution to American agriculture was to cement the known facts about soils and crops into principles that could be easily understood and used by the farmer.

---

[63] *In Memoriam Cyril George Hopkins*, p. 76.

TEN

Isabel Bevier, Lady with a Mission

I N 1872, JOHN GREGORY, who had cast the deciding vote for the admission of women students two years earlier, announced that a school "to provide a full course of instruction in the arts of the household and the sciences relating thereto" would be established the following year.[1] The School of Domestic Science and Art did not actually open, however, until 1874, when Louisa Catherine Allen joined the University faculty as an instructor. A native of Kentucky, Miss Allen had spent most of her life on an Illinois farm. After graduation from Illinois State Normal University, she had served on the staff of the Peoria County Normal School. When she came to the University of Illinois, she was twenty-two years old. Despite her youth, Louisa Allen had definite ideas about the education of women. "We discard the old and absurd notion that education is a necessity to men, but only an ornament to women," she said. "If ignorance is a disaster in the places of business where the income is won, it is equally so in the places of living where the income is expended. If science can aid agriculture and the mechanic arts to use more successfully nature's forces and to increase the amount and value of their products, it can equally aid

---

[1] *Fifth Annual Report*, p. 49. "No industry is more important to human happiness and well being than that which makes the home," Gregory said. "And this industry involves principles of science as many and as profound as those which control any other human employment."

176

the housekeeper in the finer and more complicated use of those forces and agencies. . . ."[2]

With no precedents to guide her, and with "an incredulous public opinion to contend against," Miss Allen prepared and taught what she accurately described as "the first college course of high grade in domestic science organized in the United States, if not the world."[3] Designed to "bring the aids of science and culture to the all-important labors and vocations of womanhood," the four-year curriculum combined background courses in the liberal arts (chemistry, botany, physiology, literature, history, modern languages, philosophy, and mathematics through trigonometry) with "technical studies" beginning in the middle of the sophomore year. These technical studies included food and dietetics, household esthetics, household science, "domestic economy, . . . with social usages and laws of etiquette," home architecture, and hygiene.[4] To obtain a bachelor of science degree, a student had to complete all of the courses in the curriculum and write an original thesis.

The Gregory-Allen experiment lasted only six years, and it was terminated by the actions of the principals themselves. In June, 1879, three months after her promotion to full professor, Louisa Allen married the widowed John Gregory.[5] The following June,

---

[2] *Eighth Report*, p. 67.

[3] Mrs. John M. Gregory, "The School of Domestic Science of the Illinois Industrial University," U.S. Bureau of Education, *Industrial Education in the United States: A Special Report* (Washington, 1883), p. 279. Among land-grant colleges, both Iowa State (in 1869) and Kansas State (in 1873) preceded Illinois in introducing home economics courses, but these courses were little more than cooking-and-sewing schools.

[4] *Ibid.*, p. 282. A strong advocate of "a sound mind in a sound body," Miss Allen fitted up one of the library wings in University Hall as a women's gymnasium and gave daily instruction in calisthenics. The exercises with wands and dumbbells, designed "to secure . . . physical vigor, robust health, and a graceful carriage," were "witnessed and heartily approved by some of the most eminent medical men in the State." But many parents objected to these exercises as too strenuous for the fragile creatures women were then presumed to be, and more than a third of the girls were excused from the classes. *Eighth Report*, pp. 67–68, 90, 184.

[5] At the trustees' meeting on March 12, 1879, Gregory, who was at least covertly courting Miss Allen at that time, asked that she be made a full professor with a

177

Gregory and his young wife resigned from the University. Gregory's successor as regent, Selim Peabody, considered the School of Domestic Science "an experiment in darkness," and he persuaded the Board of Trustees to abolish it in March, 1881. For the next two decades, despite an alumni movement to reinstate the School in the early 1890s, the University did not offer a course in home economics.[6] But on March 13, 1900, under combined pressure from two women trustees, Lucy Flower and Mary Turner Carriel, and the Association of Domestic Science of the Illinois Farmers' Institute, the Board voted to establish a "department of domestic science" in the College of Agriculture.

The woman chosen to head this new department, Isabel Bevier, was born on a farm near Plymouth, Ohio, on November 14, 1860. She attended the high school at Plymouth and Wooster Preparatory School, and taught in a country school for three summers before she was eighteen. After graduation from Wooster University in 1885, where she excelled in languages, Isabel was a principal and then a teacher in Ohio high schools. In 1888, the year she received her master's degree in Latin and German from Wooster, the drowning of her fiance changed the course of her life.[7] At the urging of friends, Isabel accepted a professorship of natural science at the Pennsylvania College for Women in Pittsburgh. To prepare herself for this position, she spent the summer of 1888 studying chemistry at the Case School of Applied Science

---

$300 raise in pay. The Board approved the promotion but not the salary increase. After a European honeymoon, the Gregorys returned to the University in the fall of 1879. Gregory died in 1898, and was buried on the University campus.

[6] For a detailed account of Peabody's actions and of the campaign for a home economics curriculum, see Solberg, *The University of Illinois, 1867–1894*, pp. 242–243, 351–354. This campaign was led by two members of the class of 1890, Katharine L. Kinnard and Charles H. Shamel. Miss Kinnard's letters to Shamel, located in the University of Illinois Archives, provide interesting insights into the women's rights movement at the end of the nineteenth century.

[7] "She rarely spoke of this tragic experience but when she did, you realized how vivid the memory of it was and something of the depth of her grief." Lita Bane, *The Story of Isabel Bevier* (Peoria, 1955), p. 16. Miss Bane was one of Isabel Bevier's students and later third head of the Department of Home Economics at the University of Illinois. Although unabashedly worshipful, her book (the only published biography of Miss Bevier) contains useful information not available elsewhere.

in Cleveland. The following summer, Miss Bevier's teacher at Case, Professor Albert W. Smith, convinced her that the future for women in chemistry was in work with foods. Upon Smith's recommendation, she studied summers at Harvard and with Wilbur O. Atwater, the pioneer nutritionist, at Wesleyan University in Connecticut.[8]

After resigning from the Pennsylvania College for Women in 1897, Isabel continued her education the following year at Western Reserve University and at the Massachusetts Institute of Technology, where she studied food and sanitary chemistry under the redoubtable Mrs. Ellen H. Richards.[9] In the fall of 1898, at

[8] Under Atwater's direction, Miss Bevier made dietary studies of white families in Pittsburgh and black families near Hampton, Virginia. The results of these studies, as well as those of a similar study conducted later at Lake Erie College, are reported in Bulletins 52 (1898), 71 (1899), and 91 (1900) of the U.S. Department of Agriculture Office of Experiment Stations.

[9] Ellen Richards was graduated from Vassar College in 1870 and entered the Massachusetts Institute of Technology as its first female student the following

Louisa Catherine Allen Gregory, Head of the School of Domestic Science, 1874–1880.

Mrs. Richards's suggestion, Isabel reluctantly accepted an appointment as professor of chemistry at another women's institution — Lake Erie College in Painesville, Ohio. "I had long before decided that I would not spend my years teaching in any woman's college . . . ," she said. "I had never been able to make them seem other than abnormal places of residence for me. My association with my father and three brothers, as well as my training in coeducational colleges, had made me entirely coeducational in all my sympathies." [10] During her two years at Lake Erie College, Miss Bevier taught all of the courses in chemistry and a course in sanitation and was in charge of "domestic arrangements" for the students, including the planning of menus. She had already submitted her resignation when she was invited to visit the University of Illinois in the spring of 1900 as a candidate for the newly created professorship of household science.

"I shall never forget my first impressions of Champaign . . . ," Miss Bevier recalled many years later. "I was the guest of President Draper, and after luncheon he took me for a drive. I thought I had never seen so flat and so muddy a place: no trees, no hills, no boundaries of any kind. This lack of boundaries, physical and mental, the open-mindedness of the authorities and their willingness to try experiments, indeed their desire to do so, opened up a whole new world to me. President Draper and I soon found one common bond, possibly a surprising one, our love of fine horses.

---

year. She remained at M.I.T. as an instructor of sanitary chemistry until her death in 1911 at the age of sixty-nine. During the last thirty years of her life, Mrs. Richards was a leader in home economics education. The author of many books and pamphlets dealing with food, clothing, and shelter, and a frequent lecturer on these subjects, she was a co-founder of the Lake Placid Conference on Home Economics, the forerunner of the American Home Economics Association. She served as chairman of the Lake Placid Conference from 1899 to 1908, and as first president of the American Home Economics Association from 1909 to 1911.

[10] Isabel Bevier, "The History of Home Economics at University of Illinois, 1900–1921," a fifty-page, typewritten manuscript written in 1935 and located in the Home Economics Library in Bevier Hall, Urbana. Miss Bevier used parts of this manuscript in somewhat different form in her "Recollections and Impressions of the Beginning of the Department of Home Economics at the University of Illinois," *Journal of Home Economics* XXXII (May, 1940): 291–297. The manuscript is also quoted extensively in Lita Bane's *The Story of Isabel Bevier.*

I felt almost as if I had been riding with my father." [11] On April 18, 1900, at Draper's recommendation, Isabel Bevier was appointed professor of household science at the University of Illinois.[12] Since the agriculture building, which was to house the new department, was not yet finished, she set up temporary headquarters on the fourth floor of the Natural History Building. In January, the Department of Household Science [13] was moved to the north wing of the agriculture building over the dairy.

"I had made it plain to President Draper and Dean Davenport that fine cooking was not in my repertoire," Miss Bevier said,

and both Mrs. Richards and Professor Atwater had emphasized the fact that my special training had been in the chemistry of foods and nutrition. Indeed I learned some years later that Professor Atwater had written definitely to President Draper that if the department was expected to be organized on cooking school lines, I had better not be called as I would be a misfit. President Draper had said to me, 'I don't care if you can cook or not. . . . I want you to run your department and it will be judged by the results obtained in its laboratories and class rooms and its success by the measure of University respect obtained for it.[14]

Certainly the course of study announced in the 1900–1901 University catalog made no concessions to the cooking-and-sewing school adherents. Of the 130 semester hours required for graduation, only one-fourth were in household science. Heavily weighted

---

[11] *Ibid.* Draper was mutually impressed with Isabel Bevier. "I felt far from certain about her strength," he wrote Liberty Hyde Bailey, "though not about her character or culture and accomplishments. . . ." Quoted in Bane, p. 25.

[12] *Twentieth Report*, p. 275. Elizabeth Sprague, who had taught with Miss Bevier at Lake Erie College, was appointed instructor in household science at the same meeting of the Board of Trustees. Because of illness, however, Miss Sprague was unable to accept the appointment.

[13] Draper assigned the naming of the department to Davenport, Burrill, and Miss Bevier. "The three of us wanted science as the basis and the scientific approach to the subject, but it was Dean Davenport who said, 'I believe there will be some day a science of the household. Let's get ready for it and develop it.' So the child was named 'Household Science' and thus due warning given that neither a cooking school nor a milliner's shop was being opened in the University." Bevier, "The history of Home Economics at University of Illinois, 1900–1921."

[14] *Ibid.*

with German and science courses, and with "suggested electives" in French, history, literature, psychology, and economics, the curriculum provided for a liberal as well as a professional education.[15]

Twenty girls enrolled in the three household science courses offered that first year — Home Sanitation, Elementary Household Decoration, and Principles of the Selection and Preparation of Food.[16] By the spring of 1903, when the legislature appropriated

[15] *University Catalog, 1900–1901*, pp. 126–128, 149, 238–239. Girls could specialize in household science through the general course in the College of Agriculture or earn a bachelor's degree with a major in household science from the College of Science or the College of Literature and Arts (combined in 1913 as the College of Liberal Arts and Sciences).
[16] Miss Bevier taught Home Sanitation in the fall and Elementary Household Decoration in the spring. Cornelia Simon, a graduate of the Lewis Institute in Chicago, was appointed assistant in household science on December 1, 1900. Miss Simon taught Principles of the Selection and Preparation of Food the second semester. Courses in food chemistry and dietetics, although listed in the catalog, were not given because of inadequate laboratory facilities.

Isabel Bevier, Head of the Department of Household Science (Home Economics), 1900–1921.

$80,000 for a Woman's Building, sixty students were registered in nine household science courses. The following year, enrollment increased to eighty students and the number of courses to eleven, including two for graduates.[17] "Almost daily I went to Dean Davenport to recount my successes and failures and to find out what to do next," Miss Bevier said. "There was always in Dean Davenport's mind the broadest outlook, the ability to see things in their relationships. These qualities made him a wonderful dean for a department looked upon with suspicion."[18] Andrew Draper also cooperated completely with Miss Bevier in her efforts to build up the Department of Household Science, and she felt "real regret" when he resigned as president in the spring of 1904. "He had been such a tower of strength to me," she said, "considerate and helpful in many unexpected ways, so appreciative of the difficulties and of my efforts."[19]

In the fall of 1905, the Department moved to more spacious quarters in the north wing of the recently completed Woman's building. A beautiful New England colonial structure of red brick trimmed with white stone, the Woman's Building contained a gymnasium and swimming pool, a social center for women students, and offices, lecture rooms, a model dining room, and chemical and cooking laboratories for Household Science. The building was dedicated on October 16, 1905 as a part of the installation

---

[17] The undergraduate courses were Home Architecture and Sanitation, Elementary Home Decoration, Food and Nutrition, Dietetics, Economic Uses of Food, Textiles, Hygiene and Public Health, Household Management, and a seminar for advanced students. The two graduate courses were Home Economics ("A study of the origin and development of Home Economics, with particular reference to its industrial, educational, and sociological aspects") and Special Investigation ("Problems in the application of the principles of bacteriology, chemistry, and physiology, to the ordinary processes used in the preparation of food").

[18] Bevier, "The History of Home Economics at University of Illinois, 1900–1921." Nor was suspicion limited to the Department itself. Violet Jayne, the Dean of Women and an associate professor of English, "expressed great surprise" at Isabel's desire to join a campus German club. "I could not tell her that I had had six years of German," Miss Bevier said, "and that in my college work I was supposed to have done best in languages and literature." Bevier, "Recollections and Impressions of the Beginning of the Department of Home Economics at the University of Illinois," p. 294.

[19] Bevier, "The History of Home Economics at University of Illinois, 1900–1921."

ceremonies for President Edmund James, and the first classes were held in it the following month. Since James had studied in Germany and had a German wife, Miss Bevier was afraid that he might subscribe to the "kuchen, kirchen, kinder" concept of women. But her fears proved groundless. "I came to have great admiration for President James personally and his manner of doing things," she said. "He was sometimes abrupt, but you could be too. He would listen respectfully and tell you what he thought of the procedure. . . . The subject of discussion was either for or against the good of the university and stood or fell by that standard. But you had your chance."[20]

Miss Bevier made the most of her chances. Under her direction, the Department staff, now numbering five members, prepared a syllabus for teaching household science in the high schools, and two noncredit courses for rural teachers, one dealing with foods and the other with "the plan, decoration, and care of the house," were given in the summer of 1905. A credit course for prospective teachers was offered during the regular 1905–1906 school year, and courses in Household Art and the History of Home Economics were added the following year.[21] Nellie E. Goldthwaite joined the household science staff in the fall of 1908. Formerly head of the chemistry department at Mount Holyoke College and a scientist in the Rockefeller Institute for Medical Research, Dr. Goldthwaite was the first full-time research worker employed by a home economics department. In addition to taking charge of the graduate students, she did important work in quality control in yeast breads and in determining the role of pectin in jelly-making.

On January 20, 1909, the Department opened the Experimental House. The ten-room structure, located at the corner of Wright and Daniel Streets near the Woman's Building, was the first house

---

[20] *Ibid.*

[21] A continuation of the Textiles course, Household Art dealt with "materials suitable for various uses in home and in clothing; consideration of texture, of quality, of design in relation to form; of color in relation to environment and personality; hygienic properties and cost." *University Catalog*, 1906–1907, p. 297. The textbook for the history course was *The Home Economics Movement* (1906) by Isabel Bevier and Susannah Usher. Miss Bevier wrote two other books, *The House: Its Plan, Decoration and Care* (1906) and *Home Economics in Education* (1924).

used as a laboratory for home economics classes in the United States.[22] Three new courses were listed in the 1909–1910 catalog — Special Problems in Connection with the Service of Food, Economics of the Family Group, and Problems in the Economics of the Family Group. The instructor of this last course was David Kinley, then professor of economics and dean of the Graduate School, and later to succeed Edmund James as president of the University. When Miss Bevier was organizing the household science curriculum in 1900, Kinley had asked how much credit she was going to give for baking bread, and she had answered, "Not

---

[22] Catherine Beecher, the sister of Harriet Beecher Stowe, apparently originated the idea of a "practice house" in 1852, but the house at Illinois was the first actually in existence. Students in home management studied the physical and mechanical problems of running the house, those in house planning made major improvements by changing the location of doors and windows and modernizing the lighting system, and those in interior decoration selected the furnishings to illustrate both good and bad taste. The Experimental House was widely publicized, and as many as eighty visitors came in one day to see the furniture and new electrical equipment.

Woman's Building shortly after its completion in 1905. The Horticultural (now Surveying) Building and University orchards are at upper left.

much, because we are not baking much bread."[23] The fact that Kinley was teaching a course in household science ten years later is a measure of the "University respect" the Department had achieved during the first decade of its existence. Nor was this respect limited to Miss Bevier's fellow faculty members in Champaign-Urbana. "I doubt if there is a more influential woman on this subject [home economics] in the American Colleges today," Alfred C. True, Chief of the Office of Experiment Stations, wrote of Isabel Bevier in September, 1910. "If any one should ask me to see a real college department of Home Economics I should send him first to the University of Illinois."[24]

In winning academic recognition for her department, however, Miss Bevier lost the support of the women in the Illinois Association of Domestic Science.[25] Organized in 1898 as an auxiliary of the Farmers' Institute, the Association had played a major role in establishing the Department of Household Science and in persuading the legislature to appropriate funds for the Woman's Building in which the Department was housed. The conflict between Isabel Bevier and the members of the Association, like that between John Gregory and the "narrow-gaugers" more than thirty years earlier, was a fundamental one. The leading spokesman for the Association was Mrs. Henry M. Dunlap, wife of the state senator who handled the University appropriations bills and daughter-in-law of Gregory's nemesis, Matthias L. Dunlap. Mrs. Dunlap's ideas about what she called "household economy" had been formed by the deaths of her children at early ages and by attending the lectures of Sarah Tyson Rorer at the World's Columbian Exposition of 1893. An expert cook and demonstrator with a magnetic personality, Mrs. Rorer believed that most of the ills of mankind, including alcoholism, criminality, and insanity, could be cured through a well-balanced diet. Mrs. Rorer's lectures

---

[23] Bevier, "The History of Home Economics at University of Illinois, 1900–1921."

[24] A. C. True to President James, September 26, 1910, James Faculty Correspondence, Box 13.

[25] This organization was renamed "Department of Household Science, Illinois Farmers' Institute" in May, 1908. To avoid confusion with the University Department of Household Science, the original name is used here.

struck the senator's wife with the force of revelation. Mrs. Dunlap became convinced that her children had died because of improper nutrition, and that the only way to prevent similar tragedies was to introduce cooking classes in all Illinois schools, including the University.[26]

Although Miss Bevier cooperated with the Association to the extent of sponsoring a two-week School for Housekeepers at the University and of devising a bread score card for use at county Institute meetings, she stoutly resisted any attempts to impose cooking-and-sewing-school standards upon the Department of Household Science. "I believe the University should reach down to the people from every avenue of approach possible," Mrs. Dunlap complained at the state meeting of the Association in February, 1909. "I am constantly asked if there is not a six months, a year or two years course in Household Science that is planned to give practical yet scientific training. People of limited time and means are just as important to reach as those of greater opportunities."[27] But despite pressure from Davenport himself, Miss Bevier refused to offer credit short courses in home economics, to lower the academic requirements for admission to the regular Department courses, or to accept an "advisory committee" of Association members. "Since those women and I had never spoken the same language and held such opposite ideas about the teaching of Household Science," she said, "I could not expect help from such

---

[26] "By our ignorance," Mrs. Dunlap said in February, 1898, "we may place food upon our tables in such a combination and manner of preparation that we are by degrees killing our loved ones instead of bringing to them healthy minds and bodies. . . ." *Farmers Institute* III (1898): 135. Davenport states in his manuscript autobiography that "poor Mrs. Dunlap was made to feel that she had lost her little family of four kiddies because she had not fed them properly, whereas the real cause was diphtheria." The 1918 *Alumni Record of the University of Illinois* lists only three Dunlap children: Mabel, born January 23, 1883, died April 3, 1892; Clarence, born December 26, 1886, died March 30, 1892; and Daisy, born December 13, 1894, died February 8, 1895. It is possible, of course, that a fourth child was stillborn or died unnamed shortly after birth. None of the deaths was registered either in the Champaign County Clerk's Office in Urbana or the Bureau of Statistics in Springfield, but the fact that the two older children died within four days of each other suggests the possibility of a contagious disease such as diphtheria.

[27] *Farmers' Institute* XIV (1909): 165.

a committee. I was warned by Dean Davenport if I refused this offer I must do it at my own risk. I said, 'I take the risk.'"[28]

In the spring of 1909, Isabel Bevier was granted a sabbatical leave to study with two noted nutritionists in the East, Lafayette B. Mendel of Yale and Henry C. Sherman of Columbia.[29] The members of the Association assumed that they had seen the last of Miss Bevier, and when they learned that she planned to return to the University, their smouldering resentment burst into full flame. Davenport found himself in a ticklish position. Although he respected Miss Bevier's abilities and considered her a close friend, he could not carry out his plans for the College of Agriculture without the support of the Farmers' Institute. On November 22, 1909, Davenport wrote Miss Bevier that "in the best interests of all concerned" she should resign from the University of Illinois. "There is outside of the University a widespread . . . personal dislike to yourself as head of the department," he said. "However unjustly this prejudice has come about, the fact is that it exists, and I am satisfied can neither be improved nor abated. . . . If you should sever your connection voluntarily you manage the case yourself, and while certain people might have the satisfaction of feeling that they had accomplished their purpose, yet your life and opportunity for service in your chosen field would remain unimpaired. . . ."[30]

Miss Bevier was at Columbia University when Davenport's letter arrived, and she decided to ask the advice of Andrew Draper, who was then Commissioner of Education of New York State. "I had faith in his judgment," she said, "and it was a real comfort

---

[28] Bevier, "The History of Home Economics at University of Illinois, 1900–1921."

[29] Miss Bevier was originally granted leave from July first to December 31, 1909. On December 14, 1909, the trustees extended her leave until September 1, 1910. *Twenty-fifth Report* (1910), pp. 121, 498. In addition to working with Mendel and Sherman (whom she had first known as a "fellow-laborer" in Professor Atwater's laboratory many years earlier), Miss Bevier visited a large number of industrial plants and various schools in the East, Midwest, and South. During her absence, Miss Susannah Usher was acting head of the Department of Household Science.

[30] E. Davenport to Professor Isabel Bevier, November 22, 1909, James Faculty Correspondence, Box 13.

to have the counsel of so wise a friend. . . . He said to me, 'If you leave now you can spend the rest of your life telling why you left the University of Illinois. Go back and tend strictly to your own business and I think you will be supported.' So in July I returned. President James and Dean Kinley . . . had through it all given me their cordial support, and welcomed me back."[31] Earlier

---

[31] Bevier, "The History of Home Economics at University of Illinois, 1900–1921." Shortly after receiving Davenport's letter of November 22, 1909, Miss Bevier wrote James that "it is difficult for me to see that it is either wise or just to remove a professor against whom there is no charge of inefficiency, unfaithfulness or the shadow of any difficulty with her co-workers or students, only the charge that she has not pleased a certain few whose grievances have been manufactured and nurtured for nine years. It would not seem to me desirable that the removal or retention of a professor should be left to outsiders. . . ." Isabel Bevier to President Edmund James, December 2, 1909, James Faculty Correspondence, Box 13. See also E. Davenport to Professor Isabel Bevier, February 16, 1910 and February 25, 1910, Davenport Letterbook 57, pp. 391–392, 461–462; E. Davenport to Edmund J. James, March 4, 1910, copy in College of Agriculture files; and E. Davenport to Miss Isabel Bevier, June 1, 1910, Davenport Letterbook 59, p. 81.

Mrs. Henry M. Dunlap, wife of the state senator from the University district, and a leading member of the Domestic Science Association of the Illinois Farmers' Institute.

that same month, on July 1, 1910, the executive board of the Association of Domestic Science had held a special meeting at the Dunlap estate near Champaign to discuss "the matter of cooperation with the Household Science Department in the University of Illinois. . . ." As a result of this discussion, the executive board passed a resolution requesting the board of directors of the Farmers' Institute to investigate the differences between the Association and the Department "and place the matter before the Trustees of the University in an endeavor to secure a satisfactory adjustment. . . ." Until this "adjustment" was secured, the Association would "discontinue to encourage" young women to attend the School for Housekeepers at the University, and would not make nominations for free county scholarships in the Department of Household Science.[32]

On August 10, 1910, Davenport wrote Edward W. Burroughs, president of the Farmers' Institute, that "such a course as now seems to be entered upon is extremely dangerous. Above all, it endangers the existence of our advisory committees, for there are many who have not ceased to prophesy that our close relations with outside organizations would yet bring trouble. It remains to be seen whether their prophesies are true."[33] Whatever his feelings about Miss Bevier, Burroughs had no desire to destroy the amicable relationships between the Farmers' Institute and the College of Agriculture. When the Institute board of directors met the following week, Burroughs appointed two of Davenport's friends — Frank I. Mann and Alfred N. Abbott — to serve with him on a committee to present the Association's grievances before the Board of Trustees. On December 9, 1910, Mann, the committee chairman, reported to the Institute that the University had agreed to reorganize the Department of Household Science "on a broader and more comprehensive basis, on condition that sufficient

---

[32] *Farmers' Institute* XVI (1911): 325–326. The scholarships for girls in Household Science were awarded upon the same basis as the Institute scholarships for young men in the College of Agriculture. See *Farmers' Institute* V (1900): 157; *Farmers' Institute* XII (1907): 391; and *Twenty-first Report*, pp. 69, 111–112.

[33] E. Davenport to Mr. E. W. Burroughs, August 10, 1910, Davenport Letterbook 59, pp. 346–353.

funds . . . can be secured."[34] A few months later, the legislature appropriated $5,000 to the Department "to advance the art of practical housekeeping in the State,"[35] and the war was over.

In explaining her conflict with the Association of Domestic Science many years later, Isabel Bevier wrote that "if I had not been so busy developing the department, speaking at Farmers' Institutes, writing texts for use in the department, and had had the patience and had taken the time to seek the favor of those women, the breach might have been avoided."[36] But this explanation is a simplistic one. When Miss Bevier first arrived at the University, Draper told her that he did "not care very much about your running around the country for the farmers' institutes," and she had taken him at his word. Between 1901 and 1910, she spoke at only four state meetings of the Farmers' Institute, and her attendance at county meetings was similarly dismal.[37] Moreover, tact (as she herself cheerfully admitted) was not one of her virtues, and she not only did not "seek the favor" of Mrs. Dunlap and her friends but actively discouraged their help. Davenport, who was diplomatic by nature as well as by necessity, knew that Miss Bevier could have mollified the Association women without seriously compromising the standards of the Department of Household Science, and he was understandably upset by her attitude.[38] The important point, however, is that Isabel Bevier

---

[34] *Farmers' Institute* XVI (1911): 327, 333.

[35] *Twenty-sixth Report* (1912), p. 143. The Department received $2,500 annually for 1911 and 1912.

[36] Bevier, "The History of Home Economics at University of Illinois, 1900–1921."

[37] Between 1903 and 1905, for example, Cyril Hopkins gave talks at forty-one county Institute meetings; during this same period, Miss Bevier spoke at only nine meetings. "I usually go to about four institutes a year," she told the Association members at the state meeting in February, 1907, "because once a month is about as often as I can be absent from my classes and do my work. . . . It takes one day to go, one day to stay there and one day to get home; all this when we had left a class of twenty. When we are . . . here together let us say this right out." *Farmers' Institute* XII (1907): 430.

[38] "I sustained Miss Bevier in every way I could until it became clear to me that she was ready to sacrifice anything in the interest of fighting her critics," Davenport wrote President James. "She has sacrificed the old-time high regard of her nearest associates, and I am certain that we shall have serious trouble as long

was brought to the University of Illinois to develop a home economics curriculum of genuine college caliber and she had succeeded brilliantly. Making all due allowances for the harassment Davenport suffered from the Association as a result of Miss Bevier's lack of tact, the fact remains that he sacrificed academic principle for political expediency in asking for her resignation.[39]

The controversy between Miss Bevier and the Association had had little effect upon the Department of Household Science itself. By the fall of 1910, nearly 250 students were enrolled in sixteen household science courses, and the staff numbered nine members. To meet the Department's need for more space, the 1911 legislature appropriated $125,000 for an addition to the Woman's Building. This addition, which was completed in 1913, was 200 feet long and three stories high, with a two-story colonnade between the main entrances. Unfortunately, the Woman's Building, designed by the famous New York firm of McKim, Mead, and White, had not been planned for enlargement, and the heavy "Modern Colonial Style" of the addition contrasted strangely with the pristine New England architure of the original structure.[40] But whatever its aesthetic deficiencies, the addition provided the Department with new kitchens, a dining room, classrooms, a cafeteria, and a five-room "practice apartment." The cafeteria, which occupied much of the second floor on the east side, allowed the Department to offer training in institutional food service. The practice apartment on the third floor was used as a laboratory to study the problems of the home. Each girl registered in the home management course lived in the apartment as a member of a "family" group, serving in turn as cook, laundress, and housekeeper.[41]

---

as she remains." E Davenport to Dr. E. J. James, July 26, 1910, James Faculty Correspondence, Box 14.

[39] According to Miss Bevier, Davenport later apologized for his actions: "Dean Davenport . . . said, 'You were right and I was wrong. I greatly overestimated the strength of the opposition.' " Bevier, "The History of Home Economics at University of Illinois, 1900–1921."

[40] During a conference with President James, Miss Bevier objected to the "pillars" on the addition's facade: " 'For heavens' sake, don't call them pillars,' said President James. 'The state architect nearly had a fit with the trustees calling them pillars.' 'What are they?' I asked. 'Pylons.' 'Never anything better named,' I said. 'The whole addition is a pile on.' " *Ibid.*

[41] An "evolution" of the Experimental House (which had been discontinued in

The addition to the Woman's Building was informally opened on April 25, 1913, with a luncheon for the University Senate in the cafeteria. The following spring, on May 8, 1914, Congress passed an act that provided the third leg of the "three-legged stool" of agricultural instruction, research, and extension. The Smith-Lever Act authorized cooperation between the land-grant institutions and the United States Department of Agriculture "in the giving of instruction and practical demonstrations in agriculture and home economics . . . to persons not attending or resident in . . . colleges. . . ." To finance this work, $4,580,000 was to be distributed annually among the states "in the proportion which the total rural population of each State bears to the total rural population of all the States." The states were required to match the federal funds dollar for dollar.[42]

Through the Morrill and Hatch Acts, the government had furnished money for teaching and investigation in agriculture; the Smith-Lever Act enabled the land-grant universities to organize a permanent system of county agricultural agents (called "farm advisers" in Illinois) and home economics extension workers. To qualify as a farm or home adviser, a candidate needed a degree from a recognized college or university and five years' experience as a farmer or, in the case of home advisers, in teaching or lec-

deference to the Association's wishes during Miss Bevier's absence in the East), the practice apartment is presently occupied by the offices of English as a Second Language. In 1942, Davenport House (807 South Wright Street, Champaign) was assigned to the Department for a home management house, child development laboratory, and staff offices. Four years later, the Home Management House moved to its present location at 1202 West Green Street, Urbana. At the same time, the Department acquired the former residence of President David Kinley at 1204 West Springfield Avenue for use as a Diet Research House.

[42] $480,000 was appropriated the first year, $400,000 the second year, and $500,000 for each of the following seven years until the annual appropriation was $4,100,000 in excess of the original $480,000. The Capper-Ketcham Act of 1928 authorized an additional $1,480,000 annually for extension work. The apportionment formula and matching requirement were the same as for the Smith-Lever Act, but eighty percent of the money was allocated for the salaries of county agents. The Bankhead-Jones Act of 1935 appropriated an additional $12,000,000 per year for extension ($8,000,000 the first year and annual increases of $1,000,000 until the maximum sum was reached). The states were not required to match this money. On June 26, 1953, Congress approved an act removing the statutory ceiling for extension funds.

turing and demonstrating.[43] "The haphazard, politically dominated work of the Farmers' Institute, well-intentioned but uneducational, was over," Isabel Bevier said. "Their misguided efforts
were to be transferred to non-political organizations directed by
men and women trained in educational methods."[44] But Miss
Bevier's views were colored by her unhappy experience with the
Association of Domestic Science. Far from being "misguided" and
"uneducational," the Farmers' Institute in Illinois, as well as
similar organizations in other states, had "proved the most effective agencies for bringing together the research and teaching
talent of the colleges and the highest achievements in farm practice before the development of modern extension methods."[45]

[43] Although candidates for home adviser were not required to have farm backgrounds, preference was usually given to those who did. Miss Bevier once silenced
objections to a candidate who had not lived on a farm by saying, "I'm not so
much interested in whether the young woman has lived on a farm or in town
as I am whether or not she has *lived*. I think this woman has." Bane, pp. 171–172.
[44] *Ibid.*, pp. 58–59. This statement also appears in Miss Bevier's manuscript
history of the Department, but the syntax (evidently through typing errors) is
garbled.
[45] Ross, *Democracy's College*, p. 164. On July 1, 1943, the state legislature

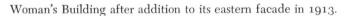

Woman's Building after addition to its eastern facade in 1913.

In the fall of 1901, Davenport had appointed Fred H. Rankin to act as a liaison man between the College of Agriculture and the Farmers' Institute. Rankin's work in encouraging young men and women to enter the College and in arranging for faculty speakers at county and state Institute meetings helped lay the foundation for the extension service in Illinois. On June 1, 1912, the first two farm advisers in the state, William G. Eckhardt and John S. Collier, began work in DeKalb and Kankakee Counties, respectively. When the Smith-Lever Act was passed two years later, ten other Illinois counties had formed "Farm Bureaus" and employed farm advisers.[46] The County Farm Bureau became the nucleus of Davenport's program for developing agricultural extension. Any county with a Bureau membership of 300 men was eligible to select a farm adviser from a list of applicants approved by the College of Agriculture. The County Bureau agreed to provide the adviser with an automobile, office, and clerical help, and to pay part of his salary. Although this arrangement proved effective for carrying out Davenport's program, it gave rise to criticism that resulted in complete separation of Farm Bureau and the cooperative extension service half-a-century later.[47]

Davenport organized extension work in Illinois with himself as director and Walter F. Handschin and Isabel Bevier as vice-directors of agricultural and home economics extension, respectively. On March 1, 1915, Miss Mamie Bunch, a 1914 graduate of the University, was appointed state leader of home economics

passed an act placing the Illinois Farmers' Institute under the management of the extension service of the College of Agriculture. Eight years later, on June 18, 1951, the legislature repealed the act of 1895 creating the Farmers' Institute, and the organization that had served Illinois agrciulture so well for so many years ceased to exist.

[46] These were McHenry, Livingston, Will, DuPage, Kane, Tazewell, Peoria, Champaign, Winnebago, and Iroquois Counties. By 1935, all of Illinois' 102 counties were represented by farm advisers. On July 1, 1961, Hamilton County became the last Illinois county organized for a home adviser. The titles of the farm and home advisers were changed in 1967 to "Extension Adviser, Agriculture" and "Extension Adviser, Home Economics."

[47] For an analysis of the relations between agricultural extension and the Illinois Farm Bureau, see William J. Block, *The Separation of the Farm Bureau and the Extension Service* (Urbana, 1960).

extension.[48] At the end of her first year in this position, Miss Bunch reported that she and her staff had served more than 16,000 Illinois women through one-week "movable schools," lectures and demonstrations, short courses, and the annual School for Housekeepers held at the University in January. The following year, home economics extension reached 50,000 people in the state, including 11,208 visitors to the "Demonstration Car." A converted Pullman, the Demonstration Car contained labor-saving devices (washing machine, mangle, cream separator, vacuum cleaner, ice cream freezer), water and electric lighting systems, a septic tank, and house furnishings ranging from kitchen utensils to color schemes and furniture for the living room and bedroom.[49] "This car," the Department of Household Science announced in September, 1916, "shows how power commonly used upon the farm may also be employed in performing a large part of the heavy labor of the home, thereby contributing to the health and comfort of the housekeeper; how to secure an adequate water supply for both the house and barn with the necessary provision for sewage disposal; and, finally, how, by attention to equipment and the principles of form and color, the essentials of comfortable living may be secured for the country home at a reasonable cost."[50]

---

[48] *Twenty-eighth Report* (1916), pp. 126, 139, 224. The County Home Bureaus (renamed Homemakers' Extension Associations in 1962) were organized independently of the Farm Bureau in Illinois. The organization of home economics extension is dealt with comprehensively in Gertrude E. Kaiser's "A History of the Illinois Home Economics Program of the Cooperative Extension Service" (doctoral dissertation, University of Chicago, 1969). For a listing of state leaders of farm and home advisers in Illinois, see Appendix G.

[49] Perry G. Holden was apparently the first man to use trains for extension work. In 1904, with the cooperation of two railroads, Holden ran special trains through Iowa to promote improved seed corn. Holden's "Seed Corn Gospel Trains" traveled 10,000 miles in 1904 and 1905, stopping 1,235 times to reach 145,363 people. Other states quickly emulated Iowa. In 1911, seventy-one trains in twenty-eight states reached nearly one million farmers.

[50] University of Illinois College of Agriculture Extension Circular 3 (Urbana, September, 1916). The Demonstration Car traveled throughout Illinois. The two demonstrators who accompanied the car, Olive B. Percival and Floyd E. Fogle, held the car open for inspection in the morning, operated the equipment in the afternoon, and gave lectures at a "suitable hall" in the evening. The organization or organizations contracting for use of the car agreed to pay twenty-five dollars

The Department of Household Science grew rapidly between 1912 and 1917, with enrollment increasing from 358 to 525 students and the faculty from nine to sixteen members.[51] On February 23, 1917, Congress passed the Smith-Hughes Act providing for the promotion of vocational education in the secondary schools. As a result of this act, the University of Illinois, in common with the other land-grant institutions, assumed responsibility for the training of high school teachers in agriculture and home economics. "As I see it," Miss Bevier said,

> the main purpose of this work [home economics] in both high school and university is the same, *viz.*, to provide, as an integral part of the girl's training, work with the materials, the processes and products of the home to the end that the girl may go from both high school and university with some appreciation of the place of woman in home and family life, with a first-hand knowledge of its processes, some technical skill in and business sense concerning them. The necessity for such work is due . . . very largely to changed conditions, to the pressure of modern life, to the evils of specialization, which provides one teacher to train the head and another the feet of the girl, and yet another to care for her morals.[52]

On April 6, 1917, the United States entered the First World War. Under Miss Bevier's direction, the Department of Home Economics (the name was changed in July, 1918) conducted special classes in the canning of fruits and vegetables, clothing renovation, home nursing, and first aid, and Miss Bunch and her

---

for an engagement of three days or less and five dollars for each additional day, to provide proper advertising, to arrange with the local railroad for placing the car on an accessible spur or sidetrack, to secure a hall for the evening lectures, and to furnish board and room to the demonstrators. It is perhaps not surprising that Miss Percival and Mr. Fogle were married in 1918.

[51] During this period, the number of undergraduate courses offered by the Department increased from sixteen to eighteen and the graduate courses from two to four. Of the 305 graduates in household science between 1901 and 1917, seventy-five were married, fifty-six were living at home, 135 were teachers, fourteen were cafeteria and tearoom directors, eight were dietitians, and seventeen were in miscellaneous occupations.

[52] Isabel Bevier, "Home Economics in the High School and in the University," typed manuscript in College of Agriculture files. Parts of this manuscript are quoted in Bane, pp. 120–121.

extension staff (with the addition of forty-five temporary workers) demonstrated the use of substitutes for meats, sugar, fats, and wheat at "food shows" throughout the state. Between September, 1917, and the end of the war fourteen months later, home economics extension reached 315,703 Illinois people through lectures, conferences, and demonstrations, and sent out 734 newspaper articles, 10,794 letters, and 127,557 bulletins and circulars dealing with the conservation of foods and materials vital to the war effort. In addition to directing the activities of the Department, Miss Bevier served as chairman of the women's conservation committee of the National Defense Council in Illinois and as a member of Herbert Hoover's Food Administration staff in Washington.[53]

53 "I recollect Miss Bevier with especial appreciation," Hoover wrote from the White House in 1932. "She was in charge of experimental work in development of substitutes which would assist in the conservation of food. She was most successful and influential in this work. Her personality was especially helpful in the dark days of the war. Her urbanity, her sense of humor and her sense of proportion were a delight to those around her." Herbert Hoover to Miss Louisan Mamer, December 16, 1932. Typed copy of letter in College of Agriculture files.

Interior of the Home Economics Demonstration Car.

During the war, home economics came of age. "The people of the United States . . . learned more of . . . home economics in one year in war time than they had learned in five years before," Miss Bevier said. "Many new lines of effort were open to women; dietitians were asked for by hotels as well as hospitals; women trained in the problems of the home were sought by banks as well as by commercial firms to help in teaching thrift. The Child Labor Bureau, the Red Cross, and the Public Health Service called persistently for women trained in home economics."[54] But neither the war nor the influenza epidemic during the fall of 1918 (when the upper gymnasium of the Woman's Building was used as a hospital for University students) caused Miss Bevier to lose sight of what she considered the true goal of home economics education. "Home Economics," she said, "in either peace or war, has a chance to teach something of the beauty of life and the unity of life, to teach that there is an art in the well-ordered home and a well-ordered life; and that perhaps is the greatest thing that home economics has to do."[55]

On September 1, 1921, Isabel Bevier resigned as head of the Department of Home Economics at the University of Illinois. She was succeeded by Ruth Aimee Wardall, one of the first three women to graduate from the Department (class of 1903) and the first to receive a master's degree in home economics (1907) from the University.[56] "Life looked very difficult for me," Miss Bevier said in giving the reasons for her resignation, "and I was physically very much exhausted."[57] Apparently she soon recovered her

[54] Isabel Bevier, "Development of the Field of Home Economics," U.S. Department of the Interior Bureau of Education Bulletin 29, *Land-Grant College Extension 1910–1920, Part V. — Home Economics* (Washington, 1925), p. 11.

[55] Association of American Agricultural Colleges and Experiment Stations. Thirty-first Annual Convention. Washington, D.C., November 14–16, 1917. *Proceedings*, p. 131.

[56] Ruth Wardall (1877–1936) served as head of the home economics departments at South Dakota Agricultural College (1903–1906), The Ohio State University (1907–1913), and the University of Iowa (1913–1921) before returning to her alma mater. At the close of Miss Wardall's administration at Illinois in 1936, thirty staff members were offering forty courses in home economics.

[57] Bevier, "The History of the Department of Home Economics at University of Illinois, 1900–1921." Miss Bevier originally submitted her resignation to take effect either July first or September 1, 1920, "as . . . the best interests of the Department

usual indomitable energy and good health. During the following five years, Miss Bevier served as chairman of the Department of Home Economics at the University of California at Los Angeles (1921–1923) and as a lecturer (1925–1926) at the University of Arizona.[58]

In February, 1928, Herbert Mumford, who had succeeded Davenport as dean of the College of Agriculture in 1922,[59] asked Miss Bevier to return to Illinois to conduct a survey of the home economics extension service in Illinois. Miss Bevier's report of this survey reflects the changes that had taken place in the lives of rural women since the early years of the century. "In the Women's Sessions of the Farmers' Institute 20 years ago," she wrote Mumford on March 20, 1929,

> the majority of the women were over 50 years old, a rather phlegmatic group somewhat wearied with the struggle, relieved that they were as far on as they were, and not keen to undertake new burdens — rather more in the mental state of the woman who announced mostly she "would druther do as she'd druther." Generally the officers were women of poise, experience, and ability, but the lay member who read her paper did it often with trembling voice and shaking hands. Now the average age I would guess is under 40, women who are in the midst of the battle. They are well-groomed, their stockings are silk, their skirts and hair are short, and their heels are too high for comfort. Their minds are eager,

---

demand." Isabel Bevier to Dr. E. Davenport, February 17, 1920. Typewritten copy of letter in College of Agriculture files. At the urging of Davenport and President David Kinley, however, she agreed to remain at the University one more year. During the twenty-one years that Miss Bevier served as its head, the Department of Home Economics graduated 630 students and offered courses to approximately 5,000 young women.

[58] "There is one thing I am sure of," she said of her stay in Arizona, "and that is that the end of the world is a long way off. The Lord has too much to do in Arizona yet." Bane, p. 82.

[59] Davenport resigned on March 14, 1922, and Mumford became dean the following September first. In November, 1928, Davenport (who had been vice-president of the University during his last two years as dean) was appointed special assistant to President Kinley. Davenport served in this position until June 30, 1929, when he retired to his Michigan farm. On May 1, 1931, Davenport was awarded a Doctor of Laws Degree by the University of Illinois. He had previously received LL.D. degrees from Michigan State College (1907) and the University of Kentucky (1913), and a doctorate of science from Iowa State College (1920).

alert, hungry for information on child care and training, on house furnishing, on dyeing, on kitchen equipment, and numberless other points. They have definite opinions on many subjects, [and] are interested in self-development.[60]

After retiring from the University of Illinois as professor of home economics, emerita in September, 1930, Miss Bevier spent the remaining years of her life in Urbana. Through her writings, research (she was the first to use a chemical thermometer in the cooking of meats), and administrative skills, she had achieved national fame in her field. "The scientific esteem in which home economics is held in any comparable institution," Professor Henry C. Sherman of Columbia said in 1933, "is closely proportional to the fidelity with which it has followed the standard set by Miss Bevier."[61] In addition to developing one of the outstanding home economics departments in the United States, Miss Bevier served as president of the American Home Economics Association (1911–1913) and as a member of the editorial board of the *Journal of Home Economics*. At various times during her career, she was also chairman of the subcommittee on human nutrition of the National Research Council, vice-president of the section on manual training and house economics of the National Educational Association, and chairman of the home economics division of the Association of Land-Grant Colleges and Universities. Miss Bevier was awarded honorary doctor of science degrees by Iowa State College in 1920 and by her alma mater, Wooster University, in 1936.

Perhaps Isabel Bevier's greatest contribution to home economics, however, is the imprint she left on the lives of her students and associates. Tall and strong, with ruddy cheeks, blue eyes, and snow-white hair, Miss Bevier was a handsome and

---

[60] Isabel Bevier, "Study of Home Economics Extension Work," signed typewritten copy in College of Agriculture files. Also quoted in Bane, p. 86. Miss Bevier served as professor of home economics from 1928 to 1929 and as acting vice-director of home economics extension from 1929 to 1930.

[61] H. C. Sherman, "Isabel Bevier: A Contribution of Chemistry to Home Economics," typewritten manuscript in College of Agriculture files. Quoted in Bane, p. 71.

majestic woman.[62] In both appearance and character, she exemplified those qualities now described by that overworked word "charisma." No one who knew Miss Bevier ever forgot her. At once tactless and charming, wistful and brusque, idealistic and practical, serious and gay, she inspired deep affection from the thousands of women who came under her influence. Among these women was Juliet Lita Bane, one of Miss Bevier's former students (class of 1912) and third head (1936–1948) of the Department of Home Economics at the University of Illinois. "How I've wished," Miss Bane once wrote, "that I might catch an inspiration that would enable me to depict . . . some of Miss Bevier's fine spirit of courage, strictest honesty, great tolerance, keen insight, illuminated by a sprightly and kindly humor that endeared her to all of us. We respected the superiority of her intellect, the accuracy of her judgment, the flavor of her words, but we loved the warmth of her understanding sympathy, the beauty of her gracious womanliness, the greatness of her generosity and human kindliness." [63]

---

[62] In the winter of 1920, Miss Bevier was painted by Louis Betts of New York City, a fashionable portrait artist of the period. This picture, although superior to most works in that genre, emphasizes Miss Bevier's winsome femininity at the expense of the forcefulness that was an equally vital part of her character. Miss Bevier herself was reportedly pleased with the portrait, but her artistic and literary tastes were conventional. Her favorite poem, for example, was the elder Oliver Wendell Holmes's "The Chambered Nautilus." The portrait, which the Department of Home Economics presented to the University on May 21, 1921, now hangs on the east wall of the student lounge in Bevier Hall.

[63] Lita Bane, "Isabel Bevier — An Appreciation," typewritten manuscript dated March 29, 1935, in College of Agriculture files. Quoted in part in *The Story of Isabel Bevier*, p. 165. Miss Bane (1887–1957) received a master of arts degree from the University of Chicago in 1919, and an honorary doctorate of science from Kansas State College in 1938. Before becoming head of the Department of Home Economics, she was assistant state leader and state leader of home economics extension in Illinois, a teacher at Washington State College and at the University of Wisconsin, associate editor of the *Ladies' Home Journal*, collaborator in parent education with the U.S. Department of Agriculture extension service, and executive secretary (1923–1925) and president (1926–1928) of the American Home Economics Association. On September 1, 1948, Miss Bane was given a leave of absence because of ill health. She never returned to active headship of the Department. Mrs. Kathryn VanAken Burns, state leader of home economics extension (1923–1956), served as acting head until September 1, 1949, when she was succeeded in this position by Dr. Janice Minerva Smith. On April 1, 1950, Dr. Smith was made head of the Department of Home Economics.

But Miss Bevier was not always kind. Easily hurt by real or fancied slights, she often passed judgment on people without full knowledge of the facts. Although she was quick to condemn, Miss Bevier was equally quick to forgive. Despite Davenport's attempts to force her resignation in 1909, she did not harbor a grudge. She realized that Davenport believed he was acting in the best interests of the College of Agriculture, and they remained close friends for many years. "Her service to the University, the state and her chosen subject," Davenport wrote in the spring of 1940, "are above the power of mere words to signify." [64] The following spring, on March 31, 1941, Davenport died of a kidney ailment at his home in Woodland, Michigan. One year later, on March 17, 1942, Miss Bevier succumbed to arteriosclerotic heart disease in Urbana. [65] Their careers had paralleled the development of agriculture and home economics during the first two decades of the twentieth century; their lives ended during a war that was to usher in a new age and unimaginable changes in both urban and rural life. But the ideals that Eugene Davenport and Isabel Bevier stood for are as valid today as half-a-century ago. Miss Bevier was speaking for Davenport as well as for herself when she said that "the new farm life means an attitude of mind that recognizes that land owners are trustees of a valuable inheritance which they should pass on unimpaired. It recognizes

---

[64] Eugene Davenport, "Agricultural Pioneering in the University of Illinois," typewritten manuscript dated March, 1940, in College of Agriculture files.

[65] Davenport was buried at Woodland, Michigan, and Isabel Bevier at Plymouth, Ohio. Miss Bevier bequeathed $5,000 to the trustees of the University of Illinois to finance a series of lectures dealing with "the scientific, economic, esthetic, and social aspects of home and family life, in order that the woman so trained may be enabled to apply this knowledge in her daily tasks in her home, family, and community life in accordance with the finest intellectual and spiritual ideals." Extracts from will of Isabel Bevier, February 11, 1938. Typewritten copy in College of Agriculture files. The first of these lectures, "Food and Nutrition Today and Tomorrow," was given by Miss Bevier's old friend and colleague, Henry C. Sherman, on May 15, 1945. Two years later, on April 17, 1947, the Woman's Building was renamed Bevier Hall. At the same ceremony, the "old agriculture building" was named Davenport Hall and the "new agriculture building" (completed in 1924) was named Mumford Hall in honor of Dean Herbert W. Mumford. When the present home economics building was completed in 1956, the name Bevier Hall was transferred to it, and the original Bevier Hall (formerly the Woman's Building) was renamed the English Building.

that people are more than land, more than machines — that the purpose of the farm home and the farm life is to produce healthy, happy, useful individuals who shall find their satisfaction, their means of expression, their place of contributing to the world's joy, bearing their share of the world's sorrow, doing their share of the world's work on the farm or in the farm home." [66]

---

[66] Isabel Bevier, "Problems and Opportunities of Farm Life," address delivered at The Ohio State University, November, 1917. Typewritten copy in College of Agriculture files. Quoted in Bane, pp. 148–149.

ELEVEN

Later Developments in the College

"T HE HISTORIAN fifty years hence," Eugene Davenport wrote in 1912, "will discharge a pleasant duty in making record of the richest half-century of human progress along agricultural and humanistic lines. . . ." During the fifty-eight years since Davenport made this sanguine prediction, the United States has suffered through a severe economic depression, two world wars, and the myriad anxieties of the nuclear age. In the light of these events, one may well question how far we have progressed along "humanistic lines." There can be no doubt, however, about our progress along "agricultural lines." The development of agriculture is perhaps this country's outstanding technical achievement of the twentieth century.

The University of Illinois College of Agriculture, along with her sister institutions in other states, has played an important part in this development. When Davenport retired as dean in 1922, the College of Agriculture was a full-fledged center of agricultural learning with coordinated research, teaching, and extension programs. Throughout the succeeding years of striking changes in agriculture — a technological revolution, mass migrations from the country to the city, and wide specialization of types of farms and farming services — the organization and direction of the College have remained essentially unchanged.

During these years, the College has made substantial contributions to state, national, and international agriculture. But in the absence of detailed scholarly works dealing with American agriculture since the 1920s, and of the historical perspective that time alone can give to the relative importance of men and events, it is not possible to present an analytical account of this period. The following summaries of what seem to be some of the major developments within the various College departments and the work of the Dixon Springs Agricultural Center and the international agricultural programs are drawn from detailed reports prepared by staff members of the College and deposited in the University Archives. These summaries may serve as a starting point for that future historian who will continue the history of the University of Illinois College of Agriculture.

AGRICULTURAL ECONOMICS

Five years before establishment of the Department of Farm Organization and Management (now Agricultural Economics) in 1917, W. F. Handschin initiated cost studies of Illinois farms. These studies, which have continued since 1912, and the cost studies and records kept by farmers in the farm business associations, give Illinois perhaps the most complete production and economic data from farms of any state in the nation. Several other cornbelt experiment stations use these data as a basis for predicting costs and returns of various farm enterprises and as standards for research in farm production economics.

In the 1920s, C. L. Stewart devised the Export Debenture Plan for making payments to exporters of farm products so that prices in the United States could be maintained above world levels. Stewart's plan became a keystone of our national farm program, and variations of it have been used for corn, wheat, cotton, and other products. Stewart and H. C. M. Case worked with the Farm Foundation in 1938 in developing the North-Central Land Tenure Committee representing twelve Midwestern states. This committee was the forerunner of later regional committees sponsored by the Farm Foundation for research in marketing, rural sociology, and farm management.

Since the Second World War, the Department has made extensive use of new research methods in agricultural economics, including electronic computers, time-and-motion studies, linear programming, the Markov chain, the flexible standard in analysis of the farm business, and the speculative error concept as a means of forecasting grain prices.

Agricultural Engineering

One of the early leaders in the fight for rural electrification, E. W. Lehmann started electric power and processing studies soon after becoming first head of the Department in 1921. In addition to developing a mechanical bunk-feed distributor for feeding livestock, Department scientists have designed and tested electrical controls, metering and blending devices, and conveyors for automatic feed-handling systems.

On October 22, 1924, the Department demonstrated the use of the combine to harvest soybeans. This demonstration, which is believed to be the first of its kind, proved that the combine harvested a much larger percentage of soybeans than the threshing machine, and played a key role in the rapid expansion of the crop in Illinois. The number of combines owned by Illinois farmers increased from nineteen in 1925 to 93,000 in 1961. During this same period, soybean acreage in the state increased from 106,000 to 5,500,000 acres.

Illinois agricultural engineers have conducted continuous research on farm tractors since 1924. Among the results of this research are one of the first reports on the use of rubber tires for tractors; the conversion of tractors from kerosene to gasoline; the installation of alcohol-water injectors to permit operation on low-octane fuels; designs for safer, more efficient, and easier-to-operate tractors; and the formulation of principles for tractor selection, improved maintenance, and lower operating costs. The Department has also carried out investigations of crop drying, farm structures, drainage, soil and water conservation, and tillage practices.

Agronomy

Under the direction of J. G. Mosier, R. S. Smith, and others, the Department has developed perhaps the most comprehensive state soil survey in the nation. Illinois soil-testing methods are used as a basis for fertilizer applications by more than two-thirds of all states testing soils. In the 1930s, Department studies of the colloid fraction in soils resulted in the separation, identification, and naming of the clay mineral Illite. E. E. DeTurk and his co-workers demonstrated potash fixation by Illite, and showed the importance of this fixation in fertility practices.

The research and extension activities of W. L. Burlison, J. C. Hackleman, and C. M. Woodworth have helped make Illinois the largest producer of soybeans in the United States. Staff agronomists have released many soybean varieties to Illinois farmers, including Illini, Ilsoy, Chief, and Viking. Since 1936, the research that has made new varieties possible has been carried out in cooperation with the U.S. Regional Soybean Laboratory. Department scientists have also developed hundreds of varieties of winter wheat and widely used hybrids and inbred lines of corn.

The Illinois Maize Genetics Laboratory, staffed by members of the Departments of Agronomy, Horticulture, Plant Pathology, and Botany, is conducting a coordinate program of basic research in maize genetics. Recent field experiments indicate that high lysine (modified-protein) corn may have major effects upon both human and animal nutrition throughout the world.

ANIMAL SCIENCE

The work of H. H. Mitchell, H. L. Rietz, and H. S. Grindley led to the adoption of statistical treatment of data in animal nutrition laboratories. Mitchell also demonstrated the correlation between the nutritive value of a protein and the essential amino acids it contained, investigated the mineral requirements (especially calcium) of animals and man, made the first analysis of the composition of the entire human body, and developed a practicable method for determining the biological value of proteins. Working closely with Mitchell, T. S. Hamilton carried out research on energy metabolism with respect to the quality and level of proteins.

Illinois animal scientists were the first to demonstrate that lamb gains were increased by adding the tetracycline antibiotics at levels of 7.5 to 10 milligrams, a practice now commonly followed in finishing rations for both sheep and cattle. W. E. Carroll studied the food requirements of pregnant swine, and L. E. Card did basic work on chick growth rates, body composition, and basal heat production. Card and Elmer Roberts showed conclusively that the resistance of chickens to pullorum disease is hereditary.

In the 1920s, the Department introduced the McLean County System of Swine Sanitation. This system greatly increased the number of pigs marketed per litter as well as the hog's efficiency in converting feed to meat. Development of a technique for surgical removal of the pituitary gland from living chickens has enabled Department poultry specialists to study the effect of individual hormones in the adult fowl, and has resulted in new findings in the physiology of egg production.

DAIRY SCIENCE

Between 1919 and 1928, the Bowlker Breeding Project provided Department scientists with valuable information about the inheritance of milk and butterfat yields and body color. Using cows from the Bowlker herd, W. L. Gaines and F. P. Sanmann proved that all of the milk obtained at one milking is present in the udder at milking time. Gaines also devised a formula for estimating energy from milk and butterfat yields that is widely used in dairy research.

Studies by H. A. Harding and M. J. Prucha indicated that dairy utensils were the principal sources of contamination of milk. Later experiments by Prucha demonstrated that the bacterial count was greatly reduced when clean utensils were disinfected with chemicals, especially chlorine. Prucha and G. F. Smith of the Department of Chemistry developed the aerosol method of whipping dairy products, and Prucha and P. H. Tracy carried out experimental work on paper milk containers that led to general public acceptance of these containers. During the Second World War, Tracy helped perfect a process for preserving powdered whole milk for use by the armed forces.

H. A. Ruehe developed a method for concentrating buttermilk that facilitated the storage and shipment of what was previously considered a waste product, and W. W. Yapp formulated a dimension-weight index for cattle and an equal-parent index for evaluating the transmitting ability of dairy bulls. More recent Department research has revealed that a single ejaculate of bull semen can, without reduction in fertility, be used to inseminate more than one hundred cows. This research is part of a broad program in the reproductive physiology of animals.

FOOD SCIENCE

Established as Food Technology in 1948, the Department has carried out studies in the use of flexible plastic film for heat-preserved foods, and has developed methods for the production of precooked, dehydrated lima beans and cream-style corn. Dairy technologists (the division of dairy manufactures was transferred from the Department of Dairy Husbandry to Food Technology in 1948) have demonstrated that the loss of flavor in cottage cheese is due to the presence of quaternary ammonium compounds used in cleaning dairy equipment, devised a procedure for studying milk protein in a synthetic medium exactly simulating its natural environment, and published data used by industry and the U.S. Public Health Service in setting standards for pasteurizing milk at higher temperatures and shorter times.

Since the invention of canning by Nicolas Appert in 1809, the heat resistance of spores of food-spoilage organisms has been a major problem. Illinois food microbiologists have conducted experiments on the details of spore germination, particularly as measured by heat resistance, and have succeeded in starting, stopping, and restarting the germination process.

As a byproduct of a study on the flavor reversion of soybean oil, Department food chemists discovered a process for the improvement of beef tallow. They have also investigated the toxicity of overheated, oxidized fats and the possible role played by lipids in heart diseases.

FORESTRY

Soon after its establishment in 1938, the Department began research on reforestation and woodland management. This research, which has been continued to the present, has provided information on the adaptability of several tree species to Illinois soils and site conditions, growth rates, and the economic returns that may be expected from forest property. Studies dealing with the growing and marketing of Christmas trees have helped many landowners increase their incomes.

Illinois foresters have also investigated the life histories and potential control measures of forest-tree insects, used aerial reconnaissance in the mapping of forest vegetation, demonstrated that the service life of posts with naturally low resistance to decay and insects can almost be trebled through chemical treatment, and have developed and patented a method for burning tree stumps with the aid of a chemical formulation.

The Department's field laboratories include six areas ranging in size from forty to 1,000 acres that are close enough to Champaign-Urbana for use in the instructional program, and a number of research properties at various locations in the state. The 2,500-acre Sinnissippi Forest in Ogle County (managed by the Department under an agreement with the owners) was recently the locus of a ten-year study in the control of oak-wilt disease.

HOME ECONOMICS

The Department conducted the first controlled research in the cooking of meats and offered the first course in family economics in the United States. With federal funds from the Purnell Act of 1925, home economists carried out studies of Illinois soft-wheat flours and the vitamin content of cereals. A 1936 project on the calcium needs of children was one of the first of its kind in this country.

Since 1938, Department research workers have contributed basic information on the comfort of human subjects at various environmental temperatures and relative humidities, saving and spending patterns of rural families, and space standards for designing work areas in homes, including a "wheelchair kitchen" for the physically handicapped.

They have also studied obesity in children; the reaction of fabrics to repeated small stresses; conservation of flavor and nutritive quality of foods under various home practices; chemical composition and uses of soybeans and soybean products; freezing of fruits, vegetables, and cooked prepared foods; chemical and physical properties of starch; ascorbic acid retention in cooked vegetables; and mineral, protein, thiamine, and riboflavin requirements in humans.

HORTICULTURE

The Department has carried out experiments on fertilizers for greenhouse crops, the continued use of old soil for carnations, and the effects of bud selection on roses and carnations. J. W. Lloyd classified vegetables according to growth season and planting practices, and M. J. Dorsey and R. L. McMunn were the first investigators to study the gross morphology of the peach fruit. R. V. Lott's work on the physiological development of peaches formed the basis for legal adoption of comparative maturity standards for the leading varieties of peach and apple fruits.

H. W. Anderson isolated the causal organism of red stele root rot in strawberries, and A. S. Colby introduced Vermilion as a resistant variety. W. A. Huelsen developed varieties of tomatoes resistant to *Fusarium* wilt as well as inbred lines of sweet corn that are used by commercial growers. The development by Illinois plant breeders of apple species immune to the apple scab disease has received wide attention.

Department scientists have also devised reliable tests for determining color, firmness, and crack resistance of tomato varieties; established that photoperiod may be used to advantage in the propagation and flowering of carnations; developed stocks of disease-free carnations for the florist industry; and introduced over one hundred varieties of chrysanthemums, including twenty-seven varieties grown extensively in the United States, and seven produced by European florists. Recent Department research in plant physiology includes studies of ion transport, nitrogen metabolism, pollen physiology, the mechanism of action of growth regulators, and low-temperature injury to plants.

PLANT PATHOLOGY

In 1869, T. J. Burrill offered probably the first course in plant pathology in the United States. Eleven years later, he proved that bacteria can cause disease in plants as well as in animals and created the science of bacterial plant pathology. It was not until 1941, however, that the Department of Horticulture organized a division of plant pathology. This division became a separate department in 1955, bringing plant pathologists from other College departments and the Illinois Natural History Survey into a single administrative unit.

Among other contributions to their field, Illinois plant pathologists have demonstrated that a protein produced by a plant pathogenic microorganism can induce symptoms of disease (wilt) in plants; identified the tobacco mosaic virus of tomatoes and new species of fungus causing strawberry leaf blight and brown stem rot of soybeans; developed genetic resistance to the fungus causing the northern corn leaf-blight disease; experimentally transmitted the peach X-disease virus by means of biovectors (presumably grasshoppers); and discovered chloromycetin, streptothricin, Endomycin, Levomycin, and Filipin. (Several of these antibiotics have proved effective in controlling human diseases.)

Research in the Department of Plant Pathology is no longer concerned solely with the identification and control of plant diseases. New research tools have allowed Department scientists to investigate the more fundamental aspects of plant diseases, including host-parasite interactions, fungus physiology, and the biochemistry of viruses.

ANIMAL PATHOLOGY AND HYGIENE

The Department of Animal Husbandry established a division of animal pathology and hygiene in 1917 that became a separate department in the College of Agriculture in 1941. This department was transferred to the newly created College of Veterinary Medicine in 1945. Robert Graham, who had served as head of both the division and Department of Animal Pathology and Hygiene, was appointed first dean (1945–1956) of the College of Veterinary Medicine. He was succeeded as dean by Carl A. Brandly (1956–1968) and L. Meyer Jones (1968—). All instruction in veterinary science is carried on by the College of Veterinary Medicine, but part of the research and all of the extension activities are administered by the College of Agriculture. Veterinary medicine, which has been a part of the University almost from the beginning (the first course in the subject was taught in 1870), deserves a history of its own.

Dixon Springs Agricultural Center

During the Depression, southern Illinois farmers, concerned about low soil fertility and severe erosion, asked the College of Agriculture to locate an agricultural experiment station in their area. These requests resulted in the Dixon Springs Experiment Station (renamed Agricultural Center in 1964) near the villages of Glendale and Robbs. The Center was established under the direction of a College of Agriculture committee composed of W. L. Burlison, W. G. Kammlade, H. W. Mumford, and H. P. Rusk, chairman. Several federal agencies were also involved in planning the Center and in purchasing lands for its use, including the Resettlement Administration, Forest Service, Soil Erosion Service (now Soil Conservation Service), and the Bureaus of Animal and Plant Industry of the U. S. Department of Agriculture. In 1940, all lands were transferred to the Forest Service. The Forest Service then leased the lands to the University of Illinois under a long-term, free-use permit that is still in effect.

The Dixon Springs station was formally dedicated on October 8, 1938, and J. H. Longwell was appointed superintendent the following year. He was succeeded in 1940 by the present head, R. J. Webb. (Webb's title was changed from superintendent to assistant director of the Illinois Agricultural Experiment Station in 1964.) Early research at the Center was directed toward reclaiming and rebuilding soils and determining the crops and livestock operations best suited to the area. From this research, Dixon Springs scientists developed farming systems that have proved profitable to the farmer while preserving soil productivity through successive years. These basic studies have been continued, although the major emphasis now is upon utilization of the crops produced, evaluation of farming systems, and disease control and management. Newer areas of investigation involve the College of Veterinary Medicine, the Departments of Forestry and Horticulture, the wildlife research, entomology, and aquatic biology sections of the Illinois Natural History Survey, and the Departments of Botany, Zoology, and Geography of the College of Liberal Arts and Sciences.

The Dixon Springs Center consists of about 4,900 acres of open land and timbered areas divided into 150 fields varying in size from a fraction of an acre to 100 acres. The buildings include an administration headquarters, a combination dormitory and meeting room, fourteen staff houses, laboratories, workshop, structures for machinery and grain storage, and livestock barns and sheds. There are 1,000 head of beef cattle, including a breeding herd of 400 cows, and 1,000 head of breeding sheep. The area also contains abundant wildlife for study and survey. The Center staff is composed of a dozen professional and about fifty nonacademic members.

INTERNATIONAL AGRICULTURAL PROGRAMS

The international programs of the College of Agriculture are largely sponsored and financed by the Agency for International Development (AID) of the United States government. The College has had cooperative agreements with India since 1952, and with Sierra Leone, Africa, since 1963. From 1963 to 1966, the College's Office of Agricultural Communications assisted the Ministry of Agriculture in setting up an agricultural information office in Amman, Jordan.

The College currently has AID contracts with Jawaharlal Nehru Agricultural University and Uttar Pradesh Agricultural University in India, and with Njala University College in Sierra Leone. These contracts involve assigning staff members to the participating countries, training foreign participants at the University of Illinois, and purchasing and delivering equipment, books, and supplies for use in India and Africa. A coordinated soybean research project has been conducted at the two Indian universities and the Champaign-Urbana campus since 1967. In 1969, this project was made a part of the Program for International Research, Improvement, and Development of Soybeans in many foreign countries. In addition to the AID programs, members of the Department of Agricultural Economics are working with the Ford Foundation in developing agricultural economics at Uttar Pradesh Agricultural University and other institutions in India.

Through bringing American agricultural technology to other countries, College of Agriculture staff members are continuing the century-old land-grant college tradition of helping people to help themselves.

APPENDIXES

Top, left, Herbert W.
Mumford (1871–1938);
right, Joseph C. Blair
(1871–1960); middle,
left, Henry P. Rusk
(1884–1954); right,
Robert R. Hudelson
(1886—); bottom, left,
Louis B. Howard
(1905—); right,
Orville G. Bentley
(1918—).

APPENDIX A

HERBERT WINDSOR MUMFORD (1922–1938)

Mumford was graduated from the Michigan Agricultural College (now Michigan State University) in 1891, and served as professor of agriculture at his alma mater from 1899 to 1901. He was head of the Department of Animal Husbandry at the University of Illinois from 1901 to 1922, and dean of the College of Agriculture from 1922 until his death as the result of an automobile accident in 1938. When Mumford became dean, the farmers were already suffering from the economic malaise that was to infect the entire nation seven years later. He saw clearly that the marketing of agricultural products would play as important a role in the years ahead as methods of increasing production had played in the past, and in 1928 he launched a series of agricultural adjustment conferences in each farming-type area of Illinois. These conferences were continued annually until the federal adjustment program was begun in 1932.

JOSEPH CULLEN BLAIR (1938–1939)

After graduation from the Provincial College of Agriculture at Truro, Nova Scotia, in 1892, Blair attended Cornell University for four years. He came to the University of Illinois as instructor of horticulture in 1896, and was made head of the Department of Horticulture in 1902. Blair served in this position until 1938, and as dean of the College of Agriculture from 1938 until his retirement the following year.

HENRY PERLY RUSK (1939–1952)

Rusk was graduated from Valparaiso University in 1904, and received his bachelor's and master's degrees from the University of Missouri in 1908 and 1911. After teaching for one year at Purdue University, Rusk joined the Department of Animal Husbandry staff at the University of Illinois in 1910. His skill as a judge of livestock and his research in cattle feeding (he was a pioneer in the use of soft corn for fattening steers) soon earned him the esteem of scientists, stockmen, and farmers. Rusk succeeded Mumford as head of the Department of

Animal Husbandry in 1922, and became dean of the College of Agriculture in 1939. During his tenure as dean, he served on a large number of national committees, boards, and commissions, including the chairmanship of the Agricultural Task Force of President Herbert Hoover's Commission on Organization of the Executive Branch of the Government.

ROBERT R. HUDELSON (1953–1954)

Hudelson received his B.S. and Ph.D. degrees from the University of Illinois in 1912 and 1939, and his M.A. from the University of Missouri in 1915. He was employed as a farm manager by the Doane Agricultural Service from 1922 until his appointment to the College of Agriculture staff three years later. In 1933, Hudelson worked with Dean Mumford in administering the Agricultural Adjustment Act in Illinois. During the following two decades, he served successively as assistant dean (1933–1943) and associate dean (1943–1951) of the College of Agriculture, acting dean (1951–1952) of the College of Commerce, and acting dean (1952–1953) of the College of Agriculture. In March, 1953, he succeeded Rusk as dean of the College. Hudelson retired from the University in 1954, and served as manager of the Farm Department of the Champaign Bank and Trust Company until 1966.

LOUIS BRADLEY HOWARD (1954–1965)

A 1927 graduate of Purdue University, Howard received his M.S. and Ph.D. degrees from the University of Chicago in 1928 and 1931. Before his appointment to the University of Illinois staff as head of the newly created Department of Food Technology in 1948, he served in various positions with the U.S. Department of Agriculture, including chief of the Bureau of Agricultural and Industrial Chemistry in Washington, D.C. Howard was appointed associate director of the Illinois agricultural experiment station in 1951, and dean of the College of Agriculture in 1954. He resigned as dean in 1965. The following year, he returned to Washington as director of the International Rural Development Office of the National Association of State Universities and Land-Grant Colleges, retiring from this position in 1968. Howard is widely known for his research work in food processing (he holds a patent on dehydrofreezing), and in 1952 the U.S. Army awarded him a Certificate of Appreciation for his contributions to the food program during the Second World War.

Appendix A

ORVILLE GEORGE BENTLEY (1965—)

Bentley was graduated from South Dakota State College in 1942, and received his M.S. and Ph.D. degrees from the University of Wisconsin in 1947 and 1950. He joined the Animal Science Department in the Ohio Agricultural Experiment Station at Wooster in 1950, and was appointed dean of the College of Agriculture and Biological Sciences at South Dakota State College in 1958. Upon Howard's resignation in 1965, Bentley was made dean of the University of Illinois College of Agriculture. A noted animal nutritionist as well as a college administrator, Bentley was one of ten agricultural specialists who accompanied Secretary of Agriculture Orville Freeman on a fact-finding mission to South Vietnam in 1966.

APPENDIX B

Agricultural Economics (established 1917; Farm Organization and Management until 1932)

Farm Organization and Management

Walter F. Handschin, Head	1917–1922
Harold C. M. Case, Acting Head	1922–1929
Head	1929–1932

Agricultural Economics

Herbert W. Mumford, Acting Head	1932–1934
Harold C. M. Case, Head	1934–1955
Lawrence J. Norton, Head	1955–1956
Garret L. Jordan, Acting Head	1956–1957
Harold G. Halcrow, Head	1957–

Agricultural Engineering (established 1921; Farm Mechanics until 1932)

Emil W. Lehmann, Head	1921–1954
Frank D. Lanham, Head	1954–

Agronomy (established 1899)

Perry G. Holden, Head	1899–1900
Cyril G. Hopkins, Head	1900–1919
William L. Burlison, Head	1919–1951
Morell B. Russell, Head	1951–1962
Acting Head	1962–1963
Marlowe D. Thorne, Head	1963–

Animal Science (established 1901; Animal Husbandry until 1947)

Herbert W. Mumford, Head	1901–1922
Henry P. Rusk, Head	1922–1939
William E. Carroll, Head	1939–1947
Leslie E. Card, Head	1947–1958
O. Burr Ross, Head	1958–1964

Robert O. Nesheim, Head   1964–1967
Donald E. Becker, Head   1967–

Dairy Science (established 1902; Dairy Husbandry until 1947; Dairy
    Production from 1947 to 1949)
    Wilber J. Fraser, Head   1902–1913
    Harry A. Harding, Head   1913–1920
    Martin J. Prucha, Acting Head   1920–1921
    Harrison A. Ruehe, Head   1921–1946
    William W. Yapp, Acting Head   1943–1947
    Glenn W. Salisbury, Head   1947–1969
    Karl E. Gardner, Acting Head   1955–1956
    Kenneth E. Harshbarger, Head   1969–

Food Science (established 1948; Food Technology until 1963)
    Louis B. Howard, Head   1948–1952
    R. Ralph Legault, Acting Head   1952–1953
    Robert M. Whitney, Executive Officer   1953–1954
    Reid T. Milner, Head   1954–

Forestry (established 1938)
    J. Nelson Spaeth, Head   1938–1965
    Ralph W. Lorenz, Acting Head   1965–1966
    Thomas E. Avery, Head   1966–1968
    William R. Boggess, Acting Head   1968–1969
                  Head   1969–

Home Economics (established 1900; Household Science until 1918)
    Isabel Bevier, Head   1900–1921
    Ruth A. Wardall, Head   1921–1936
    J. Lita Bane, Head   1936–1948
    Mrs. Kathryn V. Burns, Acting Head   1948–1949
    Janice M. Smith, Acting Head   1949–1950
                  Head   1950–

Horticulture (established 1902)
    Joseph C. Blair, Head   1902–1939
    John W. Lloyd, Acting Head   1939–1940

Maxwell J. Dorsey, Head 1940–1948
Bryan L. Wade, Head 1948–1949
Charles J. Birkeland, Acting Head 1949–1950
                            Head 1950–

Plant Pathology (established 1955)
    Manson B. Linn, Acting Head 1955–1957
    Wayne M. Bever, Head 1957–

APPENDIX C

Major Buildings

	Year completed	Original cost (dollars)
Old Agriculture Building (Davenport Hall)	1900	165,000
Agronomy Building (now Forest Science Laboratory)[a]	1905	17,000
Beef Cattle Barn (now Small Animal Veterinary Clinic)	1905	28,000
Horticultural Building (now Surveying Building)[b]	1905	18,000
Woman's Building (now English Building)[c]	1905	80,000
Farm Mechanics (Agricultural Engineering) Building[d]	1907	33,000
Floriculture and Vegetable Crops Buildings	1913	88,000
Stock-Judging Pavilion	1913	112,000
Animal Genetics Building	1916	12,000
Cattle Feeding Plant	1917	30,000
Beef Cattle Plant	1918	144,000
Horticulture Field Laboratory	1923	240,000
New Agriculture Building (Mumford Hall)	1924	493,000
Dairy Manufactures Building	1925	252,000
Horse Barn	1925	35,000
Swine Plant	1925	33,000
Dairy Barns	1926	118,000
Agronomy Seed House	1930	52,000
Administration Building, Dixon Springs Agricultural Center	1938	23,000
Agricultural Engineering Research Laboratory	1952	248,000
Animal Sciences Laboratory	1952	2,232,000
Veterinary Medicine Building	1952	1,738,000
Large Animal Veterinary Clinic	1955	572,000
Bevier Hall (Home Economics Building)	1956	3,464,000
Child Development Laboratory (Home Economics)	1956	546,000
Veterinary Medical Research Building	1961	360,000

Burnsides Research Laboratory (Food Science)	1963	900,000
Jonathan Baldwin Turner Hall (Plant Sciences Building)	1963	3,847,000

ᵃ This building, known for many years as the "Old Agronomy Storehouse," has served at various times as a horse barn, garage, seed storehouse, and photography laboratory. Since 1967, it has been the Forest Science Laboratory.

ᵇ The name is misleading. Although used to store the surveying equipment of the Department of Civil Engineering after completion of the Horticulture Field Laboratory in 1923, the so-called "Surveying Building" now houses a lithography laboratory and classroom for freehand drawing in the Department of Art.

ᶜ An $125,000 addition to the Woman's Building was erected in 1913, and the entire structure was remodeled in 1924. The building has been occupied by the Department of English since 1956.

ᵈ An addition to the Farm Mechanics Building was constructed in 1911, a tractor laboratory and garage in 1924, and an addition to the garage in 1928.

Agronomy Building (now Forest Science Laboratory), completed 1905.

Beef Cattle Barn (now Small Animal Veterinary Clinic), completed 1905.

Farm Mechanics (Agricultural Engineering) Building, completed 1907.

Horticultural Building (now Surveying Building), completed 1905.

Floriculture Building, completed 1913.

Vegetable Crops Building, completed 1913.

Stock-Judging Pavilion, completed 1913.

Animal Genetics Building, completed 1916.

Horticulture Field Laboratory, completed 1923.

New Agriculture Building (Mumford Hall), completed 1924.

Dairy Manufactures Building, completed 1925.

Agronomy Seed House, completed 1930.

Animal Sciences Laboratory, completed 1952.

Veterinary Medicine Building, completed 1952.

Bevier Hall (Home Economics Building), completed 1956.

Large Animal Veterinary Clinic, completed 1955.

Veterinary Medical Research Building (Center for Zoonoses Research), completed 1961.

Child Development Laboratory (Home Economics), completed 1956.

Jonathan Baldwin Turner Hall (Plant Sciences Building), completed 1963.

Burnsides Research Laboratory (Food Science), completed 1963.

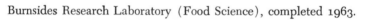

APPENDIX D

UNDERGRADUATE AND GRADUATE DEGREES, INCLUDING FOREIGN STUDENTS,
1872–1969[a]

Year	B.S. Degree		M.S. Degree		Ph.D. Degree	
	Total students	Foreign students	Total students	Foreign students	Total students	Foreign students
71–72	1	0	0	0	0	0
72–73	6	0	0	0	0	0
73–74	5	1	0	0	0	0
74–75	7	0	0	0	0	0
75–76	5	0	0	0	0	0
76–77	4	0	0	0	0	0
77–78	5	0	0	0	0	0
78–79	1	0	0	0	0	0
79–80	1	0	0	0	0	0
80–81	2	0	0	0	0	0
81–82	0	0	0	0	0	0
82–83	0	0	0	0	0	0
83–84	3	0	0	0	0	0
84–85	1	0	0	0	0	0
85–86	0	0	0	0	0	0
86–87	0	0	0	0	0	0
87–88	1	0	0	0	0	0
88–89	1	0	0	0	0	0
89–90	0	0	0	0	0	0
90–91	2	0	0	0	0	0
91–92	0	0	0	0	0	0
92–93	2	0	0	0	0	0
93–94	1	0	0	0	0	0
94–95	0	0	0	0	0	0
95–96	0	0	0	0	0	0
96–97	2	0	0	0	0	0
97–98	2	0	0	0	0	0
98–99	4	0	0	0	0	0
99–00	2	0	0	0	0	0

Year	B.S. Degree		M.S. Degree		Ph.D. Degree	
	Total students	Foreign students	Total students	Foreign students	Total students	Foreign students
00–01	4	0	0	0	0	0
01–02	4	0	3	0	0	0
02–03	9	0	0	0	0	0
03–04	16	0	1	0	0	0
04–05	18	0	2	0	0	0
05–06	25	1	9	2	0	0
06–07	43	0	4	1	1	0
07–08	38	4	6	1	0	0
08–09	54	3	8	0	1	0
09–10	49	2	7	0	0	0
10–11	52	4	3	0	1	0
11–12	67	1	10	1	3	1
12–13	95	8	11	1	0	0
13–14	142	7	11	4	1	0
14–15	136	6	7	0	4	1
15–16	188	6	12	1	0	0
16–17	235	2	26	1	3	1
17–18	140	5	8	1	0	0
18–19	64	4	8	1	3	0
19–20	151	6	12	3	1	1
20–21	176	11	9	2	2	1
21–22	183	6	16	5	1	1
22–23	189	3	13	1	3	3
23–24	149	6	17	0	1	0
24–25	145	4	15	0	1	0
25–26	116	1	13	0	3	0
26–27	105	2	17	0	3	0
27–28	110	6	12	2	4	0
28–29	119	1	13	0	7	0
29–30	122	2	25	2	4	0
30–31	105	1	13	0	5	0
31–32	109	1	18	0	4	0
32–33	130	2	24	3	9	4
33–34	118	1	11	0	3	0
34–35	130	2	16	0	5	0
35–36	168	2	7	0	1	0

Appendix D

Year	B.S. Degree		M.S. Degree		Ph.D. Degree	
	Total students	Foreign students	Total students	Foreign students	Total students	Foreign students
36–37	201	1	19	1	4	0
37–38	235	1	34	1	2	0
38–39	248	1	36	1	2	0
39–40	355	1	27	1	9	1
40–41	325	0	39	1	9	1
41–42	305	5	46	1	6	0
42–43	259	0	28	2	5	0
43–44	107	2	9	1	7	1
44–45	83	1	12	0	4	1
45–46	132	0	18	3	3	0
46–47	241	3	51	4	9	1
47–48	250	1	52	3	11	1
48–49	328	1	50	8	12	3
49–50	459	1	87	8	17	5
50–51	425	3	87	9	23	4
51–52	306	3	95	2	29	5
52–53	307	2	73	8	20	4
53–54	277	2	75	9	36	7
54–55	274	5	73	15	54	12
55–56	294	5	69	8	51	12
56–57	321	5	92	11	28	10
57–58	331	8	90	11	39	10
58–59	282	1	98	21	36	13
59–60	279	6	103	23	56	23
60–61	251	3	84	13	45	10
61–62	271	6	70	26	50	17
62–63	258	8	73	29	50	9
63–64	305	3	90	20	35	9
64–65	272	11	86	30	44	15
65–66	295	11	86	19	48	24
66–67	325	8	89	15	48	22
67–68	373	5	83	18	54	28
68–69	377	4	121	29	74	24

[a] Includes all degrees conferred in August and October of the first year shown and in February and June of the following year.

APPENDIX E

Growth of College and Agricultural Experiment Station, 1890–1921

Year	Federal funds		State appropriations		Faculty	Under-graduate students	Graduate students
	College	Station	College	Station			
90–91	$ 5,000	$15,000			3	7	0
91–92	5,000	15,000			3	6	2
92–93	5,000	15,000			3	13	0
93–94	5,000	15,000			3	5	2
94–95	5,000	15,000			3	9	0
95–96	7,000	15,000			3	14	0
96–97	7,000	15,000			6	17	0
97–98	7,000	15,000			8	19	0
98–99	7,000	15,000			9	25	0
99–00	28,000	15,000			16	90	0
00–01	28,000	15,000			17	159	0
01–02	28,000	15,000	$ 8,000	$ 54,000	23	232	0
02–03	28,000	15,000	8,000	54,000	27	284	0
03–04	28,000	15,000	61,000	85,000	37	339	0
04–05	28,000	15,000	61,000	85,000	37	406	0
05–06	28,500	20,000	61,000	95,000	44	430	9
06–07	28,500	22,000	61,000	95,000	50	462	10
07–08	31,000	24,000	71,000	102,500	61	528	17
08–09	33,500	26,000	71,000	102,500	63	531	15

		(Smith-Lever)						
09–10	36,000		28,000	55,000	138,000	74	660	23
10–11	38,500		30,000	55,000	138,000	74	729	28
11–12	41,000		30,000		$476,150[a]	100	829	27
12–13	41,000		30,000		476,150	120	905	22
13–14	41,000		30,000		470,490	137	1,014	33
14–15	41,000	$ 10,000	30,000		470,490	149	1,184	51
15–16	41,200	36,282	30,000		460,615	153	1,257	75
16–17	41,200	58,000	30,000		460,615	151	1,201	66
17–18	41,200	80,085	30,000		422,615	149	768[b]	43
18–19	41,200	101,987	30,000		422,615	131	745[b]	12
19–20	41,200	189,595	30,000		422,615	149	1,271	36
20–21	41,200	211,496	30,000		443,465	130	1,179	63

[a] Appropriations to College and experiment station made in one lump sum after 1911.
[b] Decreased enrollment reflects United States's entrance in the First World War.

241

APPENDIX F

Administrative Officers, Agricultural Experiment Station, 1888–1969

Selim H. Peabody, President of Board of Direction	1888–1891
George E. Morrow, President of Board of Direction	1891–1894
Thomas J. Burrill, President of Board of Direction	1894–1896
Eugene Davenport, Director[a]	1896–1922
Herbert W. Mumford, Director	1922–1938
Joseph C. Blair, Director	1938–1939
Henry P. Rusk, Director	1939–1952
Robert R. Hudelson, Director	1952–1954
Louis B. Howard, Director	1954–1965
Morell B. Russell, Director[b]	1965–1969
Glenn W. Salisbury, Director	1969–
Associate Directors	
William E. Carroll	1946–1951
Louis B. Howard	1951–1954
Tom S. Hamilton	1954–1962
Morell B. Russell[b]	1962–1965

---

[a] On June 9, 1896, the University trustees reorganized the agricultural experiment station. The dean of the College of Agriculture was appointed director of the station, and the Board of Direction became an Advisory Board. This organization was essentially unchanged until April 1, 1965. See footnote, Appendix H, and text, p. 114.

[b] See footnote, Appendix H.

APPENDIX G

Walter F. Handschin
   Vice Director of Agricultural Extension   1914–1922
Isabel Bevier
   Vice Director of Home Economics Extension   1915–1921
Ruth A. Wardall
   Vice Director of Home Economics Extension   1921–1936
J. Lita Bane
   Vice Director of Home Economics Extension   1936–1947
J. Clyde Spitler
   Assistant Director of Agricultural Extension   1937–1943
   Associate Director of Agricultural Extension   1943–1949
William G. Kammlade
   Associate Director of the Extension Service in
      Agriculture and Home Economics   1949–1960
John B. Claar
   Associate Director of Cooperative Extension Service   1960–1965
   Director of Cooperative Extension Service[b]   1965–
Moyle S. Williams
   Associate Director of Cooperative Extension Service   1969–

State Leaders of Farm Advisers
   Walter F. Handschin   1914–1917
   George N. Coffey   1917–1922
   William H. Smith   1922–1930
   J. Clyde Spitler   1930–1949
   William G. Kammlade[c]   1949–1960

State Leaders of Home Advisers
   Mamie Bunch   1915–1920
   J. Lita Bane   1920–1923
   Mrs. Kathryn V. Burns   1923–1956

---

[a] The dean of the College of Agriculture also served as director of the Cooperative Extension Service until April 1, 1965. See footnote, Appendix H.

[b] See footnote, Appendix H.

| Lulu S. Black | 1956–1959 |
| Florence A. Kimmelshue (Acting)[c] | 1959–1960 |

State Leader of 4-H Club Work

| Richard O. Lyon | 1961– |

Assistant Directors of Cooperative Extension Service

William D. Murphy[d]	1959–
Martha L. Dunlap[d]	1960–
Moyle S. Williams	1963–1969
Hadley Read	1966–

---

[c] The titles of State Leader of Farm Advisers and State Leader of Home Advisers were dropped in 1960.

[d] Mr. Murphy and Miss Dunlap perform the duties previously assigned to the State Leader of Farm Advisers and the State Leader of Home Advisers.

APPENDIX H

DEANS AND DIRECTORS, COLLEGE OF AGRICULTURE, 1969[a]

Dean of the College of Agriculture
    Orville G. Bentley
Associate Dean; Director of International Agricultural Programs
    George K. Brinegar
    Assistant Director
    Wilbur D. Buddemeier
Associate Dean; Director of Cooperative Extension Service
    John B. Claar
    Associate Director
    Moyle S. Williams
    Assistant Directors
    Martha L. Dunlap
    William D. Murphy
    Hadley Read
Associate Dean; Director of Resident Instruction
    Karl E. Gardner
    Assistant Deans
    Cecil D. Smith
    Warren K. Wessels
Associate Dean; Director of Agricultural Experiment Station
    Glenn W. Salisbury
    Assistant Director
        Robert J. Webb (also superintendent of Extension Programs, Dixon Springs Agricultural Center)

---

[a] On April 1, 1965, the University Board of Trustees made the following changes in the titles of four administrative officers of the College of Agriculture: Dean of the College of Agriculture, Director of the Agricultural Experiment Station, and Director of the Cooperative Extension Service changed to Dean of the College of Agriculture; Associate Director of the Agricultural Experiment Station changed to Director of the Agricultural Experiment Station and Associate Dean of the College of Agriculture; Associate Director of the Cooperative Extension Service changed to Director of the Cooperative Extension Service and Associate Dean of the College of Agriculture; Associate Dean of the College of Agriculture changed to Director of Resident Instruction and Associate Dean of the College of Agriculture. The duties and responsibilities of these four administrators remained essentially the same as before.

APPENDIX I

Awards to College of Agriculture Graduates

	Year graduated	Year received
University of Illinois Alumni Association Achievement Award		
Robert L. Latzer	1908	1960
Charles B. Shuman	1928	1957
Oliver J. Troster	1916	1967
Collett E. Woolman	1912	1959
Loyalty Award		
Karl Adams	1931	1968
Curt E. Eckert	1930	1961
Edwin E. Griffin	1924	1962
Frederic B. Hoppin	1941	1963
Elmer Roberts	1913	1969
Walton Rose	1932	1961
J. Clyde Spitler	1907	1969
Reid R. Tombaugh	1926	1969
Kenneth N. Zimmerman	1951	1966
College of Agriculture Alumni Association Award of Merit		
Louis A. Abbott	1915	1961
Joseph Ackerman	1929	1965
Ralph Allen, Jr.	1915	1966
Robert D. Armstrong	1936	1969
Edwin Bay	1921	1969
Walter G. Baysinger	1919	1964
Richard Best	1922	1969
George Bouyoucos	1908	1968
George Brauer	1947	1968
George Bruington	1924	1967
Martin G. Burris	1942	1964
Wise Burroughs	1934	1969
Eugene D. Funk, Jr.	1922	1967
Edwin E. Griffin	1924	1966
Harold W. Hannah	1932	1965
Melvin Henderson	1925	1965
James E. Hill	1916	1961

Appendix I

College of Agriculture Alumni Association Award of Merit (Cont.)	Year graduated	Year received
Frederic B. Hoppin	1941	1966
Earl M. Hughes	1929	1968
P. E. Johnson	1930	1961
Lyle Johnstone	1905	1965
Trevor Jones	1927	1969
Jake L. Krider	1939	1962
Donald O. Lee	1925	1963
Theodore N. Mangner	1937	1963
Leslie E. Mathers, Sr.	1913	1962
Walter W. McLaughlin	1920	1965
Ralph E. Nowlan	1923	1968
Harry G. Russell	1930	1964
Lawrence H. Simerl	1932	1966
Melvin E. Sims	1941	1964
Frank H. Shuman	1921	1968
Guy D. Smith	1929	1967
J. George Smith	1940	1963
J. Clyde Spitler	1907	1967
E. George Thiem	1921	1963
William N. Thompson	1940	1960
Jonathan B. Turner	1923	1962
Clarence W. Weldon	1923	1964
Paul E. Woodson	1925	1961

Bibliography

This book is based almost entirely upon unpublished and published materials in the University of Illinois Archives and the College of Agriculture files. The principal sources are listed below. Other source materials are described in the appropriate footnotes.

UNPUBLISHED

PRIMARY

Unless otherwise indicated, the following materials are located in the University of Illinois Archives.

Agriculture Experiment Station, Botanist's Correspondence, 1901–1910. Contains correspondence of Thomas J. Burrill.

Isabel Bevier Papers, 1900–1942. College of Agriculture files.

Botany Correspondence, 1879, 1894–1912. Contains correspondence of Thomas J. Burrill.

Thomas J. Burrill Papers, 1854, 1863–1912.

Eugene Davenport Letterbooks, 1888–1911.

Eugene Davenport Personal Letterbook, 1900–1911.

Andrew S. Draper Faculty Correspondence, 1894–1904.

Andrew S. Draper General Correspondence, 1894–1904.

Andrew S. Draper Letterbooks, 1894–1904.

Andrew S. Draper Personal Letters, 1892–1913.

Mathias L. Dunlap Papers, 1839–1858, 1867–1877.

"Faculty Record," 1868–1901. Proceedings of faculty meetings.

John M. Gregory Papers, 1838–1898.

Bibliography

Clark R. Griggs, Memoir, 1906. A document concerning the location of the University prepared for President James.

Cyril G. Hopkins Letterbooks, 1899–1919.

Edmund J. James Faculty Correspondence, 1904–1915.

Natural History Survey, Chief's Correspondence, 1871–1909. Contains correspondence of Stephen A. Forbes.

SECONDARY

Unless otherwise indicated, the following typewritten materials are located in the College of Agriculture files. The dates are those shown on the manuscripts.

Bevier, Isabel. "The History of Home Economics at University of Illinois, 1900–1921." 1935. Home Economics Library.

Davenport, Eugene. "The American Agricultural College." November 15, 1912.

Davenport, Eugene. "Agricultural Development and Public Welfare." January 15, 1910.

Davenport, Eugene. "Agricultural Pioneering in the University of Illinois." March, 1940.

Davenport, Eugene. "The Development of the Agricultural College and Experiment Station During the Ten Years of President James' Administration, 1904–1914." March, 1914.

Davenport, Eugene. "The Development of Agricultural Education During the Past Fifty Years." October, 1926.

Davenport, Eugene. "Early Trials of the Agricultural Colleges and Experiment Stations." 1924.

Davenport, Eugene. "Genesis of the Illinois Agricultural Experiment Station." March, 1938.

Davenport, Eugene. "How the Farmers of Illinois Developed Their College of Agriculture at the University of Illinois." n.d.

Davenport, Eugene. "Making Headway in Scientific Agriculture." Address given at dedication of new agriculture building (Mumford Hall), January 25, 1924.

Davenport, Eugene. "Rejuvenation of the College of Agriculture of the University of Illinois." November, 1933.

Davenport, Eugene. "What One Life Has Seen." Manuscript autobiography, 1936. University of Illinois Archives.

Dunlap, Henry M. "A Legislative History of the University of Illinois, 1851–1939." University of Illinois Archives.

Forbes, Stephen A. "The Life and Work of Professor George E. Mor-

249

row." Address given at memorial service in University Chapel, April 8, 1900.

Holden, Perry G. "The University of Illinois (An Important Part of My Life)." Manuscript memoir, 1944. University of Illinois Archives.

Hopkins, Cyril G. "Illinois Soils in Relation to Systems of Permanent Agriculture." n.d. [1906?]

Hottes, Charles F. "Personal Recollections of Dr. Thomas J. Burrill and the Bacteriology of His Time." Carl Stephens Papers, 1912–1951. University of Illinois Archives.

Swanson, Richard A. "Edmund Janes James." Doctoral dissertation, University of Illinois, 1966.

PUBLISHED

PRIMARY

Alumni Record of the University of Illinois. Chicago, 1918.

Alumni Quarterly. Urbana, 1909–1915.

Alumni Quarterly and Fortnightly Notes. Urbana, 1915–1922.

Annual Reports of the Board of Trustees. Springfield and Urbana, 1867–1922.

Annual Reports of the Illinois Farmers' Institute. Springfield, 1896–1922.

Champaign County Gazette. Champaign, 1867–1894.

Chicago Tribune. Chicago, 1867–1894.

Illini. Urbana, 1874–1922.

Illinois Agriculturist. Champaign, 1901–1915.

Illinois House Journal. Springfield, 1867–1922.

Illinois Senate Journal. Springfield, 1867–1922.

Prairie Farmer. Chicago, 1852–1922.

Illinois State Horticultural Society. *Transactions.* Springfield, 1870–1917.

Report of the Commissioner of Patents for the Year 1851. Part II: Agriculture. 33 Cong., 1 sess. Senate Exec. Doc. 118. Washington, 1852.

University of Illinois Agricultural Experiment Station and Extension Bulletins and Circulars. Urbana, 1888–1922.

University of Illinois Catalogs. Urbana, 1867–1922.

U. S. Department of Agriculture Bulletins and Circulars. Washington, 1867–1922.

Bibliography

BOOKS

Bane, Lita. *The Story of Isabel Bevier.* Peoria, 1955.

Bevier, Isabel. *Home Economics in Education.* Philadelphia, 1924.

Bevier, Isabel. *The House: Its Plan, Decoration and Care.* Chicago, 1906.

Bevier, Isabel, and Susannah Usher. *The Home Economics Movement.* Boston, 1906.

Block, William J. *The Separation of the Farm Bureau and the Extension Service.* Urbana, 1960.

Brown, D. Alexander. *Grierson's Raid.* Urbana, 1954.

Carriel, Mary Turner. *The Life of Jonathan Baldwin Turner.* n.p., 1911; 2nd ed., Urbana, 1961.

Davenport, Eugene. *Education for Efficiency.* New York, 1909.

Davenport, Eugene. *Principles of Breeding: A Treatise on Thremmatology.* Boston, 1907.

Davenport, Eugene. *Timberland Times.* Urbana, 1950.

Eddy, Edward D., Jr. *Colleges for Our Land and Time.* New York, 1957.

Ginger, Ray. *Altgeld's America: The Lincoln Ideal versus Changing Realities.* New York, 1958.

Girling, Katherine Peabody. *Selim Hobart Peabody, a Biography.* Urbana, 1923.

Gregory, Allene. *John Milton Gregory: A Biography.* Chicago, 1923.

Hofstadter, Richard. *Social Darwinism in American Thought.* Philadelphia, 1944.

Hopkins, Cyril G. *Soil Fertility and Permanent Agriculture.* Boston, 1910.

Hopkins, Cyril G. *The Story of the Soil.* Boston, 1911.

Horner, Harlan H. *The Life and Work of Andrew Sloan Draper.* Urbana, 1934.

In Memoriam Stephen Alfred Forbes, 1844–1930. Urbana, 1930.

In Memoriam Cyril George Hopkins, 1866–1919. Urbana, 1922.

James, Edmund J. *The Origin of the Land Grant Act of 1862 (the So-Called Morrill Act) and Some Account of Its Author, Jonathan B. Turner.* University of Illinois Studies IV, No. 1. Urbana, 1910.

Kersey, Harry A. *John Milton Gregory and the University of Illinois.* Urbana, 1968.

Lacey, John J. *Farm Bureau in Illinois.* Bloomington, 1965.

Nevins, Allan. *Illinois.* New York, 1917.

Nevins, Allan. *The State Universities and Democracy.* Urbana, 1962.

Newcomer, Mabel. *A Century of Higher Education for American Women.* New York, 1959.

Periam, Jonathan. *The Groundswell: A History of the Origin, Aims, and Progress of the Farmers' Movement.* St. Louis, 1874.

Powell, Burt E. *Semi-Centennial History of the University of Illinois I: The Movement for Industrial Education and the Establishment of the University, 1840-1870.* Urbana, 1918.

Ross, Earle D. *Democracy's College: The Land-Grant Movement in the Formative Stage.* Ames, 1942.

Sixteen Years at the University of Illinois: A Statistical Study of the Administration of President Edmund J. James. Urbana, 1920.

Tilton, Leon D., and Thomas E. O'Donnell. *History of the Growth and Development of the Campus of the University of Illinois.* Urbana, 1930.

Solberg, Winton U. *The University of Illinois 1867-1894: An Intellectual and Cultural History.* Urbana, 1968.

True, Alfred C. *A History of Agricultural Education in the United States, 1785-1925.* U.S. Department of Agriculture, Misc. Pub. No. 251. Washington, 1937.

True, Alfred C. *A History of Agricultural Experimentation and Research in the United States, 1607-1925.* U.S. Department of Agriculture, Misc. Pub. No. 251. Washington, 1937.

True, Alfred C. *A History of Agricultural Extension Work in the United States, 1785-1923.* U.S. Department of Agriculture, Misc. Pub. No. 15. Washington, 1928.

ARTICLES AND ADDRESSES

Bevier, Isabel. "Development of the Field of Home Economics." U.S. Department of the Interior Bureau of Education Bulletin 29. *Land-Grant College Extension 1910-1920, Part V. – Home Economics* (Washington, 1925), 7-12.

Bevier, Isabel. "Recollections and Impressions of the Beginning of the Department of Home Economics at the University of Illinois." *Journal of Home Economics* XXXII (May, 1940): 291-297.

Bullard, Samuel A. "Makers of the University, IV, Andrew Sloan Draper." *Alumni Quarterly* IV (April, 1910): 93-103.

Burrill, Thomas J., "Eugene Davenport," *Illinois Agriculturist* XIX (June, 1915): 735-738.

Burrill, Thomas J. "Some Early Inside History and Its Lessons." *Dedication Agricultural Building University of Illinois, May 21, 1901* (printed pamphlet).

Bibliography

"Clark Robinson Griggs and the Location of the University." *Alumni Quarterly and Fortnightly Notes* I (October 15, 1915): 17–22.

Cunningham, Joseph O. "The Genesis of Our Campus." *Alumni Quarterly* IX (January, 1915): 18–21.

Davenport, Eugene. "Early Days of the Illinois Agricultural Experiment Station." *Science* LXXXVII (June 17, 1938): 542–545. Address given at the fiftieth anniversary of the Illinois Agricultural Experiment Station, March 25, 1938.

Davenport, Eugene. "History of Collegiate Education in Agriculture." Society for the Promotion of Agricultural Science. *Proceedings* XXVIII (Lansing, 1907): 43–53.

Davenport, Eugene. "A Son of the Timberlands." *The Country Gentleman* XC (September, 1925): 17, 59–60; (October, 1925): 17, 91; (November, 1925): 23, 123–124; (December, 1925): 30, 128–129; XCI (January, 1926): 32, 132–134; (February, 1926): 38, 155–157; (April, 1926): 38, 54; (July, 1926): 30, 84; (September, 1926): 50, 53–54.

Davenport, Eugene. *Wanted: A National Policy in Agriculture* (printed pamphlet). January, 1919. Address given at the thirty-second annual convention of the Association of American Agricultural Colleges and Experiment Stations. Baltimore, Maryland, January 8, 1919.

Davenport, Eugene, *et al. Agriculture at the University of Illinois: A Statement of the Work and Needs of the College of Agriculture and Agricultural Experiment Station* (printed pamphlet). March, 1917.

Forbes, Stephen A. "Aspects of Progress in Economic Entomology." *Journal of Economic Entomology* II (February, 1909): 25–35.

Forbes, Stephen A. "The Ecological Foundations of Applied Entomology." *Annals of the Entomological Society of America* VIII (March, 1915): 1–19. Annual address given before the Entomological Society of America. Philadelphia, December 30, 1914.

Forbes, Stephen A. "The Lake as a Microcosm." *Bulletin of the Natural History Survey* XV (November, 1925): 537–550.

Forbes, Stephen A. "Thomas Jonathan Burrill." *Alumni Quarterly and Fortnightly Notes* I (July 15, 1916): 409–417.

Forbes, Stephen A. "War as an Education." *The Illinois* III (October, 1911): 3–10.

Gregory, John M. "Agricultural Graduates." *Illini*, March, 1875.

Gregory, Mrs. John M. "The School of Domestic Science of the Illinois Industrial University." U.S. Bureau of Education. *Industrial Edu-*

cation in the United States: A Special Report (Washington, 1883), 279–285.

James, Edmund J. "The Life and Labors of Jonathan B. Turner." *Journal of the Illinois State Historical Society* VIII (April, 1915): 7–22.

James, Edmund J. "The President's Tribute." *Alumni Quarterly and Fortnightly Notes* I (May 1, 1916): 336–337.

Mills, Harlow B., *et al.* "A Century of Biological Research." *Illinois Natural History Survey Bulletin* XXVII (December, 1958): 85–234.

Morrow, George E. "Agricultural Education." *Illini*, February, 1877.

Mumford, Herbert W. "A Half-Century of Achievement by the Illinois Agricultural Experiment Station." *Science* LXXXVII (June 17, 1938): 539–542.

Richmond, Charles A. "Dr. Gregory's Early Days." *Alumni Quarterly* VIII (July, 1914): 147–152.

Ross, Earle D. "The 'Father' of the Land-Grant College." *Agricultural History* XII (April, 1938): 151–186.

"Sketch of Manly Miles." *Appleton's Popular Science Monthly* LIV (April, 1899): 834–841. Also printed in Michigan State Board of Agriculture, *Annual Report*, XXXVIII (1899): 422–428.

Smith, Erwin F. "In Memoriam Thomas J. Burrill." *Journal of Bacteriology* I (May, 1916): 269–271.

Solberg, Winton U. "The University of Illinois Struggles for Public Recognition, 1867–1894." *Journal of the Illinois State Historical Society* LIX (Spring, 1966): 5–29.

Stevens, Neil E. "The Centenary of T. J. Burrill." *Scientific Monthly* XLIX (September, 1939): 288–292.

Turner, Fred H. "Misconceptions Concerning the Early History of the University of Illinois." Illinois State Historical Society. *Transactions for 1932.* Illinois State Historical Library Pub. No. 39 (n.p., n.d.): 63–90.

Index

Abbott, Alfred N., 190
Abbott, Alice A., 131n20, 136
Adams Act, 146n63
Agency for International Development, 215
Agricultural Department, 18, 19
Agricultural Economics, Department of, 154, 206, 215
Agricultural Engineering Building. See Farm Mechanics Building
Agricultural Engineering, Department of, 135n33, 207
Agricultural experiment stations, 29, 74. See also Illinois Agricultural Experiment Station
Agricultural lectures, 40, 48, 49n2; *Illus.*, 43. See also Farmers' Institutes
Agricultural press: opposition to renaming University, 61; attitude toward University, 107, 108; pressure on legislature, 122
Agricultural research: and Bill 315, 141
Agriculture: courses in, 18, 19, 31, 34n12, 55n16, 59, 60, 76; science of, 41, 52, 57; free tuition for students of, 42; experiments in, 52, 65, 69; failure of education in, 56, 57, 73; opposition to education in, 58, 59; schools of, 73; work in divided, 110; enrollment in schools of, 117n45; money appropriated for in other states,

118n46, 139n46; equipment for study of in other states, 122n56
Agriculture Building, 142, 144n60; request for, 116; estimated cost of, 113n34, 118, 126, 127; appropriation for, 129; facilities of, 136, 137; dedication of, 137n42; *Illus.*, 138, 139
Agriculture, College of: faculty of, 50, 137, 146, 150; funds for, 51, 69n15, 121, 137, 138, 141, 142n54, 143n55, 146n64, 149n71, 149n73, 150n2; decline of, 55, 65, 72; enrollment in, 56, 65, 66, 72, 76, 105, 130, 136, 137, 146, 148n70, 150; curriculum of, 59, 60, 115; equipment of in 1876, 65; first dean of, 66; and "Farmers' Course," 72; disposal of holdings, 79; conditions under Morrow, 81; "Winter School," 105; condition of in 1895, 105; growth of, 107, 145, 146, 240–241; reorganization of by Draper, 110, 114; needs listed, 113n34; need for building, 115n38; refusal of University to provide facilities for, 116; entrance requirements, 129, 130n14; Davenport's plan for, 134; and pessimism over future, 136n36; report of investigating committee in 1910, 148; major buildings of, 148n70, 150, 225, 226; *Illus.*, 227–236; land holdings, 150n3; and Department of Domestic

255

Index

Bill 315, 140n50, 143n55; provisions of, 141, 142; sponsors of, 146n66; "soils section," 163

Blair, Joseph C., 151; *Illus.*, 119, 218; background of, 154, 155; as head of Department of Horticulture, 155; love of trees, 155n18; career of, 219

Bliss, Willard Flagg, 50; as professor of agriculture, 34; background of, 34; later life, 35n13; resignation, 35; *Illus.*, 35

Bogardus, Charles, 128, 129

Botany, 84

Botany, Department of, 208, 214

Bouyoucos, George J., 174n62

Bowlker Breeding Project, 209

Brandly, Carl A., 213

Brayman, Mason: report on M. L. Dunlap, 29; mentioned, 26, 27n21, 40, 44

Breeder's Gazette, 80

Broad-gauge. *See* Education

Bullard, Samuel A., 131n20, 144n58

Bulletin 22, 167n47, 168

Bunch, Mamie, 195, 196, 197, 198

Burke, W. H., 133n28

Burlison, W. L., 208, 214

Burnsides Research Laboratory: *Illus.*, 236

Burns, Kathryn VanAken, 202n63

Burrill, Thomas Jonathan: background of, 35, 36; education of, 36, 37, 83n1; training in horticulture, 37n15; as botanist, 37n16; duties in horticulture, 38, 39; joins University staff, 38n18; *Illus.*, 39, 86, 119; and Manly Miles, 54; and experiment station Board of Direction, 74; and George Morrow, 78, 79; administrative duties of, 83, 87; work in botany, 84n2; publications of, 84n3; study of fire blight, 85–88; praise for, 89; and science of bacterial plant pathology, 89; character, 89n13, 89n14, 94; death of, 90n15; and appropriations from state legislature, 102; as regent, 102n4; and E. Davenport, 106; belief in agricultural education, 107; and development of College of Agriculture, 131; and Dav-

enport's plan for College of Agriculture, 134, 135; and phosphate property, 170; naming of Department of Household Science, 181n13; first course in plant pathology, 212; mentioned, 50, 82n50, 131n20, 137n42, 158

Burroughs, Edward W., 190

Burroughs, John C., 30n26

Cameron, F. K., 166

Capper-Ketcham Act of 1928, 193n42

Card, L. E., 208

Carriel, Mary Turner: support for College of Agriculture, 123n58; and A. S. Draper, 124; and Davenport's confrontation with Board of Trustees, 134; and funds for agriculture, 140; praise for Davenport, 142n53; efforts to retain Holden, 157; advocates home economics curriculum, 178; mentioned, 118, 122n57, 127n8, 131n20

Carroll, W. E., 208

Carter-Pennell farm, 150n3

Case, H. C. M., 206

Cattle-feeding buildings, 150

Center for Zoonoses Research. *See* Veterinary Medical Research Building

Champaign: city named, 9

Champaign County: location of University, 9–13

Champaign County Fair, 33

"Champaign ring," 11, 12

Chase, Harry Woodburn, 145n62

Chester, E. E., 111

Chemistry and Natural Science, Department of, 18

Chemistry building, 75n33, 102n2, 144n60

Chemistry, Department of, 209

Chemistry laboratory, 144n60. *See also* Noyes Laboratory

"Chemistry of the Soil as Related to Crop Production" (Bulletin 22), 166

Chicago Tribune, 17n3, 24n16, 25, 26, 40, 42. *See also* "Rural"

Child Development Laboratory: *Illus.*, 235

Chloromycetin, 213

125, 126n4; and E. Davenport, 125, 126, 127; and new agriculture building, 126, 127n9; and Funk Bill, 127n9, 128, 129; proposal to downgrade College of Agriculture, 130, 131n18; inscription on agriculture building, 137n42; resignation of, 143n56; amputation of leg, 143n57; skills as administrator, 144n60; implicit criticism of, 144; and P. G. Holden, 157; and Isabel Bevier, 181n11, 183, 189

Drill hall, 144n60

Dunlap, Henry M., 46n42, 127n9, 128n10, 137n42

Dunlap, Mrs. Henry M., 186, 187n26, 191; *Illus.*, 189

Dunlap, Matthias L.: as agricultural writer, 24n16; attacks on University, 25, 26, 27, 29, 30, 40; and J. M. Gregory, 25, 27, 42; "Rural" column, 25, 26, 27, 40; personality, 28; *Illus.*, 28; trustees' resolutions concerning, 30; and annual course of agricultural lectures, 40n26; mentioned, 10, 41, 46n42

East, Edward Murray, 160, 161n33, 161n36; *Illus.*, 162

Eckhardt, William G., 136n37, 195

Education: free, 6; for industrial classes, 13; narrow-gauge, 16–19; broad-gauge, 16–19

Electrical engineering laboratory, 144n60

Endomycin, 213

Engineering. *See* Mechanic Arts

Engineering Hall, 144n60

English Building, 203n65. *See also* Woman's Building

Entomologist, State Office of, 37, 83, 93, 97, 98, 99, 137

Ewing, C. A., 147n67

Experimental farm, 32n3, 51n8, 53, 69n17, 70, 79, 159. *See also* Farms, University

Experimental House, 184, 185n22, 192n41

Export Debenture Plan, 206

Extension service. *See* Cooperative Extension Service

Extension short course, 29

Faculty: listed in several colleges, 39, 40n23

Farm advisers, 193, 195n46

Farm Bureaus, 195

Farm Committee, 69, 70, 79

Farmers: education for, 13, 19; opposition to agricultural education, 58, 81n47, 82; hostility toward University, 60, 61, 107, 113, 114; and agricultural experiment station, 75; and condition of College of Agriculture, 117n43; confrontation with Board of Trustees, 133n26; indifference to Hopkins's system of soil fertility, 166n44

Farmers' Course, 72

Farmers' Institute: proposal for, 112, 113; meeting of, at University in 1898, 116; support for Davenport, 120n50; assistance to College of Agriculture, 130; scholarship plan, 130n16, 136; confrontation with Board of Trustees, 132–134; and Bill 315, 140, 141n51; investigation of College of Agriculture in 1910, 146, 147n67; General Agricultural Committee of, 147n67, 149; and Perry G. Holden, 156n22; and Association of Domestic Science, 178; disbanded, 194n45; mentioned, 133n28, 137n42, 146n66

Farmers' Institutes: attendance at, 66, 72; reactivation of, 66n7. *See also* Agricultural lectures

Farm Foundation, 206

Farm Home, The, 111

Farm Mechanics Building, 148n70, 225; *Illus.*, 228

Farm Mechanics, Department of, 135n33. *See also* Agricultural Engineering

Farm Organization and Management, Department of. *See* Agricultural Economics, Department of

Farms, University: extent of, 31, 32n3,

Index

Hatch Act, 74, 117, 137, 138, 193
Hatch, Frederic L., 122n57, 127n8, 131n20, 132, 148n69
Hazard, Edmund B.: *Illus.*, 23
Henry, David Dodds, 145n62
Hoard's Dairyman, 151, 152n8
Holden, Perry Greeley: joins faculty, 115n37; *Illus.*, 119; and Funk Bill, 128, 129n12; accuracy of reporting, 129n12; and confrontation with Board of Trustees, 133n26; as head of Department of Agronomy, 135; resignation, 156, 157; and Eugene Davenport, 156n22; career of, 157n23; corn-breeding experiments, 159n28; use of trains for extension work, 196n49; mentioned, 131n20, 134, 157
Home advisers, 193, 194n43, 195n46
Home economics: progress during W.W.I, 199
Home Economics Building. *See* Bevier Hall
Home Economics, Department of, 197, 198, 211. *See also* Household Science, Department of
Home Economics extension service: home advisers, 193, 194n43, 195n46; and Demonstration Car, 196n50; officers of, 243–244; mentioned, 196n48, 198
Home Management House, 193n41
Hopkins, Cyril George, 151; background, 155, 156; studies in Germany, 156; as head of Department of Agronomy, 158; *The Story of the Soil*, 158n26; corn-breeding experiments, 158–162; character of, 158n26; *Illus.*, 159, 170; relations with E. M. East, 161n36; system of soil fertility, 163n39, 164, 165n42, 166; and government theories of soil fertility, 167n47; and Poorland Farm, 168, 169n51; and phosphate property, 170n52, 171n55, 172n56; fame of, 173, 174; *Soil Fertility and Permanent Agriculture*, 174; death, 174n62; contributions to agriculture, 175; at Farmers' Institute meetings, 191n37

Horticultural Building, 148n70; *Illus.*, 228
Horticultural grounds, 38, 39, 51, 65, 87n8
Horticulture, Department of: organization of, 38n20, 155n19, 212; appropriation for, 51; contributions of, 212; mentioned, 35, 38n20, 135n33, 157n24, 208, 214
Horticulture Field Laboratory: *Illus.*, 231
Hostetter, A. B., 133
Household Science, Department of: established, 157n24; courses offered, 181, 182n15, 183n17, 184n21, 185, 197n51; named, 181n13; enrollment, 182, 192, 197; suspicions of, 183n18; and Experimental House, 184, 185n22; respect for, 186; and practical housekeeping, 190, 191; staff of, 192, 197; and practice apartment, 192n41; and Diet Research House, 193n41; and Home Management House, 193n41; Demonstration Car, 196n50, 198; graduates of, 197n51. *See also* Home Economics, Department of
Howard, Louis Bradley: *Illus.*, 218; career of, 220
Hudelson, Robert R.: *Illus.*, 218; career of, 220
Huelsen, W. A., 212
Hunt, Thomas Forsythe: *Illus.*, 70; as Morrow's assistant, 71; background of, 71; and experiment station, 75n34, 78n42; and Committee on Agriculture, 132n21; corn-breeding experiments of, 158; mentioned, 105n10, 137n42
Hurlbut, S. A., 22
Hybrid corn, 161n34, 208

Illini, 59, 60, 72
Illini Grove, 87n8
Illinois Agricultural Experiment Station, 107, 214; and Morrow Plots, 67; established, 74; and Board of Direction, 74, 111, 114, 146n66; publications of, 75; and farmers, 75; staff of, 75n34; research projects, 75, 158n28, 163; and George Morrow, 78; reorganiza-

261

Index

Levomycin, 213
Liberal Arts and Sciences, College of, 98n32
Library. *See* Altgeld Hall
Library Science, School of, 144
Liebig, Baron von, 49, 175
Llewellyn, Joseph C., 131n20
Lloyd, J. W., 212
Logan County, Illinois: bid for location of University, 10
Longwell, J. H., 214
Lott, R. V., 212

Mann, Frank I., 147n67, 149, 150, 166n44, 190
Maples, The, 109n23
Mason, J. P., 149n72
Matthews, James Newton, 20, 21n10
Matthews, William, 26
McCluer, George W., 75n34, 158, 159n28
McIntosh, Donald: *Illus.*, 119
McLean County, Illinois: bid for location of University, 10
McLean County System of Swine Sanitation, 209
McMunn, R. L., 212
McMurtrie, William, 75
Mechanical building, 144n60
Mechanic Arts, 31, 59
Mechanics: education for, 13, 19
Medicine, School of, 144
Mendel, Lafayette B., 188
Men's gymnasium, 144n60
Metal shops, 144n60
Michigan Agricultural College: and J. M. Gregory, 14; and Manly Miles, 20, 49, 54n15; compared to University of Illinois, 73, 131; and E. Davenport, 108n20, 110; and P. G. Holden, 115n37; and Herbert Mumford, 153; and experiments on corn, 159n28
Michigan Journal of Education, 15
Michigan State University. *See* Michigan Agricultural College
Miles, Manly, 20; reputation of, 49; background of, 49; as professor of agriculture, 50; knowledge of agricultural problems, 52, 53, 54; reor-

ganization of University farms, 53; *Illus.*, 53; and managing finances, 54n15; resignation of, 54; temperament of, 62; and Morrow Plots, 67n11
Military Department, 18
Miller, John A., 75n34
Mills, Charles F., 120n49; background of, 111n31; and Farmers' Institute, 112, 113; *Illus.*, 112; and A. S. Draper, 124; and financing of College of Agriculture, 138, 139
Mills, Harlow B., 99n35
Mitchell, H. H., 208
Moore, Amos F., 120n49, 121, 122
Morey, Lloyd, 145n62
Morgan County, Illinois: bid for location of University, 10
Morrill Act, 7; passage of, 4, 10; and narrow-gauge curriculum, 16, 82; funds from, 50, 51, 138, 193. *See also* Morrill Supplementary Act
Morrill, Justin Smith, 4, 13
Morrill Supplementary Act, 101n1, 117, 121
Morrison, Napoleon B., 79, 80, 116n40, 122n57
Morrow, George E.: background of, 62; character, 62, 80n45; as professor of agriculture, 62, 64, 65n4; as agricultural journalist, 63, 64; leadership in agricultural societies, 64; *Illus.*, 64; efforts to increase enrollment in agriculture, 66; as dean, 66; European trip, 66; and appropriations for agriculture, 69; and manual skills, 70, 71; appearance, 71; as lecturer, 71, 72; and decline of College of Agriculture, 72, 73; and experiment station, 74, 78; and University farms, 77, 78; health of, 78; resignation, 79, 80; critics of, 80n44; praise for, 80n45; educational practices of, 82; and E. Davenport, 106; death of, 106n13; corn-breeding experiments, 159n28; mentioned, 98, 101, 105n11
Morrow Hall, 137n41, 152
Morrow Plots: origin of, 66, 67n10, 67n11, 68; *Illus.*, 67
Mosier, J. G., 171n54, 207

Index

Richard Gordon Moores is a publications editor at the University of Illinois College of Agriculture. His diverse background includes jobs as a marine machinery buyer in New York (where he was working toward his M.A. at Columbia University); as office manager of a wholesale lumber company in Indianapolis; as reporter for the *Palm Beach Daily News* in Florida; and as English instructor at Purdue University and at the University of Illinois. His first novel, *Hell Is Not Anywhere*, was published in 1959. He is now at work on another novel.